Exodus

TEACH THE TEXT COMMENTARY

John H. Walton
Old Testament General Editor

Mark L. Strauss
New Testament General Editor

Volumes now available:

Old Testament Volumes

Exodus .... T. Desmond Alexander

Leviticus and Numbers.. Joe M. Sprinkle

Joshua .... Kenneth A. Mathews

1 & 2 Samuel .... Robert B. Chisholm Jr.

Job .... Daniel J. Estes

Psalms, volume 1 .... C. Hassell Bullock

Ecclesiastes and Song of Songs .... Edward M. Curtis

Jeremiah and Lamentations... J. David Hays

Daniel... Ronald W. Pierce

New Testament Volumes

Matthew .... Jeannine K. Brown

Mark .... Grant R. Osborne

Luke .... R. T. France

Romans .... C. Marvin Pate

1 Corinthians .... Preben Vang

Revelation... J. Scott Duvall

Visit the series website at www.teachthetextseries.com.

TEACH the TEXT
COMMENTARY SERIES

Exodus

T. Desmond Alexander

ILLUSTRATING the TEXT

Kevin and Sherry Harney
ASSOCIATE EDITORS

Adam Barr
CONTRIBUTING WRITER

BakerBooks
a division of Baker Publishing Group
Grand Rapids, Michigan

Published by Baker Books
a division of Baker Publishing Group
P.O. Box 6287, Grand Rapids, MI 49516-6287
www.bakerbooks.com

Printed in the United States of America

Library of Congress Cataloging-in-Publication Data
Names: Alexander, T. Desmond.
Title: Exodus / T. Desmond Alexander ; Mark L. Strauss and John H. Walton, general editors.
Description: Grand Rapids, MI : Baker Books, 2016. | Series: Teach the text commentary | Includes bibliographical references and index.
Identifiers: LCCN 2015045878 | ISBN 9780801092145 (paper)
Subjects: LCSH: Bible. Exodus—Commentaries.
Classification: LCC BS1245.53 A44 2016 | DDC 222/.1207—dc23
LC record available at http://lccn.loc.gov/2015045878

Contents

Welcome to the Teach the Text
  Commentary Series   vii
Introduction to the Teach the Text
  Commentary Series   ix
Abbreviations   xi

Introduction to Exodus   1
Exodus 1:1–22   8
  Standing Up for God's Kingdom
Exodus 2:1–25   14
  What Defines a Person?
Exodus 3:1–22   20
  An Awe-Inspiring God
Exodus 4:1–31   27
  The Greatest Sign of All
Exodus 5:1–6:9   33
  *Overcoming Obstacles on God's Road
  to Freedom*
Exodus 6:10–8:19   39
  Signs Pointing to God
Exodus 8:20–10:29   46
  *The Persuasive Power of a Gracious
  God*
Exodus 11:1–12:30   52
  Death Comes to Egypt
Exodus 12:31–13:16   58
  *Some Things Should Never Be
  Forgotten*
Exodus 13:17–14:31   64
  Soli Deo Gloria—Glory to God Alone

Exodus 15:1–21   71
  Someone to Sing About
Exodus 15:22–16:36   77
  Life Is More Than Food
Exodus 17:1–16   83
  Knowing the Presence of God
Exodus 18:1–27   89
  A Father-in-Law Worth Having
Exodus 19:1–25   95
  A Holy Nation for a Holy God
Exodus 20:1–17   101
  *A Radical Mission Statement
  for a Holy Nation*
Exodus 20:18–21:11   107
  *The Wide-Ranging Implications
  of Serving the Living God*
Additional Insights   114
  *The Book of the Covenant and
  Ancient Near Eastern Law Collections*
Exodus 21:12–36   116
  An Eye for an Eye
Exodus 22:1–20   122
  God's Property Values
Exodus 22:21–23:9   128
  *Religion That God Our Father Accepts
  as Pure and Faultless*
Exodus 23:10–19   135
  Making Time for God
Exodus 23:20–33   141
  You Cannot Serve God and . . .

Exodus 24:1–18 147
Feasting in God's Presence
Exodus 25:1–27:21 153
Heaven and Earth United
Exodus 28:1–29:46 159
Serving in the Presence of God
Exodus 30:1–31:18 165
Gifted by God
Exodus 32:1–33:6 171
Actions Have Consequences

Exodus 33:7–34:35 177
God, Glory, and Goodness
Exodus 35:1–40:38 183
God in Our Midst

Notes 191
Bibliography 195
Index 199
Contributors 204

Welcome to the Teach the Text Commentary Series

Why another commentary series? That was the question the general editors posed when Baker Books asked us to produce this series. Is there something that we can offer to pastors and teachers that is not currently being offered by other commentary series, or that can be offered in a more helpful way? After carefully researching the needs of pastors who teach the text on a weekly basis, we concluded that yes, more can be done; the Teach the Text Commentary Series (TTCS) is carefully designed to fill an important gap.

The technicality of modern commentaries often overwhelms readers with details that are tangential to the main purpose of the text. Discussions of source and redaction criticism, as well as detailed surveys of secondary literature, seem far removed from preaching and teaching the Word. Rather than wade through technical discussions, pastors often turn to devotional commentaries, which may contain exegetical weaknesses, misuse the Greek and Hebrew languages, and lack hermeneutical sophistication. There is a need for a commentary that utilizes the best of biblical scholarship but also presents the material in a clear, concise, attractive, and user-friendly format.

This commentary is designed for that purpose—to provide a ready reference for the exposition of the biblical text, giving easy access to information that a pastor needs to communicate the text effectively. To that end, the commentary is divided into carefully selected preaching units (with carefully regulated word counts both in the passage as a whole and in each subsection). Pastors and teachers engaged in weekly preparation thus know that they will be reading approximately the same amount of material on a week-by-week basis.

Each passage begins with a concise summary of the central message, or "Big Idea," of the passage and a list of its main themes. This is followed by a more detailed interpretation of the text, including the literary context of the passage, historical background material, and interpretive insights. While drawing on the best of biblical scholarship, this material is clear, concise, and to the point. Technical material is kept to a minimum, with endnotes pointing the reader to more detailed discussion and additional resources.

A second major focus of this commentary is on the preaching and teaching process itself. Few commentaries today help the pastor/teacher move from the meaning of the text to its effective communication. Our goal is to bridge this gap. In addition to interpreting the text in the "Understanding the Text" section, each unit contains a "Teaching the Text" section and an "Illustrating the Text" section. The teaching section points to the key theological themes of the passage and ways to communicate these themes to today's audiences. The illustration section provides ideas and examples for retaining the interest of hearers and connecting the message to daily life.

The creative format of this commentary arises from our belief that the Bible is not just a record of God's dealings in the past but is the living Word of God, "alive and active" and "sharper than any double-edged sword" (Heb. 4:12). Our prayer is that this commentary will help to unleash that transforming power for the glory of God.

The General Editors

Introduction to the Teach the Text Commentary Series

This series is designed to provide a ready reference for teaching the biblical text, giving easy access to information that is needed to communicate a passage effectively. To that end, the commentary is carefully divided into units that are faithful to the biblical authors' ideas and of an appropriate length for teaching or preaching.

The following standard sections are offered in each unit.

1. *Big Idea*. For each unit the commentary identifies the primary theme, or "Big Idea," that drives both the passage and the commentary.
2. *Key Themes*. Together with the Big Idea, the commentary addresses in bullet-point fashion the key ideas presented in the passage.
3. *Understanding the Text*. This section focuses on the exegesis of the text and includes several sections.
   a. The Text in Context. Here the author gives a brief explanation of how the unit fits into the flow of the text around it, including reference to the rhetorical strategy of the book and the unit's contribution to the purpose of the book.
   b. Outline/Structure. For some literary genres (e.g., epistles), a brief exegetical outline may be provided to guide the reader through the structure and flow of the passage.

c. Historical and Cultural Background. This section addresses historical and cultural background information that may illuminate a verse or passage.
  d. Interpretive Insights. This section provides information needed for a clear understanding of the passage. The intention of the author is to be highly selective and concise rather than exhaustive and expansive.
  e. Theological Insights. In this very brief section the commentary identifies a few carefully selected theological insights about the passage.
4. *Teaching the Text*. Under this second main heading the commentary offers guidance for teaching the text. In this section the author lays out the main themes and applications of the passage. These are linked carefully to the Big Idea and are represented in the Key Themes.
5. *Illustrating the Text*. At this point in the commentary the writers partner with a team of pastor/teachers to provide suggestions for relevant and contemporary illustrations from current culture, entertainment, history, the Bible, news, literature, ethics, biography, daily life, medicine, and over forty other categories. They are designed to spark creative thinking for preachers and teachers and to help them design illustrations that bring alive the passage's key themes and message.

Abbreviations

Old Testament

Gen.	Genesis	2 Chron.	2 Chronicles	Dan.	Daniel
Exod.	Exodus	Ezra	Ezra	Hosea	Hosea
Lev.	Leviticus	Neh.	Nehemiah	Joel	Joel
Num.	Numbers	Esther	Esther	Amos	Amos
Deut.	Deuteronomy	Job	Job	Obad.	Obadiah
Josh.	Joshua	Ps(s).	Psalm(s)	Jon.	Jonah
Judg.	Judges	Prov.	Proverbs	Mic.	Micah
Ruth	Ruth	Eccles.	Ecclesiastes	Nah.	Nahum
1 Sam.	1 Samuel	Song	Song of Songs	Hab.	Habakkuk
2 Sam.	2 Samuel	Isa.	Isaiah	Zeph.	Zephaniah
1 Kings	1 Kings	Jer.	Jeremiah	Hag.	Haggai
2 Kings	2 Kings	Lam.	Lamentations	Zech.	Zechariah
1 Chron.	1 Chronicles	Ezek.	Ezekiel	Mal.	Malachi

New Testament

Matt.	Matthew	Eph.	Ephesians	Heb.	Hebrews
Mark	Mark	Phil.	Philippians	James	James
Luke	Luke	Col.	Colossians	1 Pet.	1 Peter
John	John	1 Thess.	1 Thessalonians	2 Pet.	2 Peter
Acts	Acts	2 Thess.	2 Thessalonians	1 John	1 John
Rom.	Romans	1 Tim.	1 Timothy	2 John	2 John
1 Cor.	1 Corinthians	2 Tim.	2 Timothy	3 John	3 John
2 Cor.	2 Corinthians	Titus	Titus	Jude	Jude
Gal.	Galatians	Philem.	Philemon	Rev.	Revelation

General

AD	*anno Domini* (in the year of our Lord)		ca.	*circa* ("around," "about")
			CEB	Common English Bible
BC	before Christ		cf.	confer, compare

e.g.	*exempli gratia* ("for example")	NIV	New International Version
ESV	English Standard Version	NRSV	New Revised Standard Version
i.e.	*id est* ("that is," "in other words")	RSV	Revised Standard Version
		v./vv.	verse/verses
KJV	King James Version		

Introduction to Exodus

The second book of the Bible, Exodus derives its name from the title given to it by ancient Greek translators. The Greek word *exodos* means "going out," "departure," and is used in Exodus 19:1 to refer to the departure of the Israelites from Egypt. While the "going out" from Egypt is a highly significant event in Exodus, there is much more to the book's plot than this. Exodus is not simply a story about the Israelites coming out of Egypt, a story narrated in chapters 1–15; it is much more about God coming to dwell among the Israelites, a theme that includes chapters 19–40. This theological dimension is especially important, but unfortunately it can all too easily be overlooked in discussions that focus solely on the human side of the Exodus story.

Plot

Exodus is a book that involves movement. Firstly, there is the movement of the Israelites from Egypt to Mount Sinai. Exodus begins by placing the Israelites in the land of Egypt but ends with them camping at Mount Sinai. Most of the book's contents, chapters 19–40, describe events at Mount Sinai rather than in Egypt, with a few chapters recounting the transition from Egypt to Sinai (Exod. 15:22–18:27). Secondly, there is the movement of God, who takes up residence in the very midst of the Israelite camp. The coming together of God and the Israelites at Mount Sinai is highly significant, but the full magnitude of this convergence can be easily overlooked. It marks a partial restoration of the broken relationship between God and humanity that results from Adam and Eve's actions in the Garden of Eden, and it anticipates future developments whereby God's presence will fill a world inhabited by those who are holy as God is holy.

Authorship

Exodus itself does not at any point identify the person responsible for authoring or editing the book as we now have it. Taken at face value Exodus occasionally ascribes the composition of particular sections to individuals who are also characters within the story. In Exodus 15, it seems likely that Miriam composes the song used by the Israelites to celebrate their rescue from the Egyptian army. In Exodus 20, the Ten Commandments are attributed to God, who speaks them directly to the people. The Book of the Covenant (Exod. 20:22–23:33) is spoken by God to Moses, who subsequently records everything that God says (Exod. 24:4). Similarly, the instructions for the manufacture of the tabernacle and associated matters are spoken by God to Moses (Exod. 25–31). No specific source is given for the genealogical information in Exodus 6:14–25, but presumably this draws on known family records. The inclusion of such disparate types of material within the same narrative suggests that the author/editor incorporated into his account preexisting materials. It would require an author of exceptionally remarkable talent to compose from scratch the entire book of Exodus as a work of fiction.

A long-established tradition associates Moses with the composition of Exodus and the other books of the Pentateuch. Given his central role in the book's plot, Moses would certainly be an obvious source for most of the information recorded. However, we should also allow for the possibility that others may have contributed to shaping Exodus as we know it. For example, Exodus 16:35 clearly refers to an event that comes after the time of Moses (cf. Josh. 5:10–12).

Influenced by two centuries of studies that have ridiculed the veracity of the present biblical account, many critical scholars have constructed their own theories regarding the composition of Exodus. While these claim to be undertaken with scientific rigor, they frequently rest on questionable assumptions regarding the relative dating of passages within the Pentateuch. For almost a century the Documentary Hypothesis of Wellhausen dominated scholarly approaches to the Pentateuch, but it no longer enjoys widespread support, resulting in a morass of competing alternatives. Unfortunately, scholarly efforts to explain how and when the book of Exodus was composed have largely diverted attention away from understanding Exodus as a unified literary work of rich theological significance.[1]

Interpreting Exodus

Although the book of Exodus may be viewed as a self-contained entity, it forms part of a later literary narrative that runs from Genesis to Kings. Exodus presupposes that anyone reading it already knows the contents of Genesis.

This is evident from the book's opening sentence, which uses the names Jacob and Israel without explaining that they refer to the same person (cf. Gen. 32:28). Elsewhere in Exodus reference is made to God's covenant with the patriarchs of Genesis; this forms the basis of the expectation that God will eventually settle the Israelites in the land of Canaan (cf. Exod. 2:24; 3:16–17; 6:4–5, 8; 32:13; 33:1–3).

As well as presupposing Genesis, the book of Exodus also anticipates future developments that will be narrated in Leviticus and beyond. The instructions for the consecration of the Aaronic priests, which are given in Exodus 29, are implemented in Leviticus 8. The making of the covenant at Mount Sinai in Exodus 19–24 is presupposed at the renewing of the covenant in the Plains of Moab, as described in the book of Deuteronomy. The announcement in Exodus 15:17 that the Israelites will dwell with God on his holy mountain anticipates their settlement in the land of Canaan, a process that extends throughout the books of Joshua to Samuel.

Reading Exodus as part of the Genesis-to-Kings narrative should inform our understanding of the varied episodes that compose Exodus. When the wider canvas is taken into consideration, God's action in coming to dwell among the Israelites has every appearance of reversing, at least in part, the tragic consequences of Adam and Eve's betrayal of God in the Garden of Eden. In this reversal the Passover is central, for it involves both atonement and consecration. Through the Passover, God takes to himself the Israelite firstborn males, as they are ransomed from death, purified from the defilement of sin, and made holy. Subsequently, the firstborn males are ransomed by the Levites (Num. 3:12–13), who enjoy a special status among the tribes of Israel as those dedicated to serve God in the tabernacle/temple.

To appreciate the theological significance of Exodus, it is important to grasp that biblical narratives frequently show rather than tell what is happening. Thus, for example, although there is no specific mention of the concept of atonement in Exodus 12–13, the sacrificial animals are clearly understood to function as a ransom for the firstborn males, a point drawn out indirectly in Exodus 13:11–13, and their blood is used to purify those who pass through the bloodstained door frames of the Israelite homes. As is evident from the book of Leviticus, atonement includes both the payment of a ransom and the removal of defilement due to human sin. The same process is also reflected in the ratification of the covenant at Mount Sinai (Exod. 24:5–6), emphasizing that atonement is an essential prerequisite for the Israelites' unique relationship with God.

Although the Passover ritual involving atonement and consecration models how people may become holy, the book of Exodus underlines that perfect communion with God is not achieved. Exodus does not end with God's plans for the Israelites and all humanity being fulfilled. The tabernacle enables God to dwell in the midst of the Israelite camp, but the tent itself functions as a protective barrier between God and humanity. The construction of the tabernacle is merely a first stage toward God's glory filling the whole earth, when heaven and earth will merge into one. The developments that occur in Exodus are a significant step in the plan of divine salvation, but more has yet to take place. The events recorded in Exodus model how the broken relationship between God and humanity may be restored, implicitly indicating that a great exodus is in the future.

Key Theological and/or Narrative Themes

The convergence of God and the Israelites at Mount Sinai is a fitting conclusion to a book that has as one of its dominant ideas the theme of knowing God. Underlying the events described in Exodus is God's desire that people will come to a deeper knowledge of him, both intellectually and relationally. Through both word and action, God makes himself known, beginning with his appearance as a flame of fire to Moses (Exod. 3:2) and concluding with his glory filling the newly consecrated tabernacle (Exod. 40:34–38).

The motif of knowing God takes on special significance in the light of Pharaoh's question, "Who is the LORD?" (Exod. 5:2). The subsequent episodes involving the signs and wonders contain allusions to this question (Exod. 6:3–7; 7:5, 17; 8:10, 22; 9:4, 16, 29; 10:1–2; 11:7; 14:4, 18), indicating that the supernatural events in Egypt are specifically intended by God to make him known to both the Israelites and the Egyptians. These events, together with the destruction of the Egyptian army in the "Red Sea" (or better, "Lake of Reeds"; see the comments on 13:17–18, below), highlight the awesome power and majesty of God.

The motif of knowing God figures prominently in the covenant that is ratified at Mount Sinai, preparing for the subsequent construction of the tabernacle. The covenant establishes a special relationship between God and the Israelites, paving the way for God to come and dwell in their midst. With the making of the covenant, prominent leaders of the Israelites are given the privilege of seeing God, but not fully (Exod. 24:9–11). Yet in spite of these positive developments, even Moses, who enjoys an especially intimate relationship with God, cannot see God's face. Nevertheless, the coming of God to live among the Israelites introduces an entirely new dimension to the theme of knowing God, for he now lives in close proximity to the people, in a way that no one has experienced since Adam and Eve were expelled from the Garden of Eden. While the coming of the Lord to reside within the Israelite camp is a significant new development in God's redemptive plan, the final barrier between God and humanity will be removed only with the death of the perfect Passover sacrifice (Matt. 27:51; Mark 15:38; Luke 23:45).

In the process of coming to know God personally, the Israelites have to be set free from serving Pharaoh before they can serve the Lord. While they move from serving one master to serving another, the two masters could not be more different. Whereas Pharaoh forcibly enslaves them and subjects them to harsh servitude, the Lord invites the Israelites to accept voluntarily his rule over them, promising to treat them as his "treasured possession" (Exod. 19:5). While the Israelites are conscripted to build store cities of brick for Pharaoh, the Lord commissions and equips them to construct a royal tent as his dwelling place among them. While Pharaoh refuses to supply them with the straw necessary for their work, the Lord generously provides them with food and water during their wilderness trek. The Israelites' experience of serving Pharaoh is very different from that of serving the Lord.

Historical Setting

The events described in Exodus are undoubtedly assumed by the book's author to have a historical foundation. He writes about real events involving real people. In doing so, the author of Exodus has no qualms about attributing to God the occurrence of events and words. Throughout Exodus, God is one of the central figures, and the book itself is penned with the intention of making the Lord known to others. The supernatural events narrated provide evidence for God's existence that goes beyond what might be derived from "natural revelation."

As far as locating these events in time and history, the book of Exodus itself furnishes little specific information. Exodus 12:40–41 records that the Israelites lived for 430 years in Egypt, but no absolute date is provided for either the start or end of this period. According to 1 Kings 6:1 the exodus took place 480 years before the "fourth year of Solomon's reign over Israel." On the assumption that Solomon began his reign in 970 BC, this would give an absolute date of 1450 BC for the Israelites' departure from Egypt. However, some scholars question the accuracy of what is said in 1 Kings 6:1, preferring to date the exodus to the thirteenth century BC on the basis of other considerations, mainly archaeological.

Pointing to the lack of nonbiblical sources that mention the Israelite exodus from Egypt, some scholars believe that the Exodus version of events is largely fictitious.[2] While the absence of collaborative evidence must not be dismissed lightly, it is highly unlikely that any pharaoh would record on any stone monument a description of such events, disastrous from an Egyptian perspective. If descriptions were made on papyri and stored in the Delta region, they would have perished along with almost every other papyrus text from the New Kingdom period.

The difficulty of dating the exodus with precision is compounded by the fact that the pharaohs mentioned in Exodus are never named. This appears to be a deliberate literary feature, designed to convey the idea that these Egyptian kings are in reality nonentities, in spite of their supposed divine status in ancient Egypt. The names of the pharaohs are omitted, but ironically, those of two midwives, who bravely defied their Egyptian king, are recorded for posterity.

If there is no historical basis to the exodus, those responsible for inventing the account of Israel's remarkable deliverance from Egypt did much more than merely devise a fictional description of Israel's past. They also succeeded in establishing an annual commemorative event based on their imaginative reconstruction of the past that was embraced not only by Jews but also by Samaritans. In the light of how these two opposing religious communities celebrated the same occasion, there is good reason to question the skepticism of some modern scholars that the exodus account is merely make-believe.[3] It makes more sense to assume that the celebration of the Passover is based on an ancient reality.

Exodus and the New Testament

As the primary Old Testament paradigm for divine salvation, the exodus story informs the New Testament writers' understanding of the death of Jesus Christ at the time of the Passover (e.g., 1 Cor. 5:7). While all the Gospels draw on Exodus, John's Gospel is especially rich in highlighting parallels between Jesus's death and the Passover. John even notes that Jesus's bones are not broken, as was the case with the Passover sacrifices (John 19:33–36; cf. Exod. 12:46; Num. 9:12). John's emphasis on the Passover resonates with his belief that Jesus brings life in all its fullness. As the Passover sacrifices gave life to the firstborn Israelite males, Jesus's sacrificial death gives eternal life to those who believe in him. Moreover, to underline this link with the exodus, John records signs that Jesus performed leading up to the Passover. Like the signs performed by Moses and Aaron, Jesus's signs are also intended to promote trust in the one sent by God.

Exodus and Biblical Theology

The book of Exodus contributes in a very significant way to our understanding of God's redemptive plan for all humanity. We see in the microstory of Exodus the macrostory of the Bible. God comes as Savior and King to redeem people from satanic control, to ransom them from death, to purify them from defilement, to sanctify them so that they may be restored to the status that was lost by Adam and Eve, becoming a royal priesthood and a holy nation. Yet while God's rescue of the Israelites from Egypt models the process of salvation, it only foreshadows something greater to come, for the Sinai covenant does not enable the Israelites to obey God fully. Consequently, access to God's presence is still barred to all but the high priest, and even for him access is very restricted. A greater exodus is anticipated, one that will bring to fulfillment God's creation plan to dwell on the earth with his people. This comes through the sacrificial death of Jesus Christ, which results ultimately in the creation of the new Jerusalem, witnessed by John in Revelation 21–22.

Standing Up for God's Kingdom

Big Idea

God's people must face persecution from those opposed to the fulfillment of God's will on earth.

Key Themes

- God's people will be persecuted by those who set themselves up in opposition to God.
- A healthy fear of God prevents us from succumbing to pressure from others to do evil and produces positive results.

Understanding the Text

The Text in Context

The opening chapter of Exodus sets the background to the record of God's dramatic deliverance of the Israelites from slavery in Egypt. Eventually, this results in the Lord coming to dwell among the Israelites, having entered into a special covenant relationship with them at Mount Sinai. At the outset of Exodus, however, God does not dwell with the Israelites, and their experience of life becomes exceptionally harsh when a new pharaoh instigates a program of hard servitude designed to restrict the growth of the Israelite population.

Historical and Cultural Background

The events narrated in Exodus 1 possibly occurred during the reign of Ahmose I (1550–1525 BC), who founded a new Egyptian dynasty, known today as the Eighteenth Dynasty. During his reign, he ousted from power the Hyksos from the Delta region of Egypt. The Hyksos were foreigners of Semitic origin who controlled the northern part of Egypt from about 1650 to 1550 BC. Ahmose's success against the Hyksos may have encouraged him to suppress other non-Egyptian groups living in the Delta region.

As regards the location of the two cities named in Exodus 1:11, recent archaeological research suggests that Pithom and Rameses are to be located at

Tell el-Retabah and Qantir/Tell el-Dab'a, respectively. Both of these locations now provide evidence that cities of significant size existed on what was then a major distributary of the Nile in both the fifteenth and thirteenth centuries BC, possible dates for the exodus. If the exodus is dated to the fifteenth century BC, the name Rameses in Exodus 1:11 is anachronistic (as it must be in Gen. 47:11). The Hyksos city at Tell el-Dab'a, known as Avaris, was possibly renamed Perunefer in the fifteenth century BC, only to be renamed Pi-Ramesses in the thirteenth century BC when Ramesses II (ca. 1290–1224 BC) made this location his residence.

Interpretive Insights

1:1–6 *the sons of Israel who went to Egypt with Jacob . . . Joseph was already in Egypt.* These verses form a short prologue to the book of Exodus. Apart from setting the scene for all that follows, the prologue links together the books of Genesis and Exodus. Without a knowledge of Genesis, the prologue is unintelligible. From Genesis we know (1) that "Israel" is an alternative name for "Jacob" (Gen. 32:28) and (2) that Joseph was sold into slavery by his brothers (Gen. 37:12–36), before becoming prime minister of Egypt (Gen. 41:38–45). Since Jacob's family numbered seventy when they arrived in Egypt, their remarkable numerical growth takes on added significance.

1:7 *the Israelites were exceedingly fruitful.* Whereas verse 6 focuses on the death of Joseph's generation, verse 7 emphasizes the population explosion of the Israelites. In doing so, verse 7 echoes the language of Genesis 1, where God blesses and commands humanity to be fruitful and multiply and fill the earth (Gen. 1:28; cf. 9:1, 7). The close correspondence in language strongly implies that the Israelites are fulfilling God's creation mandate. In Genesis, the motif of numerical increase appears repeatedly in the divine promises made to the patriarchs, Abraham, Isaac, and Jacob (e.g., Gen. 12:2; 15:5; 26:4; 28:14; 48:4). The extraordinary growth of the Israelite population is a sign of divine blessing.

1:8–10 *a new king . . . came to power in Egypt.* A new era begins with the enthronement of a new monarch. Consistently, Exodus never identifies the Egyptian rulers by name. In spite of their exalted position within Egypt, they are portrayed as nonentities. In marked contrast, the Hebrew midwives are named (1:15). The Egyptian king's fear of the Israelites causes him to oppress them harshly. But this is more than xenophobia, for his actions contravene God's creation mandate. With good reason, the pharaohs of Exodus are portrayed as anti-God figures.

1:11–12 *they put slave masters over them.* Pharaoh oppresses the Israelites by having them construct cities. In doing so he usurps God's place (see "Theological Insights").

1:13–14 *worked them ruthlessly . . . labor in brick and mortar.* In describing the Egyptian oppression of the Israelites, these verses give emphasis to the Hebrew root *'abad*, "to serve," which underlies the words for "worked" and "labor." The repeated use of the root *'abad* reinforces the idea that the Israelites are Pharaoh's "slaves" (*'abadim*). Later in Exodus the Israelites will be invited by God at Mount Sinai to become his *'abadim*, exclusively committed to serving or worshiping (*'abad*) him alone (cf. 23:25). The mention of "labor in brick and mortar" reflects accurately the Nile Delta setting, where stone is not immediately available for constructing buildings.

1:15–18 *The king of Egypt said to the Hebrew midwives.* In desperation the Egyptian king pursues an additional policy, hoping to restrict the growth of the male population of the Israelites. The disobedience of the two midwives is remarkable in the light of the Egyptian king's absolute authority. These women put their own lives at risk in order to save the lives of the Israelite baby boys. The evilness of Pharaoh's plan is evident in the fact that he looks to convert into agents of death those normally associated with bringing new life.

Scholars debate the ethnicity of the midwives.[1] Were they Egyptians who served as midwives to the Hebrew women, or were they themselves Hebrews? On balance, it seems likely that they were ethnic Hebrews. The designation "Hebrew" (*'ibri*; 1:15) is associated with Abraham in Genesis 14:13 and tends to be used by foreigners to denote Israelites (e.g., Gen. 39:14, 17; 40:15). Some ancient Near Eastern texts use the term *'apiru/'abiru* to designate a group of people of lower social standing. Although it is possible to posit some link between *'apiru/'abiru* and the Hebrew term *'ibri*, this need not mean that the two words are related.

1:19–21 *The midwives answered Pharaoh, "Hebrew women are not like Egyptian women."* While some scholars suggest that the storyteller commends the deceptiveness of the midwives,[2] the narrative itself gives no reason to doubt the truthfulness of their explanation. For standing up against Pharaoh, God rewards the midwives with children of their own, a further irony in the light of Pharaoh's desire to restrict the growth of the Israelite population.

1:22 *Every Hebrew boy that is born you must throw into the Nile.* Pharaoh progresses from a disguised, but unsuccessful, policy of infanticide to one that openly involves all his people. Pharaoh probably encourages the Egyptians to implement his evil instructions on the basis of national security and self-preservation (cf. 1:9–10).

Theological Insights

The book of Exodus may be viewed as an uplifting account of how God delivers oppressed slaves from harsh exploitation, but the whole narrative takes on a deeper significance when we read it against the background of Genesis.

In particular, Pharaoh is presented as an anti-God figure, whose actions are clearly intended to curb the fulfillment of God's purposes on earth. Pharaoh's antagonism toward the Israelites is much more than xenophobia. It is an attack on God and his will for humanity. This is even more noteworthy when we recall that the Egyptian pharaohs were viewed as divine beings.

Especially important in understanding the significance of Pharaoh's anti-God behavior is the description of the Israelites' remarkable numerical growth highlighted in verse 7. At the very outset of Exodus, the Israelites are presented as fulfilling God's creation mandate for humanity by being fruitful and multiplying and filling the earth (cf. Gen. 1:28). However, they are soon enslaved by a wicked dictator, who malevolently acts to prevent the growth of the Israelite population. Pharaoh's behavior underlines that he stands against the Creator's plans for humanity as revealed in Genesis.

This opposition takes on added significance when we observe that God's creation plan is to dwell with humanity on the earth. As Revelation 21–22 reveals, the greenfield site of Eden is to become a resplendent city where God will live in harmony with his holy people. Tragically, Adam and Eve's betrayal of God in the Garden of Eden creates a major barrier to the fulfillment of God's plan. As the Tower of Babel in Genesis 11:1–9 illustrates, although human beings are innately city builders, their ambitions are decidedly anti-God. Not only does God have no place in Babel, but the city builders foolishly believe that they can access heaven itself by building a tower. Against this background, the call of Abraham anticipates that one day God will establish his holy city on the earth (cf. Heb. 11:8–16). Ironically, in opposition to God, Pharaoh sets the Israelites to building store cities, not for God's glory, but for his own. Yet the book of Exodus ends with the freed Israelites constructing a dwelling place for God on the earth. Released from the grueling task of building "store cities" (*'are misk^enot*; Exod. 1:11), the Israelites construct God's "dwelling place" (*mishkan*; e.g., Exod. 25:9 [NIV: "tabernacle"]). God's release of the Israelites from slavery needs to be seen as part of a larger story.

Teaching the Text

The initial episodes in the book of Exodus set the scene for God's dramatic intervention to rescue the Israelites from slavery in Egypt. Apart from brief references to the midwives fearing God, who in turn rewards them (1:17, 20–21), the contents of chapter 1 focus mainly on Pharaoh's mistreatment of the Israelites. As the antithesis of the one true and living God, Pharaoh is all that God is not. In large measure Exodus 1 reminds us of what the world is like when God is excluded.

The description of Pharaoh's treatment of the Israelites is a chilling reminder of how easily one people group may turn against another, harshly exploiting them under the guise of national interest. From enormous empires to the smallest nations, history teaches us that the attitude of Pharaoh toward the Israelites is not unique. How often have we seen throughout the twentieth and into the twenty-first century ethnic, racial, religious, and national interests resulting in genocide? It is all too easy for one group of people to target another. Suspicion and hatred are easily fueled, especially through fear. Only faith in God can break down the barriers that alienate people from one another.

In reflecting on the events recorded in Exodus 1, it is easy to forget that Pharaoh relied on the support of ordinary Egyptians in order to implement his policies of exploitation, oppression, and genocide. We too may unwittingly be drawn to condone behavior that is inhumane and unjust. Sadly, history reveals that, in situations where one people group has sought to dominate another, too often Christians have failed to identify clearly the evil at work. The promise of security and prosperity dulls and blinds the moral perceptiveness of people. For this reason Christians should ever be alert and quick to respond when governments advocate policies that are deliberately designed to work against the well-being of marginal communities. When such policies are clearly at odds with God's will, Christians must be prepared to take a stand.

Shiphrah and Puah honored God in the stance that they took. If we are to do God's will and see his kingdom come on earth, we must be prepared to stand up for him against hatred and injustice, even at the risk of our lives. On occasions, this may require Christians to engage in acts of civil disobedience in order to obey the moral demands of God. Such action, however, must be carefully and prayerfully undertaken and, if the present passage provides suitable guidance, in a manner that does not inflict harm to others. Not only did God reward Shiphrah and Puah immediately with families, but their names have gone down in history, in marked contrast to the perpetrators of evil.

Illustrating the Text

Throughout history, believers have taken courageous stands for life.

Biography: During World War II, as Jews were being systematically hunted down and marked for death, offering them safe haven meant risking imprisonment and death. Yet Casper ten Boom, when asked why he willingly took such a risk, commented, "It would be an honor to give my life for God's ancient people." Soon after stating this conviction, Casper, his four children, and a nephew were taken into custody after being betrayed as members of the underground in Holland. All told, they had saved an estimated eight hundred Jews. Now they faced the horror of a Nazi prison camp. Only one of Casper's daughters, Corrie, survived. This brave woman went on to inspire millions, sharing a message of God's unfailing love and the power of forgiveness. We never know where a courageous stand will lead us in this life, but we can be sure it is worth any price![3]

When we exclude God, bad things happen.

Story: Share a simple, personal experience of having left out an essential component (for instance, cooking without a key ingredient in a meal, running out of gas). It is easy to see how we do this in the small things; how much more dangerous and tragic it is when we forget the most important Person!

All too often, Christians fail to identify evil at work.

News Story: On a Sunday in February 2014, family members, noticing their absence from church, hurried over to the home of Bill and Ross Parrish, a husband and wife known to the community as loving, warm parents. During the night, as they slept, they and their two children had perished from carbon monoxide poisoning. The news report notes, "Carbon monoxide has no odor, color or taste. It diminishes your ability to absorb oxygen. Symptoms are often mistaken for something else."[4] This is why it is recommended that homes should have a carbon monoxide detector. When the signs are not identified and addressed, the consequences can be tragic. Christians must be alert to the dangerous, subtle creep of evil in our lives and world.

Be prepared to stand up against hatred and injustice, even at the risk of your life.

History: On June 5, 1989, the world outside communist China sat enthralled, watching as one man, holding two shopping bags, stopped a line of tanks headed to Tiananmen Square to break up a student-led freedom protest. This solitary figure has never been identified, yet his stand for freedom has been immortalized.[5] Shiphrah and Puah stood faithfully before an overwhelming and menacing foe. Christians, too, must be ready to stand up against hatred and injustice, even in the face of overwhelming odds and uncertain outcome.

Exodus 1:1–22

What Defines a Person?

Big Idea

Obedience to God should shape one's goals in life.

Key Themes

- God's people must not be seduced by the lure of power, prestige, and wealth.
- Faith in God should instill in his people a desire to care for the victims of human exploitation.
- God is not blind or deaf to the pain of those who are oppressed by others.

Understanding the Text

The Text in Context

Set against the background of Pharaoh's desire to kill all newborn Hebrew boys, Exodus 2 introduces Moses by focusing on three episodes from his early life. In the first of these, we learn of his birth and amazing rescue from death. In the next, we encounter Moses as an adult, deeply concerned for the well-being of his fellow Israelites. In the third episode, we see Moses as a fugitive, living in the land of Midian. These episodes provide important background information prior to God commissioning Moses to lead the Israelites out of Egypt.

The details about Moses's life do more than just explain how an Israelite comes to be herding sheep for a Midianite priest. Linking the three episodes together is the theme of Moses's identity. The first episode raises the issue of his family and ethnic identity. By the end of verse 10, two important questions are raised: Will Moses be the son of his Levite parents or of Pharaoh's daughter? Will Moses be an Israelite or an Egyptian? While the second episode goes some way toward answering these questions, the issue of Moses's identity remains. His "own people" challenge his authority to be their "ruler and judge" (vv. 11, 14). In the third episode, Moses is initially identified ironically as an Egyptian. He then marries a Midianite woman and settles in Midian. Yet he still refers to himself as a "foreigner in a foreign land" (v. 22). Against this checkered history, God's call of Moses in Exodus 3 provides clarity regarding Moses's future identity.

Historical and Cultural Background

The events recorded in Exodus 2 take place in Egypt and the Sinai Peninsula. If the birth of Moses occurred during the reign of Ahmose I (1550–1525 BC), the location of his birth is likely to be the city of Perunefer, where Ahmose I constructed a palace beside an eastern distributary of the Nile. Recent archaeological excavations and surveys provide evidence of an extensive city with a palace and harbor facilities.[1]

The land of "Midian" probably refers to a region around the Gulf of Aqaba, including part of the Sinai Desert. The name of the region may possibly derive from Midian, a son of Abraham and his wife Keturah (Gen. 25:1–2). It is a place of refuge for Moses and lies outside Egyptian control.

Interpretive Insights

2:1–2 *a man of the tribe of Levi married a Levite woman.* An unusual feature of verses 1–10 is the absence of personal names. Only Moses is named, but not until verse 10. Later, in 6:20, the father and mother of Moses are identified as Amram and Jochebed. As for Moses's sister, her name, Miriam, is first given in 15:20. We also learn later that Moses has an older brother, Aaron (4:14; 7:7).

2:3–4 *she got a papyrus basket . . . put it among the reeds along the bank of the Nile.* In the light of Pharaoh's order that every Hebrew baby boy should be thrown into the Nile River, it is ironic that the river is chosen by Moses's mother as the place of refuge. The papyrus "basket" into which Moses is placed is called a *tebah* in Hebrew. Some scholars suggest that there is a deliberate allusion here to the "ark" of Noah, the only other item called a *tebah* in the whole of the Old Testament (cf. Gen. 6:14). However, this may just be coincidental. The use of *tebah* hardly justifies the claim that the first ark is about saving humanity, whereas the second ark is about saving the chosen people.

2:5–8 *Pharaoh's daughter . . . felt sorry for him.* Since Pharaoh has issued the command to his people that they should throw every newborn Hebrew boy into the Nile, it is highly ironic that Pharaoh's daughter should rescue Moses from the river. Her compassion for this Hebrew boy sets her apart from her father.

2:9–10 *"nurse him for me, and I will pay you" . . . he became her son.* The narrative provides another unexpected twist as Pharaoh's daughter instructs Moses's mother to care for him, paying her to do so. Yet verse 10 introduces an unforeseen dimension, for Pharaoh's daughter claims Moses as her own; he becomes "her son."

She named him Moses. The name Moses is undoubtedly of Egyptian origin and means "born of," implying "child of." It comes often as an element within

Egyptian personal names (e.g., Ahmose—"child of Ah"; Thutmose—"child of Thoth"; Rameses—"child of Ra"), although it may have been used as a name in its own right. In the case of Moses, no special parentage is noted. The author of Exodus creates a wordplay on the name Moses when he describes how Pharaoh's daughter said, "I drew him out of the water." The verb "to draw out" resembles the name Moses. It is highly unlikely, however, that Pharaoh's daughter based the name Moses on the Hebrew verb. Would she have spoken Hebrew? Possibly all that is being claimed here is that she had the right to name him because she saved him from the water.

2:11–14 *he went out to where his own people were.* In spite of having grown up within the royal household, Moses distances himself from the oppressive regime of Pharaoh. He refers to the Israelites as "his brothers" (NIV: "his own people"). However, his fellow Israelites seem less inclined to accept Moses as one of their own, especially when he intervenes in a dispute. In the light of subsequent developments, the question "Who made you ruler and judge over us?" (v. 14) is highly ironic (cf. 18:13, 22).

he killed the Egyptian and hid him. Moses is passionate about caring for others, but his own attempt to bring justice results in the death of an Egyptian. While Moses will eventually deliver the Israelites from slavery in Egypt, this will be achieved through God's power, not human endeavor. Moses's action in killing the Egyptian is not presented as a model for others to follow.

2:16–18 *a priest of Midian had seven daughters.* In spite of Moses's flight from Egypt, his social conscience remains active. The "priest of Midian" is called Reuel, which means "friend of God." He is also named Jethro (3:1). While there is no evidence in Exodus 2 to suggest that Reuel worships the Lord, he is later supportive of Moses returning to Egypt (4:18) and subsequently celebrates the divine rescue of the enslaved Israelites (18:1–12). This latter passage confirms that Jethro publicly acknowledges the Lord's sovereignty due to his rescue of the Israelites from Egypt. However, the extent and nature of Jethro's faith in God remains unclear.

2:19–21 *An Egyptian rescued us from the shepherds.* The description of Moses as an Egyptian is understandable but ironic in the light of preceding events.

2:22–23 *Moses named him Gershom.* The name given to Gershom is noteworthy because it alludes to Moses's status as a foreign resident in Midian. The Hebrew noun *ger* is used to denote someone who has settled as a foreigner in another country. In Genesis, the patriarchs are perceived as foreigners in Canaan (e.g., Gen. 17:8; 19:9; 21:23; 23:4; 28:4; 37:1). Even Lot is viewed by the men of Sodom as a *ger* (Gen. 19:9). As the opening chapters of Exodus reveal, foreigners are vulnerable to exploitation. For this reason, and in the light of their own experience, God warns the Israelites not to oppress anyone who is a *ger* (Exod. 22:21; 23:9). Building on this, Moses later instructs the Israelites that they are to "love those who are foreigners, for you yourselves were foreigners in Egypt" (Deut. 10:19). By naming his son Gershom, Moses underlines his sense of separation from his own people, the Israelites.

During that long period, the king of Egypt died. Exodus 7:7 records that Moses was eighty years old when God called him to return to Egypt. According to Stephen in the book of Acts, Moses spent forty years in Midian (Acts 7:30). Since the text of Exodus is less specific, Stephen must have had access to extrabiblical traditions for this fact about Moses. The same is true for other information recorded in the New Testament concerning the exodus period (cf. 1 Cor. 10:8; 2 Tim. 3:8). We should not assume that the death of the Pharaoh comes at the end of Moses's time in Midian.

2:24 *he remembered his covenant with Abraham.* Reference is made to the covenant that God established with the patriarchs. This is probably an allusion to the covenant of circumcision initiated in Genesis 17 (cf. Exod. 6:4).

Theological Insights

For most of Exodus 1–2 God remains in the background. Nevertheless, he is fully aware of how the Israelites are being oppressed. He hears their groaning and their cries for help. Consequently, he will intervene on their behalf, as he predicted to Abraham centuries earlier (Gen. 15:13–14). God remains ever faithful to the commitments he makes. His redemptive plan will be fulfilled in his time and way.

Teaching the Text

The brief account of Moses's life prior to God's call provides an opportunity for us to reflect on the influences and choices that shape us as people. From observing Moses, we may learn something of how God expects us to live our lives.

Rejecting power, prestige, and wealth. How easy it would have been for Moses to see himself as an Egyptian and take advantage of his unique status as the son of Pharaoh's daughter. As the author of Hebrews reminds us, Moses "chose to be mistreated along with the people of God rather than to enjoy the fleeting pleasures of sin" (Heb. 11:25). Similarly, Christians often face a choice about where they will place their loyalty. Jesus recognized this and warned his followers of the need to prioritize their commitment to him before every other commitment. This applies not only to family relationships and ethnic identity but also to the acquisition of wealth. With good reason, Jesus challenges the rich young ruler to sell his possessions and be generous to the poor (Matt. 19:21; Mark 10:21; Luke 18:22). As Christians, we need courage and discernment if we are to avoid letting the world squeeze us into its mold. We are called to be servants, not those who lord over others.

Identifying with the underdog. Living for Jesus requires a willingness to stand up for the oppressed. In doing so, however, we must be careful that our actions do not in turn oppress others. To stand for equality and justice is never easy, and there will always be opposition. In challenging injustice, we must be careful that we do not leave ourselves open to the charge of doing wrong. By killing the Egyptian, Moses undermines his authority as a liberator. To his fellow Israelites it appears that Moses wants to be their ruler and judge.

Living as exiles. Moses is very conscious that he lives as a foreign resident in Midian. The book of Hebrews highlights how Abraham placed his faith in the city whose architect and builder is God. He viewed himself as a resident alien in a world that had no place for God (Heb. 11:8–10). We too as Christians need to appreciate that like Abraham our inheritance is a city that has yet to come, the new Jerusalem. As we await Christ's return in glory, we are called to be in the world but not of the world.

Illustrating the Text

Christians often face a choice about where to place their loyalty.

Church History: In the early years of the fourth century, the Roman emperor Diocletian inaugurated the Great Persecution against the church. While Christians had long been subject to persecution and injustices, these had usually been local or regional in nature. Diocletian, however, issued a series of empire-wide edicts, destroying Christian property rights, burning sacred texts, demolishing buildings, denying Christians' right of appeal, and imprisoning clergy. After the carnage, Diocletian issued a final edict, an amnesty. All arrested Christians could be freed. They only had to do one thing: sacrifice to the Roman gods. What would you have done?

We need courage and discernment to avoid letting the world squeeze us into its mold.

Props: Bring Play-Doh, a rock, and a mold or cookie cutter. Demonstrate how the Play-Doh can be easily shaped by the cutter or mold, and contrast this with the lack of malleability of the rock. (Alternatively, a wooden cross could be substituted for the rock, further emphasizing our Christ-defined shape.) Are we weak, being shaped by the world, or firm, holding strong? It depends what we are made of. What are the essential elements of our faith? Are they soft and weak conviction, or strong, rooted in the unshakable rock of God's Word?

In standing against oppression, be careful not to, in turn, oppress others.

Literature: *Animal Farm*, **by George Orwell.** A familiar theme in twentieth-century literature is the idea that the oppressed revolutionary often becomes the oppressive dictator. In a century wracked by wars and wrecked by the utopian promises of communism, there are myriad examples of this truism operative in real life. In his classic work *Animal Farm*, Orwell fictionalizes the rise of farm animals against their overlord. The revolution begins with dreams of equality and shared prosperity. It ends with some animals being "more equal than others," as one of the beloved beasts is carted off to a glue factory so that the "new bosses" can live in luxury. (The final four paragraphs of this classic tale are a particularly powerful climax.)

Christians' inheritance is a city that is yet to come, the new Jerusalem.

Science: In the 1960s, psychologist Walter Mischel at Stanford University conducted a series of experiments on the power of delayed gratification. Children were given one marshmallow, which they could choose to eat immediately or refrain from eating for several minutes. Those who delayed would be given another marshmallow. Mischel followed up with these children in adolescence and learned that those who had exercised self-control scored higher in aptitude tests and were generally noted as superior students. As believers, we are called to willingly lay aside the immediate pleasures of this fading world for the great treasures of the eternal kingdom.

An Awe-Inspiring God

Big Idea

The call of Moses provides an opportunity to witness the awe-inspiring nature of the God who invites us to serve him and other people.

Key Themes

- The God of grace may break into people's lives when they least expect him to do so.
- God's salvation is based on his prior promises and his ability to fulfill them.
- God's presence with us should transform the way we view the challenges he sets before us.

Understanding the Text

The Text in Context

After juxtaposing Moses's departure to Midian (2:11–22) and the Lord's concern for the oppressed Israelites (2:23–25), the Exodus narrative describes in chapter 3 how God commissions Moses to lead the Israelites out of Egypt. The setting for the encounter between God and Moses is significant, for Moses will later lead the Israelites back to this location in the Sinai Peninsula.

A lengthy and significant dialogue takes place in Exodus 3:4–4:17, setting the agenda for subsequent chapters. In the first half of the conversation, God informs Moses of his plans to settle the Israelites in the land of Canaan in fulfillment of his promises to the patriarchs.

Historical and Cultural Background

The events in Exodus 3 take place at "Mount Sinai," although this designation is not introduced until 19:11. At this stage, the location is merely described as the "mountain of God" and linked to the name Horeb (3:1). From the context, it seems likely that Horeb is a region within the southern part of the Sinai Peninsula. Whereas "Horeb" denotes a wider area, "Mount Sinai" designates a specific mountain. The precise location of Mount Sinai is debated, but one strong possibility is Jebel Musa. According to Deuteronomy

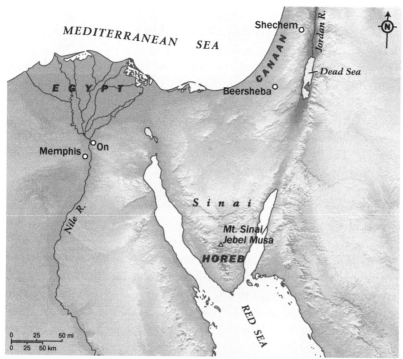

The "Mountain of God" (3:1) is later named Mount Sinai. Jebel Musa, in the southern Sinai Peninsula, is a probable location of Mount Sinai.

1:2, "It takes eleven days to go from Horeb to Kadesh Barnea by the Mount Seir road."

Interpretive Insights

3:1 *tending the flock of Jethro . . . came to Horeb, the mountain of God.* By this point in time Moses has taken on the role of shepherd. He brings Jethro's flock to Horeb, a region in the west of Midian. By describing the location as "the mountain of God"—that is, Mount Sinai—the narrative prepares for the theophany that is about to take place, as well as anticipating the grander theophany that will occur later when Moses returns with the Israelites (Exod. 19).

3:2–4 *the angel of the* LORD *appeared to him in flames of fire.* In this context, "the angel of the LORD" is probably a manifestation of God himself, rather than a messenger sent by God, although the evidence is open to debate. The fact that the ground around the bush becomes holy favors the idea that God himself is present; an angel-messenger is unlikely to have made the ground holy. There is no solid basis, however, to assume that "the angel of the LORD" is the preincarnate Christ. The expression "in flames of fire" is perhaps better translated "as a flame of fire." Here, as elsewhere in Exodus, God's presence is marked by fire and smoke (e.g., 13:21–22; 14:24; 19:18; 40:38).

3:5 *Take off your sandals.* God's presence makes the bush and the immediately surrounding area holy. Later, the entire mountain will be designated holy, when God appears before the Israelites (Exod. 19–24). By removing his footwear Moses possibly expresses an attitude of humility or respect in God's presence. Alternatively, being barefoot may be required due to the holiness of the ground. It seems likely that the Aaronic priests served barefoot within the tabernacle. The importance of being holy in order to be in God's presence is highlighted especially in the book of Leviticus.

3:6 *I am . . . the God of Abraham, the God of Isaac and the God of Jacob.* God identifies himself to Moses by referring to the patriarchs of Genesis. This provides a historical context that enables Moses immediately to know something about the person speaking to him.

3:7–10 *I have indeed seen the misery of my people in Egypt.* God has come not merely to rescue his people; he will bring them into the land of Canaan, transforming their suffering into joy. While in verses 7–9 the focus is on God's actions—note the repeated use of "I"—verse 10 introduces Moses's role in this.

a land flowing with milk and honey. The Hebrew term for "honey" probably refers not to the produce of bees but rather to "sweet syrup" from grapes, dates, and figs. The fertility of the promised land will be suitable for both animal husbandry and horticulture.

3:11 *Who am I . . . ?* The issue of Moses's identity has featured prominently in Exodus 2. As a fugitive from Egypt, Moses questions his ability to lead the Israelites out of Egypt. Given his killing of an Egyptian slave master, he is likely to be persona non grata with the Egyptians, and given his upbringing in the Egyptian court, the Israelites may well view him with suspicion.

3:12 *I will be with you.* "I will be" translates the Hebrew word *'ehyeh*, a key term in verse 14, where it is rendered "I AM." Signs will figure prominently in the chapters leading up to the Passover. However, the sign given here to Moses requires him to trust and obey God first before it will be fulfilled.

3:13–17 *What is his name?* Moses asks concerning God's name. In Genesis a variety of names are associated with God: *'el 'elyon* ("God Most High"; 14:18–20); *'el ro'i* ("God who sees me"; 16:13); *'el shadday* ("God Almighty"; 17:1); *'el 'olam* ("Eternal God"; 21:33); *'el bet-'el* ("the God of Bethel"; 31:13); *pahad yitshaq* ("Fear of Isaac"; 31:42, 53). Possibly Moses is hoping that God will reveal to him a new epithet, disclosing some special facet of God's nature. In the ancient Near East, different names attributed to a god were one way of describing the character and nature of the deity. The Israelites might possibly expect something like this if Moses has been called by God to be their leader.

I AM WHO I AM. . . . "I AM has sent me to you." God's response is enigmatic. He says in Hebrew *'ehyeh 'asher 'ehyeh*, "I AM WHO I AM." The interpretation of this remark has generated considerable discussion.[1] Most likely it conveys the idea that God will be who he is—that is, his nature does not change. This unusual expression underlines that knowledge of God comes not simply from the name attached to him but from what he does.

In verse 14 God instructs Moses to say, "I AM has sent me to you." In verse 15 God expands on this by saying, "The LORD . . . has sent me to you." "LORD" translates the Hebrew word *yhwh*, which is often pronounced "Yahweh." Out of reverence for the divine name, Jews later avoided saying *yhwh* by substituting the Hebrew word *'adonay*, which means "lord." The words *'ehyeh* and *yhwh* are related. If *'ehyeh* means "I am," *yhwh* is the equivalent "he is." Consequently, while God himself will say *'ehyeh*, "I AM," other people will say, *yhwh*, "HE IS." Already in Genesis, God has made himself known as *yhwh*, "LORD" (Gen. 15:7; 28:13; cf. 4:26).

3:19–20 *the king of Egypt will not let you go unless a mighty hand compels him.* The motif of "hand" reappears in subsequent chapters (e.g., 7:4–5; 9:3, 15; 13:3, 14, 16). In Egypt references to the "hand" of Pharaoh pointed to his authority and power.[2]

3:21–22 *I will make the Egyptians favorably disposed toward this people.* As compensation for the years of hard labor, God will cause the Egyptians to be generous when the Israelite women request items of silver and gold and clothing. The inference is that these items are given freely and not under duress. Moses later instructs the Israelites to do this (11:2–3), and the fulfillment is recorded in 12:35–36.

Theological Insights

As God chooses Moses to confront Pharaoh on his behalf and makes his plan known to him, we get a vivid insight into God's nature. Apart from a sense of his holiness, we witness something of his compassion for those who are suffering, his faithfulness to earlier promises, his patience with a reluctant Moses, and his concern for the future well-being of the Israelites.

Teaching the Text

Through Moses's encounter with God at the burning bush we can understand different aspects of God's nature. Without being fully comprehensive, we can learn the following about God from this passage.

God takes the initiative to make himself known. God manifests his presence to Moses, disclosing something of his holy nature. Likewise, in Jesus Christ, God displays his glory for us to see. To know God personally we are totally dependent on God making himself known to us. Thankfully, through Scripture God graciously continues to reveal himself to people.

Encountering the awe-inspiring holiness of God is a humbling event. Moses removes his sandals and hides his face as an act of respect in the presence of God. We too should remember the majestic glory of God when we come to worship him, recalling that corporately the church is the new temple where God is present (Eph. 2:21–22).

God promises to be ever present with his children. God reassures Moses that he will be with him throughout the whole process of rescuing the Israelites from Pharaoh's control and bringing them to Mount Sinai. We cannot presume to be in the role of Moses and so take this promise for success and guidance as one made to us in whatever we undertake. Nevertheless, it is worth recalling that the final words of Jesus to his disciples contain the promise: "And surely I am with you always, to the very end of the age" (Matt. 28:20). The assurance of God's presence with us should be an encouragement when we confront difficult situations in our lives.

The heart of God is concerned with rescuing enslaved people. God has seen the affliction and heard the cries of the Israelites as the Egyptians have exploited them. He is not oblivious to their suffering and is determined to deliver them from the grueling hardship of their daily labor. In a similar way, Christ brings freedom to those who are enslaved by the devil and sin. As John records:

> To the Jews who had believed him, Jesus said, "If you hold to my teaching, you are really my disciples. Then you will know the truth, and the truth will set you free."
>
> They answered him, "We are Abraham's descendants and have never been slaves of anyone. How can you say that we shall be set free?"
>
> Jesus replied, "Very truly I tell you, everyone who sins is a slave to sin. Now a slave has no permanent place in the family, but a son belongs to it forever. So if the Son sets you free, you will be free indeed." (John 8:31–36)

As Christians, it is important for us to live in the liberty that Christ gives us, not bound by guilt or evil habits.

God promises a better future. God's plans for the Israelites entail not merely their rescue from oppression in Egypt but their safe settlement in the land of Canaan. With God salvation is about more than just being set free; it anticipates something much better. For this reason, the author of Hebrews encourages his readers to set their hope on "the city that is to come" (Heb. 13:14), where they will live in God's presence in a world untainted by evil.

Illustrating the Text

For us to know God personally, he must reveal himself to us.

Film: Many adventure stories begin with the main character living a humdrum, "village" kind of life: small town, boring chores, average family, safe. Then someone interrupts the character's existence and calls them into an adventure they had never anticipated (e.g., *Lord of the Rings*, *Star Wars*, *Harry Potter*). Have you ever wondered what their lives would have been like if they had never been interrupted? Luke Skywalker would have probably inherited Uncle Owen's moisture farm. Frodo Baggins likely would have stayed at Bag End, growing fat and bored. Harry Potter might have ended up living as a grumpy, undereducated Muggle working at a local factory.

Everywhere we look, we see that God is seeking to "interrupt" our story. He reveals himself in the world he has made. He reveals himself in the gospel and Scripture. Through all these avenues of revelation, God is providing us an opportunity to inhabit his story.

We should remember God's majesty when we come to worship him.

Scenario: Have you ever wondered what it would be like to work at a place like the Vatican Museum? Imagine working in a place that combines some of the most majestic art ever conceived with an architectural setting memorializing centuries of pure genius. Initially, you would go to work each day overawed by the beauty of the architecture, art, and history of the place. Eventually, however, it might become just another job. Overfamiliarity can breed apathy. With God, however, it is not an overabundance of experience that would lead us to take his majesty for granted; it is a failure to behold it.

God's promise to be with us brings encouragement in difficult situations.

Lyrics: *"You Never Let Go,"* by Matt Redman. In this song, Redman celebrates the reality that God is with us through every situation. This assurance allows us to walk through any valley with the confidence that we need fear no evil.

Testimony: This point could be wonderfully illustrated by having someone share a testimony of God's presence in the midst of struggle. This could be conducted as an interview, presented live, or prerecorded on video. Here are three points you could ask the person to consider: (1) Please tell us about a time of struggle you experienced. (2) In the midst of this struggle, how did you see God's hand at work? (3) What is one thing you learned about God, having experienced this struggle?

The Greatest Sign of All

Big Idea

God graciously addresses the skepticism of unbelief by providing supernatural signs that point to him.

Key Themes

- Deeply ingrained within all of us is a latent unwillingness to obey God's call on our lives.
- God challenges the skepticism of people through extraordinary signs that demonstrate the reality of his existence.

Understanding the Text

The Text in Context

God's conversation with Moses continues in Exodus 4. By this stage, the Lord has already set out his plans for the Israelites' future settlement in the land of Canaan and issued instructions to Moses. Attention now switches to Moses and his reluctance to accept God's commission. God addresses two reasons put forward by Moses for not returning to Egypt. The first of these concerns the issue of persuading the Israelites that God has sent Moses to them. In response, God provides Moses with three supernatural signs, which Moses is to perform before the Israelites. Moses's second objection concerns his inability to speak fluently. God reassures Moses that he will equip him with the ability to speak, but Moses remains stubbornly reluctant to obey. By this stage, God's irritation at Moses's objections becomes evident. As a final concession, God promises Moses the assistance of his brother, Aaron. By the end of Exodus 4 we see that everything promised by God enables Moses to persuade the Israelite elders that God has sent him. Seeing the signs, they believe and worship.

The reports of God's call of Moses and his acceptance by the Israelites are separated by a number of short paragraphs that narrate (1) the support of his Midianite relatives (vv. 18–20), (2) further information about Pharaoh's reluctance to release the Israelites (vv. 21–23), (3) an incident involving circumcision (vv. 24–26), and (4) Moses's reunion with Aaron (vv. 27–28). The brevity of these episodes possibly indicates that Moses did not delay in obeying

God's call. Alternatively, they are deliberately kept brief so as not to distract from the main story line.

Historical and Cultural Background

Exodus 4:24–26 records a very unusual incident involving the circumcision of Moses's son by Zipporah, his Midianite wife. The brief details reported suggest that this reflects an ancient tradition. Within the context of Exodus, circumcision recalls the eternal covenant that God established with Abraham in Genesis 17. This covenant is exceptionally important because it concerns not only Abraham's immediate descendants but the nations of the earth. Very deliberately God changes Abram's name to Abraham because he is to be "the father of many nations" (Gen. 17:4–5). Through the emphasis on the importance of circumcision both here and at the Passover (Exod. 12:43–49), God's deliverance of the Israelites from the diabolical control of Pharaoh is presented as part of something much larger.

Interpretive Insights

4:2–5 *"A staff" . . . became a snake.* This is the first of three supernatural signs that God gives to Moses. His shepherd staff becomes a "snake" (*nahash*). Later, in Pharaoh's presence the staff will become a *tannin* (perhaps a snake, but more likely a crocodile; see comments on 7:9–13). Moses's staff is referred to as "the staff of God" (4:20). In the ancient world, a staff or rod was sometimes a symbol of authority derived from a deity. When Moses or Aaron uses this staff, it symbolizes God's authority and power at work (e.g., 9:20; 10:12, 21–22; 17:5, 9, 11). In the episodes to come Moses's staff is often associated with the supernatural signs that God sends (e.g., 7:9–10, 19–20; 8:5; 9:23).

4:6–8 *"Put your hand inside your cloak" . . . the skin was leprous.* The second sign involves the transformation of the skin on Moses's arm. There is no reason to assume that Moses contracts leprosy, that is, Hansen's disease. The Hebrew term *metsora'at* ("leprous") probably refers to flaky skin. Unlike the first and third signs, there is no record of this sign being performed in Pharaoh's presence.

4:9 *The water . . . will become blood.* The third sign involves water being changed into blood. Moses and Aaron will later demonstrate this sign before Pharaoh, but on a much larger scale (7:15–24). It is noteworthy that whereas the Israelites believe Moses because of these signs (4:30–31), Pharaoh remains entirely unpersuaded by them. This contrast reflects Pharaoh's stubborn opposition to God.

4:10–12 *I have never been eloquent . . . I am slow of speech and tongue.* There is no reason to doubt Moses's self-description. We may assume that he suffered from a speech defect. Less likely is the suggestion that his words mean he was no longer fluent in the Egyptian language. God's response indicates that he has the power to overcome Moses's deficiency. The form of the Hebrew verb "makes" (*sam*) in verse 11 possibly indicates that God merely claims that he has the power to influence hearing, speaking, and seeing. His remark need not be interpreted as stating that he is fully responsible for every instance of human disability.[1]

4:13–17 *Pardon your servant, Lord. Please send someone else.* Although Moses attempts to decline God's invitation as politely as possible, his words anger God, with good reason. Moses has a brother, Aaron, who is three years older (7:7). As Moses communicates, as a prophet, what God says, so Aaron will communicate what Moses says. In 7:1 Aaron is actually described as Moses's prophet.

4:18–20 *Moses went back to Jethro his father-in-law.* In spite of the brevity of verse 18, we need not suppose that Moses did not relate to Jethro all that God had said to him. God's words in verse 19 reassure Moses that it is safe for him to take his family back to Egypt.

4:21–23 *I will harden his heart.* These verses introduce the motif of Pharaoh's heart being hard. The biblical concept of a hard heart is quite different from that of modern usage. We consider a hard heart to signify a lack of compassion, a heart that is cruel. In ancient Israel, a hard heart symbolized determination or resolve. A hard heart could be either positive or negative, depending on the circumstances. It could indicate either a strong determination to stand firm or an obstinate unwillingness to change direction. The motif of Pharaoh's heart appears repeatedly throughout the episodes in Exodus 7–11. (The significance of this is discussed more fully in the "Theological Insights" in the unit on 8:20–10:29.)

4:24–26 *Zipporah took a flint knife, cut off her son's foreskin and touched Moses' feet.* This short incident continues to baffle commentators, for the Hebrew text contains various ambiguities. It probably describes how Zipporah circumcises Gershom and prevents Moses from being killed by God. Moses's failure to circumcise his son excludes Gershom from the covenant that God initiated with Abraham (Gen. 17), the very covenant that underpins the divine deliverance of the Israelites from slavery (Exod. 2:24; 6:4–5). Furthermore, coming immediately after a reference to the death of Pharaoh's "firstborn son" (v. 23), this episode possibly anticipates the Passover, when only those firstborn males who are circumcised are saved from death.

4:27–28 *he met Moses at the mountain of God.* Moses and Aaron are reunited at Mount Sinai, "the mountain of God." Once more attention is drawn to the significance of this location.

4:29–31 *Moses and Aaron brought together all the elders of the Israelites.* The story jumps to Egypt, where Moses and Aaron are received favorably.

The brevity of the narrative suggests that Moses's earlier reservations were misplaced. When the Israelites see the signs, they immediately believe that God has sent him.

Theological Insights

In spite of all that God says, Moses remains fearful that the Israelites will not believe him. In response the Lord gives him three signs designed to convince the people that God has sent him. Signs like these are rarely used by God to persuade people directly. In this instance, they are meant to authenticate Moses and his message. Similar and additional signs will be performed before Pharaoh, but he will stubbornly refuse to recognize that Moses has been commissioned by God and thus speaks with God's authority when he requests the release of the Israelites. Scripture teaches that not everyone who claims to speak for God does so. Signs are, therefore, used on limited occasions to confirm that an individual has been chosen by God for special service (cf. 1 Kings 17:22–24; John 2:11, 23).

Teaching the Text

Skepticism regarding belief in God has grown in Western society throughout the twentieth century and into the twenty-first century. This reflects an underlying desire for human autonomy that stretches back to Adam and Eve in the Garden of Eden. We witness the extent of this in Genesis 11 when those responsible for constructing the Tower of Babel either exclude God from their plans or seek to manipulate him for their own benefit (vv. 1–9). Over the centuries, little has changed as people turn their backs on the one true and living God. In the light of this, God occasionally does something extraordinary to encourage people to believe in him. The events leading up to the Israelites' release from slavery are part of one such occasion. Through a series of signs and wonders, God makes himself known. All this begins when Moses first goes to the Israelites, for they too need signs in order to believe.

Signs of judgment in Exodus. A survey of the Bible reveals that God only rarely uses signs and wonders to persuade people to believe in him. Since this is not a regular occurrence, those occasions when God intervenes in a supernatural way stand out as special. This is so regarding the deliverance of the Israelites from slavery in Egypt. The exodus is one of the major landmarks in the biblical story of salvation. Importantly, the account of the Israelites' deliverance from Egypt provides a paradigm of divine salvation. While significant in its own way, the Israelite exodus from Egypt anticipates an even greater exodus that will be achieved through Jesus Christ.

Signs of salvation in John. To draw out the exodus connection with Jesus, the apostle John records a series of signs in his Gospel that are meant to authenticate the one who has been sent by God. After the first of these, which involves changing water into wine, John comments that because of this sign "his disciples believed in him" (John 2:11). Interestingly, the next reference to signs associates them with the Passover: "Now while he was in Jerusalem at the Passover Festival, many people saw the signs he was performing and believed in his name" (John 2:23; cf. 4:48; 6:30; 12:37). Of all the signs recorded in Scripture, the resurrection of Jesus is the ultimate sign of divine power. With good reason, Christians place their hope not in a crucified Jesus but in a resurrected Lord and Savior.

The apostle John understands well that God does not perform miraculous signs all the time in order for people to believe in him. For this reason he records the signs associated with Jesus. As John states: "Jesus performed many other signs in the presence of his disciples, which are not recorded in this book. But these are written that you may believe that Jesus is the Messiah, the Son of God, and that by believing you may have life in his name" (John 20:30–31). The signs and wonders in Egypt foreshadow those performed by Jesus, who lays down his life as a Passover sacrifice, so that those who believe in him may have eternal life.

Illustrating the Text

God occasionally does something extraordinary to encourage people to believe in him.

Quote: *A Wind in the House of Islam,* by David Garrison. Garrison traces the surprising work of the Holy Spirit taking place across the Muslim world. He shares the news of one colleague, who has heard

> countless testimonies of dreams in which a "being who shone bright as light" appeared to them, beckoning them to come to him. In a recent encounter with a Muslim man who had experienced such a dream, my colleague simply opened his Bible to the story of Christ's transfiguration in Matthew 17. . . . Startled by the discovery, the Muslim responded, "That's the guy, the guy in my dreams! Who is this?"[2]

God works in mysterious, miraculous ways to draw people into his family.

The exodus from Egypt anticipates an even greater exodus achieved through Christ.

Statistics: According to the 2014 Global Slavery Index, an estimated 35.8 million people are enslaved around the globe.[3] This number includes people forced to labor against their will, trapped in sex trades, and generally taken against their will for exploitation by others. For a moment, consider the plight of these people. As stark as the total numbers are, the plight of even one person in this horrible situation is beyond imagining. God's concern, and ours, is for freedom for the oppressed, and we should work tirelessly toward that end. Imagine the joy that could come to those exploited and trapped today, a joy like that of the Israelites as they were freed from bondage in Egypt. It is also remarkable how many of those enslaved today are often unnoticed. Many in our world today live in unseen and often unacknowledged slavery to sin and death, slavery from which they can be freed through Jesus, who won an even greater freedom.

The resurrection of Jesus is the ultimate sign of divine power.

Bible: 1 Corinthians 15. Paul tells the Corinthian Christians that if Christ did not rise from the dead, "your faith is futile; you are still in your sins. Then those also who have fallen asleep in Christ are lost. If only for this life we have hope in Christ, we are of all people most to be pitied" (1 Cor. 15:17–19). Why such a bleak "if . . . then" logic? Because the resurrection is the ultimate, space-time, real-world demonstration that God is powerful and poised to put death in its place. If that keystone event is a fabrication, then any claims for our resurrection are just wishful thinking.

Overcoming Obstacles on God's Road to Freedom

Big Idea

In the light of opposition, God's people should find encouragement in his promises and the future hope to which they point.

Key Themes

- Due to the presence of evil in the world, there is always opposition to God and his plans.
- Rejection and persecution often lead to discouragement among those serving God.

Understanding the Text

The Text in Context

The account of God's rescue of the Israelites develops slowly as Moses and Aaron encounter opposition. As instructed by God, Moses and Aaron go to Pharaoh to request that the Israelites be permitted to sacrifice to the Lord in the wilderness. However, Pharaoh's reaction is not what they expected. Accusing the Israelites of being lazy, he adds to their suffering by demanding that they gather stubble in order to make bricks of clay. Disheartened, the Israelite foremen vent their anger by confronting Moses and Aaron. In frustration, Moses questions God's plan for the release of the Israelites.

Historical and Cultural Background

Although the book of Exodus plays down the idea of Pharaoh being a god, this was the status attributed to the Egyptian king. Consequently, he exercised absolute authority over his people. To challenge Pharaoh's authority not only required tremendous courage, but it was also a rejection of Egyptian beliefs regarding the gods who supposedly maintained order over their society and promised them well-being.

Interpretive Insights

5:1-3 *Moses and Aaron went to Pharaoh.* Probably encouraged by the positive response of the Israelites (4:29–31), Moses and Aaron go to the Egyptian king as instructed by God. Although in verse 1 Moses and Aaron claim to report what God said, they appear to modify God's original words (3:18). Their message comes across as a blunt demand rather than a polite request. Moreover, they initially make no mention of a three-day journey, and they speak of celebrating a festival to the Lord, rather than offering sacrifices. Ironically, when they are challenged by Pharaoh, their response in verse 3 echoes more closely God's original instructions. Yet even here they add something new, stating that God will strike the Israelites with disease or the sword if they fail to obey him. In saying this, Moses and Aaron portray God as fierce and vindictive.

I do not know the LORD. Pharaoh's response in verse 2 is noteworthy, highlighting one of the major themes in the book of Exodus. His question, "Who is the LORD, that I should obey him and let Israel go?" introduces the concept of knowing God, a motif that recurs frequently in subsequent chapters (e.g., 6:7; 7:5, 17; 8:10, 22; 9:14). At this stage Pharaoh expresses ignorance of Israel's God, but subsequent events will gradually enlighten him. The Israelites too will learn much about the Lord, but more important, they will come to know him in a personal way. To have knowledge about the Lord is not sufficient; we must know him personally.

I will not let Israel go. Pharaoh's initial reaction to Moses signals his intransigence. He is not prepared to concede anything to the enslaved Israelites, even though God's request is quite limited, requiring the Israelites to cease working for only a short period of time. Pharaoh will persist in refusing God's demand that the Israelites should be permitted to worship him in the wilderness.

5:4-5 *why are you taking the people away from their labor?* If Moses and Aaron hoped to gain Pharaoh's sympathy by portraying God as vindictive in verse 3, they have failed. Pharaoh, who was viewed as a deity, is not prepared to grant the wish of an unknown, foreign god.

5:6-14 *You are no longer to supply the people with straw for making bricks.* The Delta region of Egypt lacks natural stone for building. Consequently, bricks made of clay mixed with straw are essential for constructing buildings. Conscripted to manufacture bricks, the Israelites are supervised by foremen from within their own population. The Hebrew term denoting these foremen (NIV: "overseers," vv. 6, 10, 14, 15, 19) suggests that they were record keepers or scribes. They in turn are answerable to Egyptian overseers. To add to the burden of brick making, the Israelites have to scavenge for "stubble," rather than gathering "straw" (v. 12). Not surprisingly, they struggle to meet their quota of bricks. Because it is attached to the ground, stubble is much more difficult to collect than straw.

5:20–21 *May the* LORD *look on you and judge you!* The Lord sent Moses and Aaron to rescue the Israelites from slavery, but ironically the foremen call on the Lord to punish Moses and Aaron for making their lives even more difficult.

5:22–6:1 *because of my mighty hand he will drive them out of his country.* By indicating that Pharaoh will "drive them out of his country," God confirms that the future of the Israelites lies outside the land of Egypt. Pharaoh will do more than merely allow them to go into the wilderness for three days.

6:2–8 God's speech to Moses falls naturally into two parts. Verses 2–5 are addressed to Moses himself, whereas verses 6–8 record God's message for the Israelites. Four times God repeats the phrase "I am the LORD" (vv. 2, 6, 7, 8) with two of these framing his message to the Israelites. The repeated use of God's personal name, Yahweh (translated as "the LORD"), is significant, especially given Pharaoh's earlier question, "Who is the LORD [Yahweh]?" (5:2).

6:2–5 *by my name the* LORD *I did not make myself fully known to them.* The interpretation of verse 3 has prompted much discussion.[1] The wording of some English translations implies that the patriarchs did not know God's personal name Yahweh ("the LORD"). For example, the ESV reads: "I appeared to Abraham, to Isaac, and to Jacob, as God Almighty, but by my name the LORD I did not make myself known to them." However, this seems to contradict what Genesis says, because the patriarchs did know the name of Yahweh (e.g., Gen. 15:7). The NIV translation of verse 3 reflects an alternative approach. According to this interpretation, the patriarchs of Genesis knew God's personal name Yahweh ("the LORD"), but they did not understand all that it meant. Now through the exodus God will make himself known more fully. Although it is undoubtedly true that the events in Egypt reveal more about God, the Hebrew text of verse 3 does not explicitly say, "know fully." Consequently, it may be preferable to adopt an alternative translation for the second half of the verse: "My name is Yahweh [the LORD]. Did I not make myself known to them?"[2] Whichever interpretation is adopted, verses 3–5 stress that the divine deliverance of the Israelites from slavery in Egypt is part of a much larger process that builds on God's promises to the patriarchs.

I have remembered my covenant. Looking to the past, God underlines for Moses his commitment to the covenant established with the patriarchs, beginning with Abraham in Genesis 17. Through the everlasting covenant of circumcision God assured the patriarchs that their descendants would inherit the land of Canaan (Gen. 17:8). God emphasizes to Moses that he will be faithful to this commitment.

6:6–8 *I will free you from being slaves . . . I will redeem you.* In verses 6–8 God lists how he will help the Israelites. The focus in God's speech shifts from the past to the future. Throughout his message for the Israelites the emphasis is on what God himself will do; note the frequent use of "I." The Lord's words move from speaking of liberation from slavery, to the establishment of a special relationship with God, to taking possession of the land of Canaan. His words in verses 6–8, oriented toward the future, are clearly intended to reassure the Israelites. Of particular note is God's reference to redeeming the enslaved Israelites. The Hebrew verb *ga'al,* "to redeem," is often associated with a family member who comes to the assistance of a relative in need. This could entail rescuing a relative who has become a debt slave because of poverty. Since God speaks of Israel as his son (4:22), he may be pictured as a father who comes to redeem his enslaved child.

Theological Insights

It was not uncommon in the ancient world for someone to become enslaved because of poverty. In such circumstances it was permissible for a relative to come and redeem an individual by paying a ransom. In the story of the exodus, God is portrayed as a father who comes to redeem his son from slavery. In this instance, however, no payment is made to the Egyptians, because they have exploited the Israelites unjustly. Nevertheless, the concept of redemption is helpfully used to describe God's role in releasing the Israelites from slavery.

Teaching the Text

Although God has already warned Moses that Pharaoh would not release the Israelites unless compelled by a mighty hand (3:19), Moses is quickly discouraged when the Israelite foremen turn against him. Their criticism of Moses causes him to question what God is doing. In the light of this, the present passage is instructive regarding the nature of opposition to God's purposes, the reality of discouragement when serving God, and the reassurances that God gives to those who are discouraged.

Opposition to God's purposes. As the book of Exodus highlights in its opening chapters, we inhabit a world that is dominated by those who oppose the fulfillment of God's will on earth. At all levels, those who have no personal relationship with God are likely to live in opposition to him and his purposes. A consequence of this disconnection with God is violence toward others, which may take many and varied forms. When individuals promote their own self-serving agenda, they make life for others a grim experience. Evil oppressors take delight in destroying the well-being of other people. Sadly, the oppressed can become so conditioned that it is difficult for them to believe that God may have something much better planned for them.

Discouragement when serving God. Although Moses and Aaron have been commissioned by God to bring about the release of the Israelites from brutal slavery, the initial result of their message has the opposite effect. For the Israelites, the good news of God's concern for them turns sour as Pharaoh rejects it. With good reason, Jesus warned his followers that they and their message would not always be received enthusiastically. As the book of Acts graphically portrays, persecution was a recurring experience for the followers of Jesus. In the light of such opposition, Jesus's followers may easily become discouraged. Anticipating such difficulties, Acts highlights various occasions when believers were encouraged (Acts 4:36; 13:15; 14:22; 15:31–32; 16:40; 18:27; 20:1–2; 27:36). Times have not changed. Anyone serving God today must be prepared to face discouragement.

Reassurances from God. In the midst of life's difficulties, it is easy to focus on our troubles and to lose sight of the one who is sovereign over all. Consequently, it is vitally important to be always centered on the true God. We can easily substitute another god for the one who is the only living and real God. Like the Israelites, who described themselves as Pharaoh's servants, we too can look to appease a false deity. In the face of criticism Moses turns to God. Without condemning Moses, God comforts and reassures him. In doing so, he reminds Moses of the importance of remaining God centered. Like Moses, those who look to God will find reassurance in his promises regarding the future. As Jesus tells his disciples,

> Truly I tell you, at the renewal of all things, when the Son of Man sits on his glorious throne, you who have followed me will also sit on twelve thrones, judging the twelve tribes of Israel. And everyone who has left houses or brothers or sisters or father or mother or wife or children or fields for my sake will receive a hundred times as much and will inherit eternal life. (Matt. 19:28–29)

Illustrating the Text

The world is dominated by those who oppose the fulfillment of God's will on earth.

Literature: *The Lord of the Rings,* **by J. R. R. Tolkien.** In *The Lord of the Rings,* Aragorn, also called Strider, is being called out from obscurity to take his rightful place on the great throne of Gondor, an ancient city with a proud race. For many years, that throne has stood empty. Ruling in place of the king has been a line of stewards. Over time, these stewards have come to love their place of power and control. Though originally called to rule temporarily in the rightful king's stead, they have come to believe that they should take the king's rule for themselves. The last of this line, Denethor, ultimately commits suicide rather than enter a future under the leadership of Aragorn, his returning king. At the heart of human rebellion is a refusal to surrender rule to the rightful king, a desire to claim dominion rather than embrace stewardship.

Our message will not always be received enthusiastically.

History: In the buildup to World War II, a voice rang out in Great Britain. It was a lonely voice, warning of Hitler's intentions, sounding the alarm on the Reich, calling on Britain to "Stop it! Stop it! Stop it now!" Yet England ignored Winston Churchill. Following World War I, the British had determined that nothing would drag them into war again. A strategy of appeasement was adopted instead. In such a context, voices like Churchill's were unwelcome, sounding discordant notes that were easy to discount. Then Germany struck.

Sometimes, not only the world, but some people in the church will resist the message that we are in a battle. Often, people will label the Christian call for absolute allegiance to God as a simplistic worldview. But God demands our ultimate surrender. Any power that opposes him must be resisted.

We must be prepared to face discouragement, but a focus on the destination can sustain us.

Human Experience: Remember when we were young, heading out with the family on a road trip? Maybe it was to Disney World or the Grand Canyon or some other gem in the Americana treasure trove. There was the excitement of rising early, loading up the car, and setting out. Usually, however, at some point, the reality sank in: between our starting point and destination there is a long, hard journey. Numb knees. Bored stares out the window. Occasional war with a sibling. Way too many stops at way too many gas stations. A focus on the destination made the discouragements of a long car ride worth it. The journey to our heavenly destination, the new Jerusalem, can also be long and hard, but if we keep our focus on where we are headed, we will realize that the end result of the journey is worth the hardships along the way.

Signs Pointing to God

Big Idea

Even when God demonstrates his power through extraordinary signs, there will always be those who will continue to deny the reality of his existence.

Key Themes

- God sometimes reveals himself in history through extraordinary actions.
- Not all miracles originate with God; spiritual powers opposed to God may perform similar miracles.
- People who ask for signs from God do not necessarily want to believe that God exists.

Understanding the Text

The Text in Context

This section of Exodus marks the beginning of the series of signs and portents that Moses and Aaron will perform before Pharaoh. These signs begin in 7:8 and climax with the death of firstborn males in chapter 12. Apart from the final sign, which is described in more detail, the accounts of these signs follow a certain pattern (see "Outline/Structure" in the unit on 8:20–10:29), with some variety to avoid monotony. All the episodes need to be interpreted together as a literary unit, because subtle variations between them are used to advance the story. Consequently, teaching this section of Exodus is quite a challenge.

After failing to have the Israelites released, Moses and Aaron now return for a second audience with Pharaoh. They do so in obedience to God, having been told that Pharaoh will remain stubbornly opposed to setting the Israelites free, even when confronted with extraordinary signs and wonders. In spite of all of Pharaoh's resistance, however, the Egyptians will learn that the Lord is God over all the earth.

Outline/Structure

The narrative describing Moses's encounters with Pharaoh is interrupted briefly by the insertion of selected genealogical information in 6:14–25. This

Signs and Portents—Not Plagues

God's speech in 7:1–5 anticipates the events narrated in 7:8–14:31. Running through these chapters, but especially in chapters 7–11, is a series of extraordinary occurrences intended to persuade Pharaoh to release the Israelites. Each episode begins with the words "the LORD said to Moses" (7:8, 14; 8:1, 16, 20; 9:1, 8, 13; 10:1, 21; 11:1) and ends with a reference to Pharaoh's heart (7:13, 22; 8:15, 19, 32; 9:7, 12, 34–35; 10:20, 27; 11:10).

These demonstrations of God's power have become known as the "ten plagues." This designation, however, is never used in the Bible and is somewhat misleading. The term "plague," meaning "pestilence/disease," is not an appropriate label for most of the astonishing events that occur. In sixteenth-century English the word "plague" had the meaning "blow" or "strike" (derived from the Latin noun *plaga*, which means a "blow" or "strike"). The concept of "strikes" reflects more closely the Hebrew terminology used throughout these chapters and is linked to how the staff or hand of Moses or Aaron is used

to initiate the supernatural happenings. In Jewish tradition these events are the "ten strikes."

While the term "strike" is preferable to "plague," Exodus 7:3 introduces the expression "signs and wonders" to describe the miraculous events that will occur in Egypt. These words occur separately in chapters 8–12 to denote different events. Elsewhere in the Old Testament, the expression "signs and wonders" is the most commonly used label for God's miraculous actions in Egypt (Deut. 4:34; 6:22; 7:19; 26:8; 29:3; 34:11; Neh. 9:10; Pss. 105:27; 135:9; Jer. 32:20). As signs and wonders (or portents), the supernatural events in Egypt are designed to point to God's power. Thinking of them as signs rather than plagues makes it easier to see how they are linked to the signs performed by Jesus that are recorded in John's Gospel. The two sets of signs are closely related. When the staff becoming a snake/crocodile (Exod. 7:9–13) is counted with the other signs, Exodus records eleven signs, not ten.

material is carefully incorporated into the larger story using a literary technique known as resumptive repetition. Most of what is said in 6:10–13 is repeated in 6:26–30, picking up the story line again after the digression in 6:14–25. The insertion of information regarding the family of Levi confirms that Moses and Aaron are brothers, descended from Levi.

Interpretive Insights

6:10–12 *why would Pharaoh listen to me, since I speak with faltering lips?* Seeking to evade God's call, Moses once more stresses his limitations at speaking (cf. 4:10). Previously, God responded to Moses's objection by assigning Aaron to be a spokesman for Moses (4:14–16). For this reason, particular attention is given to Aaron and his descendants in 6:14–25.

6:14–25 *These were the clans of Levi.* The genealogical material preserved in these verses focuses on selected descendants of Levi, naming the parents of Moses and his brother, Aaron. Some other descendants are specifically named, ending with Phinehas. Verses 14–25 are clearly not a comprehensive genealogy but one designed to highlight how certain people are related to one another. The family details fall into two parts: verses 14–19a and 19b–25. This allows for the possibility that several generations are omitted in the middle of the genealogy and that the name Amram refers to two different men in verses 18 and 20. It is not uncommon in families for names to be reused, and the repetition of Amram maintains the continuity of the genealogy. The assumption that two relatives were called Amram prevents Levi from being the great-grandfather of Aaron and Moses, a fact that is difficult to reconcile with both the length of the Israelite stay in Egypt and the numerical growth of Levi's descendants by the time of their departure from Egypt. According to Numbers 3:39, the "sons of Levi" (NIV: "Levites") numbered twenty-two thousand when the Israelites departed from Mount Sinai. Such growth is inconceivable in only four generations. Moreover, according to Exodus 12:40, the Israelites were in Egypt for 430 years.

6:26–30 *It was this Aaron and Moses to whom the* LORD *said.* The preceding genealogical information corroborates that Moses and Aaron are Levites, anticipating the special role that this tribe will play in future events. These verses, which echo 6:10–13, resume the story line.

7:1 *your brother Aaron will be your prophet.* The designation of Aaron as a "prophet" underlines that he will act as Moses's spokesman. While prophets sometimes predict future events, their primary function is to communicate God's message to others.

7:3 *I will harden Pharaoh's heart.* The motif of Pharaoh's heart being hardened recurs throughout chapters 7–11, appearing in each episode involving a supernatural sign or portent. Unfortunately, the English idiom "hard-hearted" conveys connotations that are not present in the Hebrew idiom. For ancient Israelites, a heart that is hard, heavy, or strong is resolute or stubborn, and this can be viewed as either a positive or a negative quality. (See the fuller discussion in the "Theological Insights" in the unit on 8:20–10:29.)

7:5–7 *the Egyptians will know that I am the* LORD. Earlier, Pharaoh denied any knowledge of the Lord (5:2). The theme of knowing the Lord recurs frequently in the "signs and wonders" episodes (7:17; 8:10, 22; 9:14; 10:2; 14:4, 18). God intends that these supernatural events will cause the Egyptians and the Israelites to gain a better understanding of who he is. Ultimately, God's intention is that people everywhere should not just know *about* him but know him personally through an intimate relationship with him. Through the covenant at Mount Sinai, God establishes a special relationship with the Israelites, preparing the way for him to come and dwell in their midst.

7:9–13 *"Perform a miracle" . . . it will become a snake.* Anticipating Pharaoh's request for an omen, God instructs Moses to respond by changing his staff into a "snake." This resembles what Moses did earlier (4:2–4), but a different Hebrew term is used here to denote the reptile. In this context, the staff becomes a *tannin* rather than a *nahash*, "snake." Since the term *tannin* is linked to water in some Old Testament contexts (Ps. 148:7; Ezek. 29:3; 32:2), some scholars favor the translation "crocodile" in this context.[1] This helpfully indicates that this may be a different type of reptile from that mentioned in Exodus 4:2–4. Interestingly, this is the only occasion when Pharaoh asks for a sign. However, he swiftly dismisses what happens when his own "magicians" do the same thing "by their secret arts" (v. 11). The Hebrew word translated "magicians" refers to sorcerer-priests, whose religious practices were closely associated with magic. The religious aspect of their activity is important to note, because the conflict between God and Pharaoh involves the gods of Egypt (cf. 12:12). We can only surmise that some kind of occult activity on the part of the sorcerer-priests is involved here.

7:15–24 *all the water was changed into blood.* The second sign performed by Moses and Aaron, involving the transformation of water into blood, repeats what Moses did previously before the Israelites (4:9, 30–31). The Israelites believed Moses, but Pharaoh remains resolute in rejecting Moses's request to release the Israelites, especially when his own sorcerer-priests duplicate the extraordinary sign. We must take at face value the narrator's claim that the water became blood. This would appear to be a transformation that cannot be explained by purely natural causes, on a par with Jesus changing water into wine (John 2:9). Water becoming blood would be an ominous sign, warning of something more terrible to come.

8:1–15 *The Nile will teem with frogs.* For the first time in the sequence of "strikes," Pharaoh asks Moses and Aaron to intercede with God (v. 8). While Moses responds graciously, Pharaoh's true nature shows through when he reneges on his offer to let the Israelites go (v. 15).

8:16–18 *the dust will become gnats . . . gnats came on people and animals.* Dust is transformed into insects, which the NIV translates as "gnats," but they could be lice, a view that may be traced back to the first-century AD Jewish historian Josephus and rabbinic sources. In this episode the insects are described as being "on people and animals," whereas in 8:20–32 the insects appear to fly and fill houses.

8:19 *the magicians said to Pharaoh, "This is the finger of God."* The inability of the sorcerer-priests to duplicate this supernatural sign causes them to attribute it to the "finger of God." The sorcerer-priests acknowledge a divine power at work, but their comment may be intentionally worded to avoid offending Pharaoh. By speaking of God's finger, they possibly play down the significance of what has happened. Pharaoh, as a divine king, may continue to believe that his hand is more powerful. Alternatively, the reference to a "finger" of a deity may reflect Egyptian usage, whereby a deity's finger denotes danger and power.[2]

Theological Insights

God's deliverance of the Israelites from slavery in Egypt is quite unique within the Bible, for on no other occasion does God use a series of "signs and wonders" to bring salvation to a nation as a whole. As will become clearer, the Passover provides the main Old Testament paradigm of divine salvation. The signs and wonders preceding the Passover are preliminary warnings of the terrible judgment that will come upon the firstborn male Egyptians. In the light of these warnings, Pharaoh and his supporters are without excuse when punishment finally comes through the death of their firstborn sons. Even to those who deserve judgment, God may send warnings to prompt a change of heart.

Teaching the Text

How can we best convince someone that God really exists? Might a miracle persuade them to believe? Should Christians expect God to perform miracles today in order to persuade other people to believe in him? Such questions are likely to receive very differing answers in different Christian traditions. The place of miracles in the church today is not something on which all Christians agree.[3]

The story of God's deliverance of the Israelites from slavery in Egypt provides an opportunity to reflect on the significance of miracles or supernatural signs for Christians today. Several observations may be helpful in clarifying how we might view miracles.

Miracles are possible. We should not automatically deny the possibility of miracles. The Bible bears witness to the reality of supernatural events taking place. God may on occasion do something of an unexpected nature to demonstrate his extraordinary power. Some miracles may fall into the category of "signs" that are intended to point to the reality of God's existence.

Not all miracles originate with God. The initial episodes involving supernatural signs in Egypt reveal that the ability to perform miracles is not unique to God. The Egyptian sorcerer-priests have the power to replicate the miracles performed by Moses and Aaron. This should be a reminder that those hostile to God may have spiritual powers that go beyond the ordinary.

And such powers may be used to produce counterfeit signs and wonders. For this reason, Jesus warns his followers about "false prophets" who might even cast out demons in his name and do many mighty works in his name (Matt. 7:15–22). Although they might disguise themselves in "sheep's clothing," these "ferocious wolves" will be recognized by their fruit of immorality. The ability to perform miracles of itself is not necessarily a credential of genuine Christian discipleship.

People who ask for signs may not want to believe. Although God has preplanned the series of signs and wonders, the first is given in response to a request from Pharaoh. Yet when Moses and Aaron give him a sign, Pharaoh contemptuously dismisses it. The opponents of Jesus also ask for a sign, but they do so with no intention of believing. For this reason, Jesus remarks: "A wicked and adulterous generation asks for a sign! But none will be given it except the sign of the prophet Jonah. For as Jonah was three days and three nights in the belly of a huge fish, so the Son of Man will be three days and three nights in the heart of the earth" (Matt. 12:39–40).

Illustrating the Text

The ability to perform miracles is not necessarily a credential of genuine Christian discipleship.

Bible: **Acts 16:16–24.** The Bible is clear that an ability to perform miraculous signs does not prove God's anointing. Consider, for instance, Paul's experience with a slave girl who has been empowered to predict the future (Acts 16:16–24). For many who have seen this power in operation in her, it seems a clear demonstration of the gods' favor. For Paul, however, there is a much more insidious force at work. He reveals the demonic origins of the supernatural ability when he turns, rebukes the spirit, and sets the girl free from slavery to the enemy.

Even those who witness a miracle might refuse to believe.

Quote: When asked what he would say one day when God asked him, "Why didn't you believe in me?" British philosopher Bertrand Russell, replied, "Not enough evidence, God! Not enough evidence!"[4] The reality is, we are all surrounded every day by evidence that this world was created and is ruled by a sovereign God. Every sunrise and starry night speaks of his glory and majesty (Ps. 19; Rom. 1). For a heart set on rebellion, even a miracle can be explained away. For a God of amazing grace, even a heart hard as stone can be melted. This is good news.

Science: **"Can a Scientist Believe in Miracles?," by Jacalyn Duffin.** Duffin, a medical expert, shares a fascinating account of personally witnessing and documenting miracles yet (tragically) remaining an atheist in her convictions. She concludes:

> I have published two books on medicine and religion. . . .
>
> [My] research uncovered dramatic stories of recovery and courage. It revealed some striking parallels between medicine and religion in terms of reasoning and purpose, and it showed that the Church had not shrunk from science in its deliberations over the miraculous.
>
> Though still an atheist, I believe in miracles—wondrous things that happen for which we can find no scientific explanation.[5]

The Persuasive Power of a Gracious God

Big Idea

God makes himself known through a series of extraordinary events that underline his power over nature.

Key Themes

- God's power is demonstrated through signs and wonders that impact water, land, and sky.
- Although he is omnipotent, God acts graciously, even toward those who are openly opposed to him.

Understanding the Text

The Text in Context

This section of Exodus continues the series of signs and wonders that began in 7:8. Each sign follows a certain pattern, although the narrator skillfully avoids a sense of monotony by varying every report. Subtle variations between episodes give a sense of progression, although this is always tempered by a concluding remark about Pharaoh refusing to release the Israelites. The signs increase in intensity, bringing greater discomfort to the Egyptians, including the death of their livestock and physical suffering due to festering boils. From beginning to end, however, God initiates all that occurs, demonstrating his sovereignty over everything.

Outline/Structure

The signs and wonders in 7:14–10:29 fall into three sets of three that parallel each other (see table 1). While there is repetition, there is also progression, indicated by minor variations between episodes. With each successive sign in chapters 8–10, Pharaoh appears to concede a little more as Moses repeatedly requests the release of the Israelites to sacrifice to the Lord in the desert. In 8:8 Pharaoh states that he will release the Israelites if Moses prays for the removal of the frogs. When Moses does this, Pharaoh immediately reneges (8:15). In 8:25 Pharaoh states that the Israelites may sacrifice to God within the land of Egypt. Later he is prepared to let them go a little way into the desert (8:25–28), but once more he reneges (8:32). In 9:28 Pharaoh says he will permit the people to go, but this does not happen. Later, Pharaoh is willing to let the adult Israelites offer sacrifices to the Lord but not their children (10:8–11). In the next episode, Pharaoh offers to release the men, women, and children but not their livestock (10:24). These concessions portray a gradual change of heart by Pharaoh as the signs and wonders intensify, but by the end of chapter 10 the Israelites are still enslaved in Egypt.

Table 1. Parallel Sets of Signs and Wonders in Exodus 7–10

Blood (7:14–25)	Flies (or mosquitos; 8:20–32)	Hail (9:13–35)	"In the morning" occurs in 7:15; 8:20; 9:13.
Frogs (8:1–15)	Death of livestock (9:1–7)	Locusts (10:1–20)	"Go to Pharaoh" occurs in 8:1; 9:1; 10:1.
Gnats (or lice; 8:16–19)	Boils (9:8–12)	Darkness (10:21–29)	Note that there is no instruction to confront Pharaoh in 8:16; 9:8; 10:21.

Historical and Cultural Background

Some scholars have suggested that the individual signs and wonders performed in Exodus deliberately target different Egyptian gods in order to undermine belief in them. While it can be argued that some of the signs and wonders show the impotence of particular Egyptian deities, this cannot be demonstrated consistently for all the supernatural events that occur.[1]

Other scholars have suggested that the signs and wonders may be the result of a series of interrelated natural events (e.g., the flooding of the Nile causes the water to look like blood). This approach, however, cannot explain all of the story's details, and it undermines the theological basis of the narrative, which claims that these events are due to the activity of God himself.[2]

Interpretive Insights

8:21 *I will send swarms of flies on you and your officials.* The Hebrew term translated "flies" in the NIV may possibly refer to mosquitoes or other insects that bite. Since the Hebrew term *'arob* is used only with reference to this event, scholars have been unable to ascertain with any certainty the type of insect involved. Most English translations opt for "swarms of flies." On the basis that Psalm 78:45 describes these insects as feeding on the Egyptians, "mosquitoes" may convey more meaningfully for most readers the menace caused by these insects.

Exodus 8:20–10:29

8:22–24 *I will deal differently with the land of Goshen, where my people live.* God deliberately restricts the movement of these flying insects so that the Israelites are not affected by them. This distinction occurs automatically with all the signs, apart from the Passover.

8:25–27 *Go, sacrifice to your God here in the land.* Although Pharaoh is influenced by the "flies," he is prepared to let the Israelites sacrifice to God only within the land of Egypt. It is not altogether clear why the sacrifices of the Israelites would have been detestable to the Egyptians. Perhaps they feared that sacrifices to a "foreign" God would anger the gods of Egypt.

8:28–32 *I will let you go to offer sacrifices to the* Lord *your God in the wilderness.* Pharaoh's words cannot be trusted, unlike those of the Lord.

9:3–7 *a terrible plague on your livestock in the field.* While previous "strikes" brought a variety of hardships to the Egyptians, God's actions were not designed to cause any deaths (on "strikes," see the sidebar "Signs and Portents— Not Plagues" in the unit on 6:10–8:19). With this sign, Egyptian livestock in the fields are struck dead. Once again, however, God distinguishes between the Egyptians and the Israelites.

9:8–10 *festering boils will break out on people and animals.* This sign is a further intensification of God's actions against Pharaoh and his people. The Egyptians themselves are physically affected by boils.

9:11–12 *The magicians could not stand before Moses.* Previously, the sorcerer-priests were able to replicate some signs. Now they cannot even protect themselves.

9:15–19 *by now I could have stretched out my hand and struck you and your people.* From the outset God intended that there should be a series of signs and wonders (7:3). Had he wished, God could have wiped out the Egyptians with one strike. The signs, however, are a testimony to people throughout the earth of God's power. God wants people everywhere to come to a knowledge of him.

9:27–35 *The* Lord *is in the right, and I and my people are in the wrong.* Pharaoh's words lack integrity, as Moses points out. In spite of this, Moses graciously asks God to halt the thunder and hail. God's willingness to end each strike shows that he takes no pleasure in afflicting the people. His sole concern is to persuade Pharaoh to release the Israelites, but Pharaoh must do this of his own free choice. He must make this decision when not directly under duress from God.

10:1–3 *I have hardened his heart . . . tell your children and grandchildren.* On the hardening of Pharaoh's heart, see "Theological Insights." Once more God underlines that the signs performed in Egypt are meant to instruct others about him. In this instance, God tells Moses that these signs will educate future generations of Israelites about the Lord.

10:4–7 *I will bring locusts into your country.* The locusts will attack the wheat and spelt crops that survived the hail (9:32). While attacks by locusts may have occasionally occurred in Egypt, the one threatened by the Lord will be the most severe to have ever happened. As to the source of these locusts the narrator remains silent. On the one hand, it is possible that God created them in an instant out of nothing. On the other hand, it is equally possible that these locusts, having hatched from eggs, had grown to full size before being blown by the wind into Egypt. With either option, God is responsible for ensuring that the forces of nature bring a terrible destruction on the crops of Egypt.

10:16–20 *I have sinned against the LORD your God and against you.* The devastation wreaked by the locusts causes Pharaoh to confess his wrongdoing to Moses and Aaron. Modern accounts of locust plagues underscore the devastation that these insects can bring. Each insect can eat its own weight in a day. Swarms containing tens of millions of locusts are not unknown.

10:24–26 *Go, worship the LORD.* Although with each new sign Pharaoh concedes a little more to Moses and Aaron, he consistently refuses to grant their request in full. The darkness that envelops the Egyptians for three whole days is clearly more terrifying than even the locusts that have invaded the land.

10:28–29 *The day you see my face you will die.* In spite of everything that has taken place, the Egyptian king arrogantly threatens Moses with death. Pharaoh, however, will be powerless to prevent the death of the firstborn Egyptian males.

Theological Insights

Each episode in chapters 7–10 concludes with a reference to Pharaoh's heart. Although there are subtle variations in wording, on each occasion the reference to Pharaoh's heart is linked to his refusal to release the Israelites. This connection needs to be interpreted very carefully, because it can easily be misunderstood. Unfortunately, most English translations speak of Pharaoh's heart being hard, which is usually understood as implying that he lacks compassion. This is not how ancient Israelites would have understood the concept. For them, the various verbs associated with Pharaoh's heart imply that he is resolute. His heart or will is strong. In spite of the signs and wonders, Pharaoh remains committed to his initial rejection of God's request for the release of the Israelites.

Although it is sometimes suggested that God forces Pharaoh to act against his own will in order to continue the series of signs and wonders, the opposite is true. God attempts to persuade Pharaoh by bringing pressure to bear on him, but this pressure is always removed. When not under duress, Pharaoh is free to choose what to do. Remarkably, the Lord does not impose his will on Pharaoh, and he does not encroach on Pharaoh's freedom to reject him.

Ironically, God even strengthens Pharaoh's resolve, enabling the Egyptian king to remain faithful to his own inner convictions, even though these are against God and the Israelites.

Unlike the tyrannical pharaohs of Egypt, God does not impose his will on others by force. While he uses extraordinary signs in order to persuade Pharaoh, these are limited in both scope and time. Although Pharaoh occasionally indicates a willingness to release the Israelites, he reverts to his original position when each sign is removed. This is a sad reminder of how ingrained is human enmity toward God.

Teaching the Text

The account of the signs and wonders in Egypt describes events that are far removed from the experience of most modern readers. Even ancient readers would have marveled at the series of "blows" delivered by God on Pharaoh and his people (on "blows," see the sidebar "Signs and Portents—Not Plagues" in the unit on 6:10–8:19). Through these extraordinary events God discloses something of his awe-inspiring nature.

A testimony to God's power. These omens are a testimony to God's existence and power. Their astonishing nature points to the sovereignty of God over all of nature. The Lord is no family or national deity restricted to a particular geographical region. His authority in Egypt is no less than elsewhere. Before him, the so-called gods of Egypt are impotent. Centuries later, Jesus Christ will also perform "signs" as a testimony to his divine power (John 20:30–31), but in keeping with his mission these are signs of salvation, bringing life rather than death.

A testimony to God's graciousness. The signs-and-wonders episodes provide an interesting insight into the gracious nature of God when confronted by obstinate human rebellion. How easy it would have been for the Lord to obliterate Pharaoh when he first rejected God's request! Yet, God shows great restraint in graciously offering Pharaoh repeated opportunities to release the Israelites. Even when his own officials encourage him to act otherwise, Pharaoh remains stubbornly resistant. When judgment finally strikes Pharaoh, he is without excuse.

A testimony to God's patience. Running through the episodes, there is clear evidence of Pharaoh's two-faced attitude. He petitions God to remove various hardships, yet he ignores God when each petition is answered. He promises to submit to God's wish, only to recant soon afterward. In spite of this, God remains consistent in his dealings with Pharaoh. What more could God have done to persuade Pharaoh, without encroaching on his freedom to determine his own destiny? With great patience God refrains from using his absolute power to achieve his purposes. In this regard, he stands apart from every human dictator and tyrant.

Understanding how God treats Pharaoh with graciousness and patience is important for appreciating how God deals with people, especially those opposed to him, in our day. While God's power is unlimited, he does not coerce people into serving him against their will. Ultimately, those who knowingly refuse to acknowledge the sovereignty of God will have only themselves to blame.

Illustrating the Text

God is sovereign over all nature.

Quote: *Chosen by God*, **by R. C. Sproul.** Professor Sproul famously wrote,

> If there is one single molecule in this universe running around loose, totally free of God's sovereignty, then we have no guarantee that a single promise of God will ever be fulfilled. Perhaps that one maverick molecule will lay waste all the grand and glorious plans that God has made and promised to us. . . . I remember my distress when I heard that Bill Vukovich, the greatest car driver of his era, was killed in a crash in the Indianapolis 500. The cause was later isolated in the failure of a cotter pin that cost ten cents.
>
> Bill Vukovich had an amazing control of race cars. He was a magnificent driver. However, he was not sovereign. A part worth only a dime cost him his life. God doesn't have to worry about ten-cent cotter pins wrecking his plans. There are no maverick molecules running around loose. God is sovereign. God is God.[3]

Those who stubbornly refuse to repent are without excuse.

Human Experience: Have you ever received a "recall" letter for a product? It lets us know that a problem has been discovered with the item we own. It puts us on notice and shifts responsibility to us. If we choose to do nothing with the notice, then the responsibility is ours alone. Sometimes, ignoring such a notice is no big deal, involving a product with little potential for injury. At other times, it can mean the difference between life and death. In much the same way, all humanity has been put on notice that we are fatally flawed, due not to a manufacturer's defect but to our sin, and the consequences of ignoring the implications are dire and eternal.

Death Comes to Egypt

Big Idea

God mercifully provides a Passover sacrifice to save from death those who trust in him.

Key Themes

- God warns of coming judgment and provides the means of evading death due to human sinfulness.
- God graciously enables people to atone for their sin and sanctify themselves through the Passover sacrifice.

Understanding the Text

The Text in Context

The series of signs and wonders comes to a climax with the Passover. The distinctive pattern created by the episodes in Exodus 7–10 is now broken as the account of the final sign is reported. Whereas in chapters 7–10 the Israelites are largely invisible, attention is now given to describing how they should prepare for the final sign. On this occasion they must actively distinguish themselves from the Egyptians by marking their homes with blood sprinkled on the door frames. Remarkably, the threat of death hangs over the Israelites as much as it does over the Egyptians. This has an important bearing on how the Passover should be understood. It is not simply a punishment inflicted on the Egyptians. There is something of deeper significance taking place as the Israelites obey God's instructions concerning the Passover. The implications of what they do relate back to the expulsion of Adam and Eve from the Garden of Eden, when they were expelled from God's presence. The Passover ritual addresses the consequences of human rebellion against God, restoring this broken relationship.

Historical and Cultural Background

Although Exodus 12 clearly associates the origin of the Passover and the Festival of Unleavened Bread with the Israelites' divine deliverance from Egypt, since the nineteenth century critical scholarship has rejected this idea, arguing that the Passover originates in a pastoral context, whereas the Festival of

Unleavened Bread has an agricultural background. Although this theory is widely held, both of these proposals lack substance. The month of Aviv is too early for the barley harvest to have been completed, and it is highly unlikely that agriculturalists would have celebrated a weeklong festival at the very start of a harvest period.

Of greater significance for understanding the Passover are the parallels that exist between it and the process by which Aaron and his sons are consecrated as priests (Exod. 29). While some of the details differ, the overall ritual is quite similar. This suggests that the Passover was intended to consecrate or sanctify the Israelites. This correlates well with God's pronouncement in 19:6 that the Israelites are to be a "kingdom of priests and a holy nation."

Interpretive Insights

11:1–2 *Now the* Lord *had said to Moses.* The NIV translation implies that God's message in verses 1–2 was given on a prior occasion. While a pluperfect reading is possible, it is not necessary to assume that God said this to Moses previously. God's words make good sense as a new message given in the light of Pharaoh's threat to Moses in 10:28.

I will bring one more plague on Pharaoh and on Egypt. The Hebrew noun *negaʿ*, which the NIV translates as "plague," is better rendered "strike/blow" (see the sidebar "Signs and Portents—Not Plagues" in the unit on 6:10–8:19). God indicates that this will be the final blow against Pharaoh and the Egyptians. As mentioned previously in 6:1, Pharaoh's eventual response in driving out the Israelites goes beyond Moses's request that the Israelites be permitted to undertake a three-day journey into the desert to worship God (3:18; 5:1–3).

11:4–8 *Then you will know that the* Lord *makes a distinction between Egypt and Israel.* Although the NIV indicates that God's words stop in the middle of verse 7, it is more likely that they end in verse 8 with the statement, "After that I will leave." This final remark balances God's initial comment that he will go throughout Egypt. The Hebrew text provides no clear indication that the speech in verses 7b–8 ceases to be a divine message communicated by Moses. At no point does the subsequent narrative record that Pharaoh's own officials bowed down to Moses.

12:2 *This month is to be for you the first month . . . of your year.* The exodus from Egypt will be a new beginning for the Israelites. It is fitting, therefore, that the spring month of Aviv (later called Nisan) should be designated the first month of the year. The Israelites adopted the Egyptian calendar system involving lunar months, with the first day of the month occurring when the old crescent of the moon could no longer be seen before sunrise. At this stage in their history the Israelites considered the day as starting with sunrise. Only from the Babylonian exile onward did Jews reckon the day as starting with sunset.

12:3–11 *on the tenth day of this month each man is to take a lamb for his family.* The Hebrew term *seh*, translated "lamb," may refer to either a sheep or a goat. The fully grown year-old animal is set apart for several days before being sacrificed. The Passover occurs on or close to the full moon. The sacrifice takes place in the evening, after the Israelites have finished working. Special instructions describe how the meat should be cooked, and every effort is to be made to ensure that no meat is left over. The eating of the sacrificial meat is an important part of the Passover ritual. This is not merely food to sustain the Israelites on their journey out of Egypt. By eating sacrificial meat, the Israelites are made ritually holy. Through being dressed for a journey, the Israelites demonstrate their faith in God's power to deliver them from Egypt.

12:12 *I will pass through Egypt and strike down every firstborn.* To avoid this "strike" (see the comments on 11:1–2), the Israelites must actively set themselves apart from the Egyptians. Previously, God himself distinguished between the Israelites and the Egyptians.

12:14–20 *for the generations to come you shall celebrate . . . eat bread made without yeast.* Due to their swift departure from Egypt, the Israelites have no opportunity to celebrate their deliverance. Future celebrations will involve the eating of unleavened bread, a reminder of their swift departure from Egypt. Baking bread with leaven or yeast requires additional time.

12:21–22 *slaughter the Passover lamb . . . hyssop, dip it into the blood.* These verses highlight the significance of the sacrificial blood in saving the Israelite firstborn males from death. The Passover ritual atones for the sins of these Israelites. In Leviticus, atonement comprises both paying a ransom and the removal of defilement through cleansing. The lamb dies as a substitute, especially for the firstborn males (see also 13:11–16 and the comments on those verses below). The use of hyssop suggests that the blood has a cleansing or purifying role. The sprinkling of the blood on the door frames is probably intended to cleanse those who have passed through the door into the house from the defilement caused by their sins.

12:23 *he will not permit the destroyer to enter your houses.* It is sometimes assumed that the destroyer is an angel, but the evidence for this is weak. The Hebrew term *mashhit* may denote "destruction" and not the person who destroys. Even if the concept of a destroying angel is retained, the first half of verse 23 indicates that the one who ultimately strikes dead is the Lord himself (cf. 12:29).

12:27 *It is the Passover sacrifice to the Lord.* This statement underlines the sacrificial nature of what took place. The slaughter of the animals is not simply to provide blood to mark the houses and food to nourish the people. The sacrifice atones for the sins of the people, ransoming the firstborn males from death.

12:29–30 *the* L<small>ORD</small> *struck down all the firstborn in Egypt . . . not a house without someone dead.* The final strike brings death to every Egyptian household. The Hebrew term *bayit*, translated "house" in verse 30, could equally be rendered "household." There is no need to assume, as some commentators have suggested, that someone else died in those houses that lacked a firstborn son.

Theological Insights

The importance of the Passover cannot be overstated. This event forms the apex of God's deliverance of the Israelites from enslavement to Pharaoh. The Passover night was to be reenacted annually. In doing so, the Israelites recall regularly that their very existence as a nation depends on God's actions in Egypt. Yet this raises difficult theological issues. Why does God strike dead all the Egyptian firstborn sons? Are God's actions fair and just?

These are difficult questions to address, for the narrative provides no detailed explanation of God's actions. However, several observations may shed light on these issues. Firstly, it should be noted that responsibility for the death of the Egyptian firstborn rests not with God but with Pharaoh. Had he permitted the Israelites to leave Egypt on a short pilgrimage to sacrifice to God, the Egyptian firstborn would have been spared from death. It is Pharaoh's intransigence, supported by his own people, that leads to their death. Secondly, it is often noted that earlier in Exodus, Pharaoh instructed the Egyptians to drown in the Nile all newborn male Israelites (1:22). In the light of this, it is suggested that the death of the firstborn Egyptian males represents an appropriate punishment. Yet it is striking that in Exodus 12 the death penalty is also pronounced on the firstborn Israelite males. This is especially noteworthy because with the first signs God distinguished clearly between the Egyptians and the Israelites; the latter were spared from the hardships of the different signs. This suggests that the death of the firstborn is more than merely a punishment for what the Egyptians did to the Israelites. Something of greater significance is taking place. Thirdly, God's pronouncement that all firstborn males will die is a stark reminder that all human beings are under the penalty of death because of sin. The Israelite firstborn males deserve to die like the Egyptians, but God inaugurates a process by which they are saved from death. By obeying God's instructions, the Israelites save their firstborn sons. Had the Egyptians obeyed God, their sons would also have lived.

Teaching the Text

Exploring the Passover provides an important opportunity to consider how God transforms sinners into saints. The Old Testament event is the type of which Christ's death on the cross is the antitype. Although the Passover builds on the preceding signs and wonders in chapters 7–10, it differs in various respects. Most noticeable is the need for the Israelites to distinguish their homes from those of the Egyptians through a complex ritual that involves the offering of a sacrifice, the sprinkling of blood on the door frames of their homes, and the consumption of sacrificial meat. These elements are important pointers to how the Passover functions in protecting the firstborn Israelite males from death.

Before unpacking the meaning of the Passover ritual, we should observe that on this occasion God does not automatically exclude the Israelites from the "deathblow" that is about to descend on the Egyptians. In spite of all that has happened to the Israelites and their subjugation by the Egyptians, they too are under the threat of death. Only the grace of God prevents their firstborn sons from being struck dead. This is a reminder that all human beings stand condemned to death due to their sin. Of necessity, God must provide for the Israelites a means by which they may escape from the domain of death.

In the light of this, the sacrificial nature of the Passover makes good sense. The process of transforming the Israelites from slaves to Pharaoh into servants of the Lord requires both atonement and sanctification. The Passover lambs/goats atone for their sins in two ways. Firstly, they provide a ransom payment, dying in the place of the firstborn males. Secondly, their blood cleanses or purifies those who are stained and defiled by sin. Finally, the Passover sacrifice sanctifies those who eat it. By eating holy meat, the Israelites become holy. Remarkably, the Passover prepares the Israelites to be God's holy nation. This process of consecration resembles that used to set apart the Levitical priests for service within the tabernacle (Exod. 29).

The Passover is especially significant because it is about much more than deliverance from slavery. Within the context of the book of Exodus, through the Passover God transforms the status of the Israelites by atoning for their sins and consecrating them as holy. Without the benefits of the Passover, the Israelites could not experience God's presence with them in the future. Importantly, the Passover provides a paradigm for divine salvation, revealing how those estranged from God may become his people. The Passover both models and anticipates a greater exodus that comes through Jesus Christ's death on the cross.

When the theological significance of the Passover is recognized, it is no surprise that John the Baptist portrays Jesus as the lamb who takes away the sin of the world (John 1:29, 36). Not only does Jesus die at the Passover, but in doing so he promises life to those who believe in him. Affirming this interpretation of Jesus's death, the apostle Paul writes: "For Christ, our Passover lamb, has been sacrificed" (1 Cor. 5:7).

Illustrating the Text

Apart from grace, human beings stand condemned to death due to their sin.

Popular Culture: What is one of the sights that regularly greets grocery-store shoppers on their way through the checkout lane? The celebrity mug shot. It is amazing how often one of the gossip magazines plasters the face of a celebrity, usually looking the worse for wear, holding a placard, looking sullen or flashing an impudent smile. How strange that our culture loves to see our shining lights in moments of obvious guilt.

What visual image would we put on the opposite side of the guilt-innocence scale? A pastor in the pulpit? A civil-rights advocate marching for justice? A child playing with toys? The truth is that, despite appearances (and good acts), we are all sinful and in need of God's gracious provision of forgiveness and reconciliation and deliverance from death.

The Passover models and anticipates a greater exodus through Christ's death on the cross.

Art: In 2013, the Los Angeles Architecture and Design Museum featured an exhibition called "Never Built Los Angeles." This fascinating exhibit contained architectural sketches and models of transformative and potentially culture-defining plans that, if they had been enacted, would have set Los Angeles apart as a paragon of innovation. The collection of images haunted the display space like dreams one wishes to meet in the waking world. The Passover, unlike this display, is an image of something that *has happened*. It is not simply an inspiring picture of redemption. It is a picture that points to the Redeemer. He really did come. The image has been fulfilled in reality.

Some Things Should Never Be Forgotten

Big Idea
Constantly recalling how God has saved us is vital to nurturing our relationship with him.

Key Themes
- The Passover builds on God's covenant with the patriarchs regarding the blessing of the nations.
- The Passover creates a special relationship between God and the firstborn Israelite males.

Understanding the Text

The Text in Context

Continuing the story of how God delivers the Israelites from slavery in Egypt, this section reports what happens immediately after the death of the Egyptian firstborn males. Specific details are given in 12:31–42 about the departure of the Israelites from Egypt. These are immediately followed by several speeches that contain instructions outlining how in the future the Israelites are to commemorate their rescue from Pharaoh's control. These instructions apply to the reenactment of the Passover (12:43–49), the celebration of the Festival of Unleavened Bread (13:3–10), and the setting apart of all firstborn males, both people and animals (13:11–16). The use of three different ways to commemorate the Passover underlines the importance of what occurs. No other event in Israel's history receives similar recognition, although future generations are not always faithful in keeping God's instructions concerning the Passover.

Interpretive Insights

12:31 *During the night Pharaoh summoned Moses and Aaron.* The death of all the firstborn males forces Pharaoh to summon Moses and Aaron, in spite of Pharaoh's earlier pronouncement that he would not see Moses again

(10:28–29). As happens in earlier episodes, Pharaoh reneges on what he has said. However, to give the impression that he is still in charge, he fires a salvo of orders at Moses and Aaron.

12:34 *So the people took their dough before the yeast was added.* This underlines the haste with which the Israelites leave Egypt. Subsequently, unleavened bread becomes the hallmark of the seven-day festival that God institutes to celebrate the exodus from Egypt.

12:35 *The Israelites . . . asked the Egyptians for articles of silver and gold and for clothing.* This fulfills God's earlier instructions (3:22; 11:2). The Israelites are now suitably rewarded for their many years of service to the Egyptians.

12:37 *about six hundred thousand men on foot, besides women and children.* This brief statement about the number of Israelites who leave Egypt has prompted much discussion.[1] If "six hundred thousand" refers to men of military age, as most commentators assume, then the total population of Israelites was probably in the region of two million. Although some scholars have argued, with good reason, that "six hundred thousand" denotes the total population, this is difficult to reconcile with the census recorded at the start of Numbers, where a total of 603,550 is given for the men of military age, excluding the Levites (Num. 1:46; 2:32).[2] Yet this latter figure sits uncomfortably alongside the 22,273 firstborn males mentioned in Numbers 3:43. These numbers produce a ratio of one firstborn male Israelite to about thirty-six adult males, requiring each married couple to have about seventy children when females are included. This statistic suggests that the numbers preserved in the earliest Hebrew manuscripts may have become corrupted in the process of transmission. This is highly possible, since there is clear evidence elsewhere in the Old Testament of numbers being corrupted (e.g., compare 2 Sam. 10:18 and 1 Chron. 19:18).

Apart from internal difficulties regarding the large number of Israelites in verse 37, most scholars balk at the idea of around two million people leaving Egypt in the second millennium BC to invade the land of Canaan. Recent estimates of the population of the central hill country in Palestine in the twelfth century BC conclude that about fifty-five thousand people lived there. This estimate cannot be easily reconciled with an exodus population of six hundred thousand, far less two million. Additionally, it is difficult to conceive of two million people journeying together for forty years through the Sinai Peninsula. Moreover, various remarks in Exodus and Deuteronomy imply that the Israelite population was not particularly large (Exod. 23:30; Deut. 7:1, 22).

All these factors suggest that we should be cautious about assuming the accuracy of the numbers recorded in the earliest surviving Hebrew manuscripts. While alternative explanations have been proposed to reduce the size of the

Israelite population, none has gained widespread support. One factor that may have a bearing on this issue is the possibility that the Hebrew term *'elep*, normally translated "thousand," may on occasions denote a small military unit.[3]

12:41 *At the end of the 430 years, to the very day, all the Lord's divisions left Egypt.* The Hebrew expression translated in the NIV "to the very day" does not imply that the Israelites were in Egypt for exactly 430 years. Rather, rightly understood it indicates that the Israelites departed on the day immediately following the Passover night (cf. 12:51). On that very day they began their journey out of Egypt.

12:43–49 *These are the regulations for the Passover meal.* These instructions appear to be relevant for both the first Passover and later commemoration. This may explain why they are recorded at this stage in the story. Particular emphasis is given to the issue of non-Israelites participating in the Passover. By emphasizing the importance of circumcision, these verses bind together God's covenant with the patriarchs (see especially Gen. 17) and his deliverance of their descendants, the Israelites, from slavery.

13:2 *Consecrate to me every firstborn male.* Every firstborn male belongs to God in a special way. The implication of this is developed in Moses's speech to the people, especially 13:11–16.

13:11–16 *give over to the Lord the first offspring of every womb . . . Redeem every firstborn.* These instructions center on the fact that as a result of the Passover all firstborn males belong to God in a unique way. The rationale for this rests in the concept of "redemption." It might be better to speak of "ransom," since the Hebrew verb used in verse 13, *padah*, differs from the verb *ga'al*, "to redeem," that occurs in 6:6 and 15:13. Although both verbs are very similar in meaning and overlap semantically, they are not full synonyms and probably have different nuances when used in Exodus. Whereas the verb *ga'al* conveys the idea of a kinsman-redeemer acting to reverse an injustice, in this instance the prolonged enslavement of the Israelites, the verb *padah* recalls how someone under the sentence of death may save his or her life by paying a ransom (cf. 21:30). As verse 13 illustrates, a lamb may be used to ransom a donkey, the former becoming a substitute for the latter. In the light of this, the Passover sacrifices are probably viewed as ransoming the firstborn males from the power of death. Because they are ransomed by sacrifices given to God, they now belong to him.

Theological Insights

God's instructions regarding the Passover in 12:43–49 highlight the necessity of circumcision. At the heart of the covenant of circumcision is the idea that the nations will be blessed through a future royal descendant of Abraham. From the outset circumcision is given not as a mark of ethnicity but rather as a sign pointing forward to how God's covenant with the patriarchs will be fully established through Jesus Christ (Gal. 3:8–18). The linking of the Passover with circumcision reminds the Israelites that their divine salvation from slavery in Egypt depends on God's covenant with the patriarchs. This link between circumcision and the Passover may also shed light on the enigmatic passage involving Moses in Exodus 4:24–26. The short statement in 12:46 about not breaking a bone of the sacrificial lamb or goat is later picked up by the apostle John when he describes the crucifixion of Jesus (John 19:36). This is part of a much wider typology in John's Gospel, associating Jesus with a new exodus.

The special status attributed by God to the firstborn males confirms that the Passover ritual resembles the process by which Aaron and his sons are consecrated as priests (cf. Exod. 29; Lev. 8). The firstborn males are made holy and so belong to God. By highlighting how a donkey may be ransomed from death through the substitution of a lamb, 13:13 indirectly indicates that the concept of substitution is a feature of the Passover itself. Remarkably, at a later stage the Levites become a substitute for all firstborn Israelite males (Num. 3:12–13). As a result they receive a holier status than other Israelites. This enables them to have a unique role in serving God by undertaking duties associated with the tabernacle (Num. 3:6–10). This distinctive privilege, however, finds its origin in the deliverance of the firstborn males from death at the Passover.

Teaching the Text

This section of Exodus records different ways in which the Passover is to be commemorated by future generations of Israelites. No other event in their long history enjoys such prestige. For the Israelites, it was a defining moment, not only preparing them for an independent existence as God's holy people, but also modeling how people are saved from the consequences of human sin. Two features are especially noteworthy.

The Passover builds on God's earlier covenant with Abraham, Isaac, and Jacob. As the instructions in 12:43–49 highlight, only those who are circumcised may participate in the first Passover or share in later celebrations. If circumcised, even gentile males may share in the commemoration of the Passover. By emphasizing the importance of circumcision, the Passover regulations connect what happens in Egypt with God's earlier covenant with Abraham. This is noteworthy, because God's covenant with the patriarchs concerns the blessing of the nations. As Genesis 17:3–4 states, Abraham is to be the father of many nations. This is true, however, not in a biological sense, but spiritually (cf. Gal. 3:6–9). While the Passover in Egypt is about the creation of Israel as a holy nation, this has to be understood in the light of God's greater plan for all the nations of the earth.

The Passover recalls how God ransoms to himself all firstborn males. The commemoration instructions in 13:11–16 highlight the concept of ransom. By doing so, these instructions imply that the Passover sacrifices ransom all the Israelite firstborn males. By being a substitute, and dying in the place of the Israelite males, the Passover lambs and goats rescue them from death. This concept of substitution is reflected in Jesus's remark: "For even the Son of Man did not come to be served, but to serve, and to give his life as a ransom for many" (Mark 10:45). The high priest Caiaphas also alludes to something very similar:

> "You know nothing at all! You do not realize that it is better for you that one man die for the people than that the whole nation perish." He did not say this on his own, but as high priest that year he prophesied that Jesus would die for the Jewish nation, and not only for that nation but also for the scattered children of God, to bring them together and make them one. (John 11:49–52)

At the heart of the Passover is the concept of substitution. This is an important concept for understanding the Christian view of how people are restored to a right relationship with God.

Illustrating the Text

God's plan of salvation does not stop with Israel but includes all nations.

Object Lesson: It is amazing how energy can be transferred from one object to another. A simple exertion of force, exercised on the right object, can have massive effect. For example, consider the domino rally. A little push on one object can impact thousands of other objects. These fun exercises in energy transfer can range from a very small three-domino crash to a mind-bending collection of patterns, side-rallies, and rolling marbles. But it all starts with a single push. Have you ever seen one of these elaborate constructions halted midway through, or, even worse, close to the finale? One domino won't go down. So frustrating! God wants to transfer his blessing to many through us.

The ransom provided by the Passover lamb buys freedom from death.

History: Over a period of twenty-six years, prior to the fall of the Berlin Wall in 1989, the West German government paid for the release of 33,755 dissidents who had been jailed in East Germany. The average price paid for the release of a prisoner was about 4,000 deutsche marks. In all, the West German government paid over 3.4 billion deutsche marks. Payments were made both in cash and in kind. Payments were sometimes made using items that were in short supply in East Germany, including fruit, like oranges and bananas, as well as medical supplies. This remarkable scheme of ransom payments, known as *Freikauf* ("the buying of freedom"), was largely kept secret from the general population of West Germany until after the two countries were reunited. In a similar way, Passover celebrates God's deliverance of his people from death through the substitutionary death of the lamb and also points forward to the way Jesus buys our freedom from bondage and death with his very life. Thus the New Testament picks up on the image of Jesus as the Passover lamb in numerous ways, from the use of the image in the Passion Narratives to Revelation's depiction of the slain Lamb; Jesus's death in our place provides a ransom from sin and death and brings healing and life that we could never secure for ourselves.

The idea of substitution is at the heart of salvation.

Theological Reference: Conduct a brief theological aside, explaining a term that theologians use to capture exactly how Jesus was a substitute for us: "propitiation." This powerful, multisyllabic word is one that every Christian can and should grasp. A simple working definition is "turning away wrath with an offering."[4] Jesus stood in our place, as our substitute offering. God's righteousness demands that the guilty party be offered up for punishment. Yet Jesus stood in our place and said, "Father, I shall bear the punishment instead." Jesus absorbs the hammer strike of justice on our behalf.

Soli Deo Gloria—
Glory to God Alone

Big Idea

Through the destruction of the Egyptian chariot force God once more demonstrates his extraordinary power to deliver the Israelites.

Key Themes

- God's people will be persecuted by those hostile to God.
- Those who set themselves against God will suffer the consequences of their actions.
- God reveals his sovereignty over nature by using wind and water to destroy Pharaoh's elite troops.

Understanding the Text

The Text in Context

While the death of the firstborn Egyptian males prompts Pharaoh to drive out the Israelites, God plans one further demonstration of his power, a solemn reminder that the forces of evil will be punished for their exploitation of others. God intentionally creates the circumstances that encourage Pharaoh to pursue the Israelites. This is the final display of God's power in Egypt and brings to a climax God's rescue of the Israelites.

Historical and Cultural Background

Some scholars have suggested that the story of the crossing of the "Red Sea" (or better, "Lake of Reeds") resembles other ancient Near Eastern accounts that describe how the god Baal brings cosmic peace by overcoming Yam, the god of the sea.[1] While some general similarities exist, it is noteworthy that in Exodus 14–15 the sea is not hostile in any way toward God. Indeed, there is nothing to suggest that the sea is anything other than an inanimate object.

Interpretive Insights

13:17–18 *God did not lead them on the road through the Philistine country.* To avoid military conflict, the Lord guides the people away from the shorter route into Canaan along the Mediterranean coast. This route was guarded by a series of Egyptian forts designed to prevent invasions from Canaan.

toward the Red Sea. Although it has become customary to translate the Hebrew phrase *yam sup* as "Red Sea," this is misleading if it is taken in this context to refer to the Gulf of Suez. A literal rendering of *yam sup* would be "sea of reeds" or "lake of reeds." The term *yam* denotes a body of water and is usually translated "sea," but it could refer to a lake, for which biblical Hebrew has no distinctive term (cf. Deut. 33:23; Job 14:11). The most credible recent assessments of the route taken by the Israelites associate the *yam sup*, "Lake of Reeds," with a system of marshy lakes, known as the el-Ballah Lakes, which lie relatively close to the Mediterranean Sea (see map). In the time

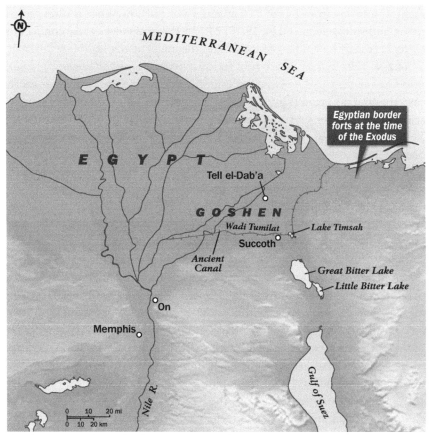

The phrase commonly translated as "Red Sea" likely refers to a series of marshy lakes that lie relatively close to the Mediterranean Sea. Most sites on the journey to Sinai have not been clearly identified.

of Moses there was one major lake; over subsequent centuries this became a series of interconnected lakes.

went up out of Egypt ready for battle. The Hebrew word *hamushim*, translated "ready for battle," might better be rendered "equipped for travel." It is unlikely that the Israelites, as newly freed slaves, are armed for military conflict, especially given what God says at the end of verse 17 regarding the prospect of war. If they were armed, they might not be quite so fearful of the Egyptian army that pursues them.

13:19 *Moses took the bones of Joseph with him.* This fulfills the request that Joseph made centuries earlier (Gen. 50:25) and confirms the confidence that he had in God's promises to the patriarchs concerning their descendants taking possession of the land of Canaan.

13:20–22 *they camped at Etham . . . pillar of cloud . . . pillar of fire.* The precise location of Etham is not known. It may have been at the eastern end of Wadi Tumilat, close to Lake Timsah. Throughout the account of the Israelites' journey from Egypt to Canaan, the Lord's presence is often linked to fire and smoke (e.g., 14:24; 19:18; 24:17). In Exodus 14 a close connection exists between the "pillar of cloud" and the angel of the Lord (see 14:19).

14:2–4 *Tell the Israelites to turn back . . . harden Pharaoh's heart . . . know that I am the* Lord. The Israelites might have expected to travel in a southeasterly direction from Egypt into the Sinai Peninsula. God deliberately instructs them, however, to journey in a northwesterly direction toward the Mediterranean Sea. As regards the places named in these verses, none has been identified with any certainty, although a number of possibilities seem feasible. Of the various options, the most likely location is the region to the west of Lake Ballah, as it existed in the second millennium BC (see map). On the hardening of Pharaoh's heart, see the "Theological Insights" in the unit on 8:20–10:29. In verse 4 we encounter once more the important theme of knowing the Lord (cf. 5:2; 6:7; 7:5, 17; 8:10, 22; 9:14; 10:2).

14:5–9 *Pharaoh and his officials changed their minds . . . six hundred of the best chariots.* As God has anticipated, the Egyptian king rues his decision to send away the Israelites. Although the Israelites have already been traveling for several days, they remain within relatively easy reach of Egyptian soldiers on chariots. Early evidence for the use of chariots in Egypt comes from the sixteenth century BC, when Ahmose I used them to overthrow the Hyksos. If the Israelites' exodus occurred in the middle of the fifteenth century BC, war chariots would have been an integral and important part of the Egyptian army. To emphasize the strength of the Egyptian force, verse 9 mentions "all Pharaoh's horses and chariots, horsemen and troops."

14:10–12 *They were terrified and cried out to the* Lord. Although 14:8 speaks of the Israelites "marching out boldly," the sudden appearance of the

Egyptian army undermines not only their self-confidence but, more important, their trust in God. Confronting Moses, the people quickly forget how God has delivered them from slavery in Egypt. Their yearning to return to Egypt features as a recurring motif during the wilderness journey and is always associated with a lack of trust in God (Exod. 15:23–25; 16:3; 17:3; Num. 11:1–6; 14:1–4; 16:13–14; 20:2–5; 21:4–5).

14:14–18 *The LORD will fight for you; you need only to be still.* Moses confidently affirms that God will once more rescue the Israelites. Importantly, Moses stresses that God alone will defeat the Egyptians, for the Israelites will take no part in the battle. They will merely be spectators. All the glory will go to the Lord.

14:19–20 *Then the angel of God . . . withdrew and went behind them.* Verse 19 links the "pillar of cloud" with the "angel of God," and there is good reason to view them as one and the same. A similar identification occurs in 3:2, where the "angel of the LORD" appears as "flames of fire." As in Exodus 3, the "angel" is a manifestation of God himself. In the light of 14:24, it seems likely that "the pillar of fire and cloud" is a theophany.

14:21–23 *Moses stretched out his hand . . . drove the sea back with a strong east wind.* Moses's action resembles what he and Aaron did when they initiated each supernatural sign in Egypt. The use of a strong east wind recalls what happens in 10:13, 19.

14:24–29 *the LORD looked down from the pillar of fire and cloud at the Egyptian army.* Having stood between the Israelites and the Egyptian army, God disables the Egyptians' chariots before closing the waters over them. This further underlines God's extraordinary power to control the natural environment.

14:30–31 *the Israelites saw the mighty hand of the LORD . . . feared the LORD.* God's actions cause the people to reverence and trust him. The destruction of the Egyptian army is a further testimony to God's sovereignty over the forces of nature.

Theological Insights

From beginning to end the defeat of Pharaoh's army is an event planned by God to be a testimony to his power, bringing glory to him alone (14:4). To this end God even strengthens Pharaoh's resolve when he decides to pursue the Israelites. However, as throughout the signs and wonders episodes, God does not cause Pharaoh to act in a way that is contrary to what the Egyptian king desires. Rather, God gives Pharaoh the courage to fulfill his own wishes.

In spite of everything that has happened in Egypt, Pharaoh's final response to the departure of the Israelites reveals that he still has not grasped and accepted the Lord's true identity. Ironically, the Israelites also appear to have only a partial understanding of God. Their fearful reaction to the arrival of the Egyptian army reveals that they have not fully recognized the magnitude of God's authority and power.

Teaching the Text

This section of Exodus underlines God's power to both save and destroy. While the primary focus is on God and all that he achieves on behalf of the Israelites, four themes may be helpfully explored.

Hostility toward God's people. Pharaoh's reluctance to see the Israelites depart from Egypt is not due to any affection for them. On the contrary, he is aggressively hostile toward them, a hostility fueled because of their commitment to worship the Lord. Unfortunately, it is one of the sad realities of human existence that those who live in obedience to God will suffer persecution for doing so. As Cain killed his own brother, Abel, so Jesus warns that on his account brother will betray brother to death, and children will persecute their parents (Matt. 10:21–22). Because of the reality of persecution, Jesus encourages his followers with these words:

> Blessed are those who are persecuted because of righteousness,
> for theirs is the kingdom of heaven.

> Blessed are you when people insult you, persecute you and falsely say all kinds of evil against you because of me. Rejoice and be glad, because great is your reward in heaven, for in the same way they persecuted the prophets who were before you. (Matt. 5:10–12)

Defeat of tyranny. Pharaoh's decision to dispatch a military force against unarmed civilians brings about the death of the soldiers. Pharaoh and his army suffer the consequence of opposing God's will. Those who set themselves against God will experience the reality of judgment and punishment. This may not come on them immediately, for during the era of grace God keeps open the possibility for evildoers to repent. Nevertheless, when Jesus Christ returns in glory, he will judge the living and the dead, rewarding everyone as he or she deserves (Matt. 25:31–46).

God's sovereignty over nature. The remarkable events at the Lake of Reeds are a further illustration of God's authority over the natural world. His ability to part the waters of the lake using a strong wind defies any natural explanation, especially given the timing of this event. If God has the power to control the wind and the water, this should engender confidence in his people that he has the power to care for them in all circumstances. As the apostle Paul affirms: "For I am convinced that neither death nor life, neither angels nor demons, neither the present nor the future, nor any powers, neither height nor depth, nor anything else in all creation, will be able to separate us from the love of God that is in Christ Jesus our Lord" (Rom. 8:38–39). The knowledge of God's sovereignty should be for Christians a source of reassurance and comfort, even in the face of persecution and death.

For God's glory. It is not uncommon for Christian authors or composers to dedicate a book or composition to God using the words "*Soli Deo Gloria.*" They do so hoping that their creative efforts will bring glory to God. While the defeat of the Egyptian army is also intended to bring glory to God, human involvement is minimal, with God himself taking the main role. This is another reminder that our salvation rests not on what we can achieve but on what God has achieved for our benefit.

Illustrating the Text

Those who live in obedience to God will suffer persecution.

Scenario: Imagine the scene. It is summer 1975, 7:23 p.m. Every seat in the movie theater is filled. People mindlessly pack popcorn in their mouths, heedless of the fact that three-quarters of it is falling to the floor. Eyes are wide. Hearts are beating. On the screen, swimmers are frolicking a bit too far from shore. A fin moves through the water. Under it all an orchestra slowly builds. It's the premiere of Stephen Spielberg's *Jaws*, and the crowd's nerves are at peak levels, having been prepped by movie trailers and gossip of the scariest movie ever.

Now, imagine this: at the height of the drama, someone bursts into the theater and shines a powerful light into everyone's faces! How do you think the crowd would react? Shouts of outrage, irritation, and confusion would probably ensue. Someone might even pelt the intruder with a tub of buttered popcorn. Why? The answer is simple: because an unwelcome, outside illumination has entered the theater and disrupted the fantasy world inside.

As Christians, we believe that the world is caught in an illusion. We are called to be a light. Very often, that light will be unwelcome, because nobody likes to be disillusioned. At times, people may even react with outrage. That is a price we have to pay.

Though justice may be delayed, it will never be denied.

Human Experience: Many people can relate to memories of Mom, exasperated with our behavior, saying, "You just wait till your father gets home." Far from being a comforting delay of punishment, this usually led to a day of dread. The reality is, unless we repent, we will be facing judgment. Our Father will make sure that no injustice will remain in eternity. The scales will be balanced.

God's sovereignty should be reassuring, even in the face of persecution and death.

Hymn: "How Firm a Foundation." The fourth verse of this hymn says, "When through fiery trials thy pathway shall lie, my grace, all sufficient, shall be thy supply; the flame shall not hurt thee; I only design thy dross to consume, and thy gold to refine." Behind this promise of comfort is the reality of God's sovereignty. Trials do not represent the triumph of evil. We can rely on the will of our good God, who promises not only to give us grace for the trial but to use it to refine us.

The focus of salvation is not on what we can do for God but on what he has done for us.

Applying the Text: This simple truth that *God* is the primary actor in the drama of salvation is also a powerful tool for evangelism. A popular approach ("Do" vs. "Done") to sharing the gospel can be quickly summarized: some world religions tell us what we have to *do* to be right with God. Christianity tells us what God has *done* for us in Jesus Christ.

Someone to Sing About

Big Idea
God's people have every reason to sing the praise of the one who is majestic in power and holiness.

Key Themes
- God's people should rejoice when God decisively intervenes to defeat the forces of evil.
- The ultimate purpose of divine redemption is that people should cohabit the earth with God.

Understanding the Text

The Text in Context

This section of Exodus brings to completion the account of God's deliverance of the Israelites from Pharaoh's tyranny. In the light of everything that God has done for them, the Israelites fittingly worship him in song. The poetic nature of the song recorded in verses 1–18 clearly sets it apart from its prose surroundings. Coming after chapter 14 this song celebrates rather than narrates God's victory over Pharaoh's army. The reader of Exodus, having witnessed the defeat of Pharaoh's army, as well as the earlier signs and wonders, is invited to share in this exuberant celebration, a fitting tribute to God for all that he has done in rescuing the Israelites from slavery.

This celebration does not dwell simply on the past. The song looks with optimism to the future, anticipating the settlement of the Israelites in the land of Canaan. In doing so, the emphasis is on the people dwelling in close proximity to God himself. This is an indication that the exodus is about much more than setting slaves free. It is about the establishment of a harmonious relationship between God and those redeemed from bondage to evil. As a paradigm pointing forward, the annihilation of Pharaoh's army heralds God's ultimate defeat of the powers of evil.

Historical and Cultural Background

It was customary for women to welcome victorious soldiers, returning from battle, with songs and dance (e.g., 1 Sam. 18:6–7). On this occasion men join them in praising the Lord, for he alone has defeated the enemy. In spite of the present literary order, the similarities between verse 1 and verse 21 suggest that Miriam composed the song in verses 1–18. She takes the lead and invites the people to sing: "Sing to the LORD, for he is highly exalted" (v. 21). Each person responds: "I will sing to the LORD, for he is highly exalted" (v. 1). The author of Exodus possibly places the details about Miriam's role after the song in order to create a frame with chapters 1–2, where women play an important role at the start of the exodus story.

Scholarly opinion on the dating of this song ranges from the late second millennium BC to the fourth century BC. The song itself undoubtedly contains archaic features, but some scholars argue that these are artificial, designed to make the poem appear ancient. There is no compelling reason, however, to reject an early date of composition.

Interpretive Insights

15:1–2 *Then Moses and the Israelites sang this song to the* LORD. The distinct form of the Hebrew text indicates that the Israelites sang this song more than once. Its repeated use would solidify within the people's memory the significance of what God did for them at the Lake of Reeds.

I will sing to the LORD. The repeated use of the first person strongly suggests a firsthand experience of what God has done. The wording suggests that verses 1–5 are addressed to other people, whereas the remainder of the song addresses God himself.

15:3–5 *The* LORD *is a warrior.* These verses assume a knowledge of the more detailed narrative recorded in chapter 14. By describing God as a "warrior," the song highlights another important aspect of God's nature. He is a God willing to fight against the forces of evil and tyranny.

15:6–12 *Your right hand,* LORD. God is addressed directly in verses 6–12. The form and content of verses 6–7 indicate that they describe God's activity in general and are not restricted to the destruction of Pharaoh's army. In marked contrast, verses 8–10 clearly allude to the events of chapter 14. Verse 9 in particular highlights the arrogance of the Egyptian soldiers as, with excited pleasure, they anticipate killing and plundering the fleeing Israelites.

15:13 *you will lead the people . . . you will guide them to your holy dwelling.* The translation of the verbs in verse 13 is problematic. Whereas the NIV opts for the future tense, the KJV and ESV prefer the past tense, which would seem to be the more likely rendering. Does verse 13 refer to what

God has already done, or does it anticipate what he is yet to do? This choice takes on added significance due to the final phrase: "your holy dwelling." What is meant by this, and how does it relate to the "sanctuary" mentioned in verse 17? This issue has engendered much discussion, and no scholarly consensus exists.[1] Those commentators who assume that both verses refer to the same place tend to favor a location in Canaan, possibly Jerusalem. More likely, however, the Hebrew expression *n^{e}weh qod^{e}sheka,* "your holy dwelling," in verse 13 denotes the encampment by the Lake of Reeds. This expression is found only here in the whole of the Old Testament, and the noun *naweh* is most often linked with shepherds and the place where they rest when on a journey with their flock. Since verse 13 also speaks of God leading and guiding the people, it seems natural to assume that his "holy dwelling" refers to where the Israelites are resting after crossing through the Lake of Reeds. Verse 13, therefore, looks back, along with verses 8–12, to how God has led the Israelites to safety, rescuing them from the tyranny of Pharaoh.

you have redeemed. This probably conveys the sense of redemption from slavery (see the comments on 6:6–8), whereas "redeem" in 13:13 denotes ransom from death.

15:14–16 *The nations will hear and tremble.* From this point onward, the song looks to the future, anticipating the Israelites' settlement in the land of Canaan. In the light of God's victory over Pharaoh, the Israelites may be confident that the nations of Canaan will not prove to be a barrier to the fulfillment of God's plans for them.

15:17 *on the mountain of your inheritance—the place, LORD, you made for your dwelling.* The expressions used to describe the destination to which God will bring the Israelites are so nonspecific that various locations are possible (e.g., Shiloh; Zion/Jerusalem; Canaan). Less likely is the suggestion that the destination is Mount Sinai. Since Shiloh and then Jerusalem served as central sanctuaries in Canaan, it may be more helpful to interpret verse 17 in a general way, embracing both locations. More important than the identity of the location is its function as a dwelling place for the Lord. Verse 17 affirms that the Israelites themselves will live in close proximity to God. Within the book of Exodus itself, the sealing of the covenant at Mount Sinai and the construction of the tabernacle are important steps toward the fulfillment of God's plan to dwell permanently among the Israelites in Canaan. This is the goal toward which everything in Exodus moves.

15:18 *The LORD reigns for ever and ever.* This final affirmation underlines the everlasting nature of God's rule. Although the forces of evil have usurped God's place as ruler of this world, God's reign over his creation will one day be fully established.

15:19 *When Pharaoh's horses, chariots and horsemen went into the sea.*
This summary statement, echoing closely 14:28–29, picks up the story line at that point chronologically.

15:20 *Then Miriam the prophet, Aaron's sister, took a timbrel in her hand.*
Miriam is possibly designated a prophet because the content of her song predicts the establishment of the Lord's sanctuary in the land of Canaan.

Theological Insights

By concentrating on what the Lord has done, the song places God at the center of everything that takes place. Even Moses receives no mention in the song, for God alone has been responsible for the Israelites' rescue from the deadly aspirations of Pharaoh's soldiers. Rightly, this song gives emphasis to God as the Divine Warrior, who is majestic in power and more than able to destroy the greatest of human armies. Yet God does not use his incomparable power in a tyrannical manner. It is only in defending the Israelites that he destroys the Egyptian forces. While God is ultimately committed to defeating all the powers of evil, this does not necessarily mean that he will do so by resorting solely to the use of power. This celebration of God's redemption of the Israelites mirrors the greater redemption that comes through Jesus Christ, leading ultimately to the creation of the new Jerusalem, where the redeemed will live eternally with their Redeemer. Yet although Christ will overcome every power that stands in opposition to God, the establishment of his kingdom is secured by self-sacrificial love and not military might.

Teaching the Text

Readers of Exodus are invited to share in the Israelites' celebration of their divine rescue from Pharaoh's elite troops. Apart from rejoicing exuberantly in gratitude to God, the song recalls the greater purpose behind God's defeat of the Egyptian chariot force. By looking back with thanksgiving and looking forward with hope, the song highlights the Israelites' dependence on God. Both their past and their future have been and will be shaped by God's actions.

Gratitude for redemption. With song and dance Miriam leads the Israelites in heartfelt praise of the Lord. The people have witnessed firsthand their dramatic deliverance from a violent military assault, no doubt motivated by the prospect of taking revenge for the death of the Egyptian firstborn males. The Israelites owe their lives to God. Gratitude for divine salvation should be the natural response of all of God's people. If the Israelites are exuberant in their praise of God, Christians have even more reason to rejoice in Christ's victory over Satan and the powers of evil.

Anticipation of future life with God. Celebration of what God had already done for the Israelites turns from looking to the past to anticipating the future. Building on God's promises, verse 17 predicts that the Israelites will dwell with God at his earthly sanctuary. This reflects a significant reversal of the disruption caused by Adam and Eve's betrayal of God in the Garden of Eden. The image of humanity residing in harmony close to God captures well the essence of the goal of divine salvation. As Jesus himself reminds the disciples, he goes to the Father to prepare a dwelling place for them (John 14:1–3). Ultimately, this comes to fulfillment in the new Jerusalem (Rev. 21–22).

This is not a song that glories in military victory and the death of enemy soldiers. Rather, it highlights how human aggression and greed will not be tolerated by the God of justice and mercy. Those who enhance their own lives by mercilessly exploiting others will reap their due reward. Those who show no mercy to others cannot expect mercy from God. Having already witnessed the devastating power of God, Pharaoh and his soldiers are without excuse when they seek to enslave the Israelites again.

Illustrating the Text

Gratitude for divine salvation should be the natural response of all of God's people.

Bible: **Jesus Heals Ten Lepers.** While traveling to Jerusalem, Jesus encounters ten men with leprosy. He took pity on them, and they were cleansed. But of the ten, only one of them, a Samaritan, returns to thank Jesus. The story illustrates that gratitude for what God has done is not always given.

God's decision to dwell with us is a reversal of the curse of the fall.

History: On April 26, 1986, a Ukrainian town was ripped apart. A fiery explosion, escaping steam, and a fallout plume rose over Chernobyl, which was forever changed as nuclear radiation spread from the nuclear power plant in meltdown. Though Soviet officials initially tried to downplay the incident, it soon became clear that the area would need to be evacuated. Eventually, more than ninety-one thousand people would be moved. In order to protect people from deadly radiation, authorities formed an "exclusion zone" stretching a thousand square miles. It is there to this day. Dikes, to prevent contaminated silt from escaping, secure rivers flowing out of the area. Experts estimate that the area will not be safe for habitation for twenty thousand years.

Our sin radically separates us from God. It is like contamination. God cannot, and will not, dwell side by side with sin. Only through his work of redemption can we have any hope to live with him.

We worship a God who executes powerful justice.

Quote: **Charles Spurgeon.** Spurgeon reminds us that our rejoicing should be in *God's sovereign justice*, not in the death of the unrighteous:

> I, for one, am perfectly satisfied with everything that God does. . . . I make bold to say that I would have praised God as the waves went over Pharaoh; for the Lord did it, and he did right. I would have cried with Moses, "I will sing unto the Lord, for he hath triumphed gloriously: the horse and his rider hath he thrown into the sea." I expect to be among the number, though some seem as if they would decline the service, who shall for ever bless God for all his dealings with mankind—the stern as well as those that seem more tender. The Lord God, even Jehovah, the God of the Old Testament, is the God whom I worship.[2]

Life Is More Than Food

Big Idea

People live not on food alone but by trusting and obeying God.

Key Themes

- God amazingly provides the means to transform the bitter into the sweet.
- God patiently uses the wilderness to disciple/train the Israelites.
- God generously supplies all that is needed for as long as it is needed.

Understanding the Text

The Text in Context

This section of Exodus reports the next stage of the Israelites' trek away from Egypt. Their journey into the Sinai Peninsula brings them into an arid region where fresh water and food are not readily available. As they journey by stages through this region, God uses the harsh conditions to train the people to trust and obey him. By presenting the people with various challenges, God intentionally prepares them so that they will understand the consequences of entering into a covenant relationship with him at Mount Sinai.

Exodus 15:22–27 forms a bridge between the Israelites in Egypt and in the wilderness. By describing how Moses, in obedience to God, transforms bitter water into sweet, these verses capture something of the exodus experience. Through Moses, the bitter experience of the Israelites' time in Egypt is made sweet. Implicit, however, in the reporting of this short episode is the importance of obeying the Lord.

Interpretive Insights

15:22 *Moses led Israel from the Red Sea and they went into the Desert of Shur.* Moses is the principal subject of 15:22–26. This is marked initially by how he is introduced as leading the Israelites into the wilderness. The name Shur refers to a region in northern Sinai that stretches from Egypt to Canaan. During their three-day trek in this arid region, the Israelites encounter no source of water. This explains their considerable disappointment when they discover that the water at Marah is undrinkable. The name Marah comes from the Hebrew adjective *mar*, meaning "bitter." Interestingly, this description recalls how life in Egypt was also bitter (1:14; 12:8).

15:24–25a *the people grumbled against Moses.* Understandably, the people confront Moses, looking for help. Their grumbling introduces a motif that recurs in various wilderness episodes (Exod. 16:2, 7–8; 17:3; Num. 14:2, 27, 29, 36; 16:11, 41; 17:5, 10). While this motif is passed over quickly in this episode, it becomes more prominent in those that follow.

the LORD showed him a piece of wood. The narrative lacks an explanation of how the wooden object transforms the water. It is not even clear what Moses throws into the water; the Hebrew noun *'ets* may refer to either a piece of wood or a tree.

15:25b–26 *the LORD . . . put them to the test. He said, "If you listen carefully."* Although the NIV, like most other English translations, interprets these verses as applying to the Israelites in general, it is more likely that Moses alone is tested here by God. Throughout God's speech in verse 26 "you" is always singular. As leader of the Israelites, Moses is under a special obligation to obey God's commands and observe his decrees.

15:27 *they came to Elim, where there were twelve springs and seventy palm trees.* The mention of palm trees at Elim indicates that this oasis has a permanent supply of water. By introducing Elim so soon after the incident at Marah, the narrator underlines God's ability to guide the people to water. They should not have become impatient at Marah.

16:1 *set out from Elim and came to the Desert of Sin.* The Hebrew term "Sin" is unrelated to the English word "sin." This is one of seven wildernesses mentioned in connection with the Israelites' journey from Egypt to Canaan. They probably arrive at this location two and a half months (or 70 days—28+28+14) after the Passover. By this stage the Israelites have exhausted all their supplies and have little prospect of finding new supplies in the wilderness.

16:2–3 *If only we had died by the LORD's hand in Egypt!* Ironically, the Israelites state that they would have preferred a swift death in Egypt by "the LORD's hand." Their memory of life in Egypt is skewed; they quickly forget their hard labor under the Egyptian slave drivers. Their anger is directed at Moses and Aaron, whom they hold responsible for bringing them into the desert. They forget that the Lord has been leading and guiding them (cf. 15:13).

16:4–5 *I will rain down bread from heaven for you.* Having already tested Moses (15:22–26), the Lord tests the obedience of the Israelites. In this context testing may also imply training. Through the provision of manna, God will train the Israelites to obey him. Part of the purpose of the wilderness trek is to develop the Israelites' trust in God.

16:6–8 *you will know that it was the LORD who brought you out of Egypt.* Countering what the people have said, Moses and Aaron remind them that the Lord has brought them out of Egypt. The Israelites' accusations indict God for failing to provide for them.

16:11–12 *the grumbling of the Israelites . . . "Then you will know that I am the* LORD." The theme of knowing the Lord reappears. The Israelites' grumbling implies that they have a deficient knowledge of the Lord.

16:13–14 *That evening quail came and covered the camp.* Some commentators mistakenly assume that God provided quail on a daily basis for the Israelites. The present passage indicates clearly that quail are supplied only on the first day. Later, in Numbers 11, after the Israelites complain about having had only manna to eat for years, God sends quail for a second time. Manna alone is the regular diet of the Israelites. Although some scholars suggest that the provision of manna may be explained as a natural phenomenon, this seems unlikely, especially when none appears on the seventh day.[1]

16:15–18 *"What is it?" . . . "Take an omer for each person."* Because the Israelites have no prior knowledge of the white flake-like substance, they give it the name "manna" (16:31), which conveys the sense "What is this?" God's instructions discourage greed. Those who gather more than others discover that everyone receives one omer, that is, about two liters (see 16:36).

16:19–21 *No one is to keep any of it until morning.* Those who store manna overnight do not believe that God will provide fresh manna each day. Their action springs from a lack of confidence in him.

16:22–23 *On the sixth day, they gathered twice as much.* The Israelites are surprised to discover that they are able to gather two omers on the sixth day. When they consult with Moses, they discover that the seventh day is to be a day of rest. This suggests that the Israelites are unfamiliar with the concept of the Sabbath. Since there is no prior mention in Genesis or Exodus of people keeping the Sabbath as a day of rest, it seems likely that it is introduced here for the first time. By doing so, God prepares for the sealing of the Sinai covenant, the sign of which is the Sabbath (31:13–17; cf. 20:8–11). Through the provision of extra manna on the sixth day, God trains the Israelites to rest on the seventh day.

16:27 *Nevertheless, some of the people went out on the seventh day.* Yet again, some Israelites disregard God's instructions.

16:28–30 *How long will you refuse to keep my commands and my instructions?* The Lord expresses his disappointment at the disobedience of the people, especially given his extraordinary provision of manna for them. By commanding the Israelites to rest on the seventh day, the Lord demonstrates his concern for their welfare. This contrasts sharply with how Pharaoh mistreated them in Egypt.

16:31 *It was white like coriander seed.* The NIV translation does not quite reflect the Hebrew text, which states that the manna was both "like coriander seed" and "white." The individual pieces of manna resemble coriander seeds, which are three to five millimeters in diameter.

16:32–36 *Take an omer of manna and keep it for the generations to come.* These verses describe events that take place after the construction of the tabernacle. Verse 35 must have been written in the postwilderness era; the Israelites have settled in the land of Canaan. Manna kept overnight would normally become infested with maggots (cf. 16:20). An omer was the daily allowance for an individual (cf. 16:16). This chapter is the only place in the whole of the Old Testament where the term "omer" is used. (It should not be confused with another measurement known as a "homer.") The need to explain the size of an omer points to the antiquity of this passage.

Theological Insights

God deliberately leads the Israelites into the wilderness in order to prepare them for life in Canaan. Their time in the wilderness is a period of training for them. By confronting the Israelites with a lack of food and water, God tests their trust in him. Their obedience in these circumstances reflects the degree to which they trust him. The instructions concerning the manna both measure their faith in God and train them to trust him more. At this initial stage disobedience is not punished, as happens when they travel from Mount Sinai toward the land of Canaan. Through his treatment of the Israelites, God reveals his patience and tolerance as he seeks to encourage them to trust him more. Contrary to popular caricatures of God, he is not a vengeful tyrant, eagerly seeking every opportunity to punish people.

Teaching the Text

Much of life revolves around food. We cannot live without it. Yet as the French playwright Molière remarked, one should eat to live, not live to eat.[2] Remarkably, our attitude toward food may give an interesting insight into our spiritual relationship with God. Exodus 16 provides an amazing opportunity to explore this issue, as God uses food to test and train the Israelites to trust and obey him more fully.

Trusting God to provide. The Israelites' lack of food raises the issue of God's care for them. Although they direct their accusations at Moses, underlying this is a lack of confidence that God will provide for them. Even when the manna is given, there are still those who hoard some of the manna because they are unsure that God will supply food on a daily basis. Centuries later the devil tests Jesus regarding the absence of food in the wilderness (Matt. 4:1–4; Luke 4:1–4). In response, Jesus quotes from Deuteronomy 8, where Moses alludes to Exodus 16 in order to teach that "man does not live on bread alone but on every word that comes from the mouth of the LORD" (Deut. 8:3).

Sharing what God gives. God's instructions to the Israelites regarding the gathering of the manna underline that they are to collect only what is needed for each person. God ensures that everyone gets the same quota, regardless of how much is gathered. Those motivated by gluttony and/or anxiety regarding the future are trained to curb their greediness. Interestingly, the apostle Paul quotes Exodus 16:18 when teaching about generosity in 2 Corinthians 8. He writes,

> Our desire is not that others might be relieved while you are hard pressed, but that there might be equality. At the present time your plenty will supply what they need, so that in turn their plenty will supply what you need. The goal is equality, as it is written: "The one who gathered much did not have too much, and the one who gathered little did not have too little." (2 Cor. 8:13–15)

God's provision of food for the Israelites is a reminder of the need to be generous to others. We need to keep our desire for food, and other material possessions, in a healthy perspective. We should never be greedy for more, and we should never place these things before obedience to God.

Illustrating the Text

The complaints we direct at people cloak a deeper dissatisfaction with God's provision.

Nature: Anyone who has tried to get rid of crabgrass knows how irritating it can be. Once it takes root, it seems impossible to remove. Part of the problem is that crabgrass can grow together, forming a mat of interconnected leaves and roots. Its seeds survive the winter and emerge again in the spring. Taking out one plant does not take out the entire organism. Each plant, in fact, is part of something much bigger, a survival system perfectly adapted to destroy a nice, green lawn.

In the same way, we may know someone (or *be* someone) who is prone to complaining. It happens in various situations and at various times; the instances might not all seem connected. But very often, this kind of constant critique and complaining is really part of a deeper, more sinister system: dissatisfaction with God. We are unhappy with him. We resent his way of handling us, the circumstances he ordains, and the position he gives. A spirit of complaining has deep, dangerous roots. Only a work of the Holy Spirit can bring true transformation—revealing, removing, and replacing dissatisfaction with gratitude.

God calls us to trust him for our daily bread.

Church History: During the Protestant Reformation, two leaders penned the Heidelberg Catechism to help the church teach basic Christianity to believers. One section of this catechism helps explain the Lord's Prayer. Here is what it says about the phrase "give us this day our daily bread": "Be pleased to provide for all our bodily need; that we may thereby know that Thou art the only fountain of all good, and that without Thy blessing, neither our care and labor, nor Thy gifts can profit us; and may therefore withdraw our trust from all creatures, and place it alone in Thee."[3] In other words, "Lord, help us to remember that you are the Source! Help us not to place our trust in our own efforts or anything else in this world."

We need to keep our desire for food, and other possessions, in healthy perspective.

Popular Culture: Americans love their pets . . . a lot. According to the National Retail Federation, our country was projected to spend $330 million on pet costumes for Halloween 2013. This leads us to consider just how much we love our Halloween festivities—enough to lay out $6.9 billion.[4] So that pet costume budget really doesn't seem so exorbitant when put in context. It is easy (though not illegitimate) to point out frivolities that pervade Western culture. And it provides a good occasion for us to examine our generosity: Are we only generous with ourselves, or do we truly share what we have been given in a way that shows genuine generosity toward others, a generosity that includes restraint toward ourselves?

Knowing the Presence of God

Big Idea

When God's people confront major challenges in life, they need to unite in trusting the one who is ever present with them.

Key Themes

- A lack of trust in God may cause quarreling among God's people.
- God's people need to be united to withstand the hostility of their enemies.

Understanding the Text

The Text in Context

This section of Exodus describes two separate incidents that arise during the Israelites' journey from Egypt to Mount Sinai. Both reflect the challenge of journeying through a hostile environment that lacks easily accessible supplies of food and water and provides opportunities for ruthless raiders to enrich themselves by attacking vulnerable travelers. Once again the Israelites' reliance on God is tested. In challenging circumstances the people need to learn that God is always with them. Through these incidents God continues to train the Israelites, preparing them for their future settlement in the land of Canaan.

Interpretive Insights

17:1 *set out from the Desert of Sin . . . camped at Rephidim, but there was no water.* The region of Rephidim lies between the Desert of Sin and the Desert of Sinai (cf. 19:1–2). The exact location cannot be identified with certainty, but it may possibly be in the area of Wadi Refayid. The name Rephidim would appear to designate a wide area rather than a particular location. This explains why Moses gives a specific name to the place where the water appears. The circumstances at Rephidim have parallels with Marah, but there the water was initially undrinkable (15:23).

17:2–3 *So they quarreled with Moses.* The people are quick to blame Moses for the absence of water. Once again they accuse him of leading them out of Egypt in order to bring about their death (cf. 16:3). The Hebrew term *rib* (NIV: "quarreled"), used to describe their accusation, implies that Moses has intentionally sought to harm them and so must bear full responsibility. Moses obviously considers his life under threat (cf. 17:4).

Why do you put the LORD *to the test?* As revealed earlier, in 16:4, God has brought the Israelites into the desert to test their obedience to him. However, by their attack on Moses the people test the Lord. This motif of testing God reappears in Numbers 14:22. While it is appropriate for God to test the Israelites' obedience, it is clearly inappropriate for them to test the Lord's faithfulness. By testing the Lord, the Israelites not only imply that he is less than perfect, but they also set themselves up as judges who are in some way superior to God. Only God, as the supreme judge over all, can truly test others. The KJV reads "tempt" where the NIV and other modern translations have "test" or "try"; this reflects how the meaning of "tempt" has changed in the English language since the seventeenth century. The Hebrew verb *nissah* does not have the negative connotation associated with the modern English term "tempt." There is no reason to assume that God does something unacceptable when he "tests" people.

17:4 *What am I to do with these people?* Exasperated by the Israelites, Moses looks to God for help, as he did previously at Marah (15:25).

17:5–6 *by the rock at Horeb. Strike the rock, and water will come out of it.* The name Horeb means "dry/desolate." As an apt description of the desert location, the designation Horeb implies that this is not likely to be a suitable place for finding water. This makes the divine provision of water all the more remarkable. Some scholars assume that Horeb is a synonym for Sinai.[1] It is more likely, however, that Horeb denotes a wider region within which are located the Desert of Sinai and Mount Sinai itself.[2] Taking the staff that he and Aaron used in Egypt, Moses strikes a large rock. Some scholars suggest that the sudden appearance of water may be explained due to a natural phenomenon: Moses uses the staff to crack the crust of soft, porous limestone to release water from the saturated rock. However, given the arid location, the sudden appearance of water stored in limestone seems most unlikely. This event is yet another example of God's power to control the natural environment.

17:7 *he called the place Massah and Meribah.* This double-barreled name means "test and quarrel." Recalling the two verbs used in verse 2 and repeated in verse 7, the name captures well the concepts of quarreling and testing that figure prominently in this incident. Numbers 20:1–13 describes a similar incident, but with an unfortunate outcome for Moses. This latter incident is known as the "Waters of Meribah" (Num. 20:13, 24; 27:14). Knowledge

Christ the Spiritual Rock

In writing to the church at Corinth, the apostle Paul refers to the wilderness experience of the Israelites. In particular, he makes reference to them eating and drinking, alluding specifically to this passage in which they drink water from a rock (1 Cor. 10:1–4). The NIV translation reads: "They all ate the same spiritual food and drank the same spiritual drink; for they drank from the spiritual rock that accompanied them, and that rock was Christ" (1 Cor. 10:3–4). Unfortunately, this translation gives the impression that the wilderness rock from which they drank was Christ. Other translations say that "they drank from the spiritual rock that followed them" (e.g., NRSV; cf. ESV). Paul is not claiming that Christ followed (or accompanied) them as they journeyed in the wilderness. Rather, he thinks of Christ following them chronologically. Paul means that in the physical drinking and eating of the Israelites in the wilderness, they share spiritually with those who centuries later feast on Christ (cf. 1 Cor. 10:16–17).

of the "Massah and Meribah" episode in Exodus 17 explains why Moses, without divine permission, strikes the rock twice in Numbers 20:1–13. The concluding question in verse 7, "Is the LORD among us or not?" takes on added significance when viewed in the light of the whole book of Exodus, which describes how the Lord comes to live among the Israelites.

17:8–9 *The Amalekites came and attacked the Israelites.* The Amalekites are associated with the descendants of Esau, according to Genesis 36:12, 16. The present passage does not explain why the Amalekites attack the Israelites. Deuteronomy 25:17–19 states that the Amalekites harass those at the rear of the Israelite expedition, presumably because they travel more slowly and are more frail. Even after the Israelites settle in Canaan, the Amalekites continued to attack them (Judg. 3:13; 6:3; 10:12; 1 Sam. 14:48).

Moses said to Joshua. Joshua, from the tribe of Ephraim (Num. 13:8), is introduced here for the first time in the Pentateuch. Undoubtedly, Moses was confident of Joshua's leadership skills (cf. Exod. 24:13; 32:17; 33:11; Num. 11:28). The Ephraimites, as descendants of Joseph, saw themselves as appointed by God to exercise leadership over all the other tribes.

17:10–13 *Moses, Aaron and Hur . . . Moses held up his hands.* These verses concentrate on Moses, Aaron, and Hur, who survey the battle from the top of a hill. The narrator is especially interested in Moses's struggle to hold up the staff of God. Hur and Aaron are later appointed deputies by Moses when he ascends Mount Sinai (24:14). Hur is the grandfather of Bezalel (31:2) and is from the tribe of Judah.

With little experience of warfare, the Israelites struggle to overcome the Amalekites. The staff of God is first mentioned in 4:20. Moses and Aaron use this staff to initiate the signs and wonders in Egypt. It is sometimes suggested that Moses holds up his hands in prayer. According to 9:29, prayer involves outstretched hands, rather than upraised hands. The raised staff is more likely to signal that divine power is used against the Amalekites. The Lord gives victory to Joshua and his troops; they do not win the battle through their own strength.

17:14–16 *I will completely blot out the name of Amalek from under heaven.* Due to the Amalekites' aggressive attack on the Israelites, God indicates that he will destroy the Amalekites over a period of time. The Amalekites come under God's judgment for attacking his people. Conflict between Israel and the Amalekites continues to the time of Saul (1 Sam. 15:1–33) and later (1 Sam. 30:18). Moses commemorates the Israelite victory over the Amalekites by building an altar and naming it "The LORD is my Banner." Normally a banner was a rallying point for troops prior to battle.

Because hands were lifted up against the throne of the LORD. The meaning of the quotation in verse 16 has engendered much discussion, and a wide variety of opinions have been expressed regarding whose hand (the Hebrew is singular, but the NIV renders it plural) is meant and what the hand does in connection with the Lord's throne.[3] Most likely, as the NIV implies, the hand is that of Amalek, and it is raised in defiance against God.

Theological Insights

The two episodes placed side by side in chapter 17 insightfully illustrate the capability and reliability of God in both providing for and protecting his people. Even when the Israelites display blatant distrust in God, the Lord nevertheless is gracious and generous in dealing with them. This response is in keeping with his plan that the Israelites' wilderness experience should be a time of training for them. To this end, he causes them to confront the prospect of dying of thirst in the desert. Ironically, on this occasion the Israelites test God by questioning the sincerity of his commitment to their well-being.

Teaching the Text

The incidents recorded in this chapter provide an interesting opportunity to explore two contrasting situations that illustrate the impact of unity and division among God's people. While the two episodes have certain features in common—a wilderness crisis for the Israelites that is resolved through Moses using his staff to invoke the power of God—they differ significantly in portraying the Israelites as first disunited, threatening to stone Moses, and then second united, supporting Moses practically.

Divided we quarrel. The Israelites' lack of trust in God manifests itself in disunity as they quarrel with Moses. Confronted with a lack of water in the desert, they blame Moses. Were they truly honest, they would direct their fury at God. Moses, however, is immediately available and an easy target. Remarkably, God graciously provides water, vindicating Moses in the process. Yet the incident is remembered for the negative attitude of the Israelites, and the place is aptly named "Quarreling and Testing." Within the life of local congregations, tensions between members and opposition to those in leadership may sometimes spring from a lack of true faith in God.

United we stand. When the Amalekites attack, the Israelites unite together, as Moses gives instructions for Joshua to assemble an army. During the battle those on the hilltop are at one with those in the valley. Together they fight the Amalekites, but in different ways. Importantly, their unity is God focused. As Aaron and Hur support Moses's tiring arms, the staff of God is held aloft, symbolizing God's empowering of Joshua and his troops. God supports his people when they are united in him.

The attack of the Amalekites is a solemn reminder that God's people come under assault from the forces of evil. We need to be unified in defending those who are most vulnerable to attack from others. This episode, however, provides no justification for Christians to initiate the taking up of arms against their enemies. The actions of Moses and the Israelite army are purely defensive, for it is the Amalekites who start this conflict.

The name given to the altar proclaims that the source of the Israelite victory is the Lord. Throughout the exodus story God's power over both nature and human forces is constantly highlighted. In the present ordering of these incidents, is there a possibility that the Israelites may have learned from the first episode to be more unified and supportive of their God-appointed leadership?

Illustrating the Text

When we stop trusting God, we cease standing together.

Quote: **Benjamin Franklin.** Upon signing the Declaration of Independence, Benjamin Franklin purportedly said, "We must all hang together or assuredly we shall all hang separately."

Props: Hold up a kite. Explain all the basic parts. The sail is the front and is usually the decorated part; it catches the wind. The spars are the "skeleton" of the kite, helping the kite hold its form. The tail prevents the kite from spinning wildly. Each part of the kite is necessary for the overall function, and none could fly alone. And, of course, what is the most important part of the kite? The flying line! It connects the kite to the anchor point, stationed on the ground, holding the kite in tension so it can stay aloft. Without the anchor, the kite would simply flutter and fall. Jesus is the anchor point of the church. As we hold together and trust in him together, we soar. (This image could be connected to the body-of-Christ image Paul uses in Rom. 12; 1 Cor. 12; Eph. 1; and Col. 1.)

God supports his people when they are united in him.

Bible: **Colossians 1:17.** In Colossians 1:17, Paul says of Jesus, "He is before all things, and in him all things hold together." Here, Paul affirms that God in Christ is the organizing principle of reality. *Everything* finds its terminus in him. Any attempts to exist independently of his lordship are an exercise in reality denial. When God's people stand together in Christ, we are placing ourselves squarely in line with the world as it really is. We are placing ourselves in the circuit of God's power, which will flow unbroken through any system that is aligned with him.

We must be unified in defending those who are most vulnerable to attack.

Applying the Text: Psalm 82:3 says: "Give justice to the weak and the fatherless; maintain the right of the afflicted and the destitute" (ESV). Challenge your congregation to consider who might be the most vulnerable within your community. For instance, who are the weak in your local schools? Who are the "destitute" where you live? It can become all too easy to pass by the very people Scripture calls us to protect. For this illustration, consider connecting with a local social-services provider and gathering data about those who struggle to make ends meet within your local community.

A Father-in-Law
Worth Having

Big Idea

God demonstrates his supremacy through his redemption of those who are enslaved to Egypt.

Key Themes

- God's rescue of the Israelites from slavery is a compelling testimony to his greatness.
- God may use the insights of others to guide his people concerning how to best organize their community life.
- God's people should be willing to delegate and accept responsibilities that will benefit everyone.

Understanding the Text

The Text in Context

Exodus 18 forms a distinctive section within the book of Exodus, framed by the arrival (v. 1) and departure (v. 27) of Jethro, Moses's father-in-law. The presence of Jethro in chapter 18 recalls the events described in 2:11–4:26 and forms an interesting frame around Moses's role as the one divinely commissioned to lead the Israelites out of bondage in Egypt. Having previously asked Jethro for permission to return to Egypt (4:18), Moses now encounters again his father-in-law near Mount Sinai.

Chapter 18 comprises two distinctive parts that form a hinge, linking together the two halves of Exodus. Verses 1–12 emphasize how Jethro affirms the Lord as the savior of Israel. This half of the chapter looks back to the events that have already taken place and provides, from a non-Israelite perspective, a very positive assessment of all that God has done for the enslaved Israelites. In contrast, verses 13–27 record how Jethro advises Moses concerning the creation of a more efficient judicial process for the Israelite community. This half of chapter 18 prepares for future developments, possibly anticipating how God will give illustrative case laws as part of the Sinai covenant (21:1–22:20).

Interpretive Insights

18:1–4 *Now Jethro, the priest of Midian and father-in-law of Moses.* Although Jethro is introduced in verse 1 as a Midianite priest, throughout the rest of this chapter he is always described as Moses's father-in-law. His relationship to Moses, not his religious status, primarily defines who Jethro is in this passage. The reintroduction of Zipporah as Moses's wife and the naming of his two sons recall the events narrated in 2:11–4:26. Eliezer was not named previously, but 4:20 states briefly that Moses has "sons." The explanation of Eliezer's name, "My God is help" (cf. NIV note), recognizes how God helped Moses to escape from Egypt after he killed an aggressive Egyptian slave driver. Gershom's name recalls Moses's status as an exile in Midian. The explanations of the boys' names convey something of the plot of the exodus story up to this point. The Israelites as exiles in Egypt are helped by God to escape from the "sword of Pharaoh." A few commentators interpret the expression "had sent away his wife" (v. 2) as implying divorce (cf. Deut. 22:19, 29). Yet nothing in the present context indicates that Zipporah is anything other than Moses's wife. Moses probably asked her to return to Midian from Egypt in order to ensure her safety and that of their sons.

18:5–7 *Jethro . . . came to him in the wilderness . . . near the mountain of God.* Moses welcomes his father-in-law warmly, recalling how years earlier Jethro extended hospitality to Moses. Previously, the Lord commissioned Moses while he was shepherding Jethro's flock near the mountain of God in Horeb (3:1). Now, "near the mountain of God" Jethro learns how God has used Moses to shepherd the Israelites out of Egypt.

18:8–11 *Moses told his father-in-law . . . how the LORD had saved them.* Moses testifies to all that God has done for the Israelites. This includes the signs and wonders in Egypt and the Israelites' subsequent journey to Horeb. Fittingly, Jethro rejoices because of the Lord's deliverance of Israel. Four times the verb *natsal*, "to rescue/deliver/save," is used in verses 8–10 to highlight the Lord's salvation. From the call of Moses onward, the Lord alone has been responsible for delivering the Israelites from slavery in Egypt. God merits all the praise. Jethro's remark "Now I know that the LORD is greater than all other gods" (v. 11) recalls how the motif of knowing the Lord comes frequently in chapters 5–14. Moses's testimony prompts Jethro to affirm positively that the Lord is superior to all other gods.

18:12 *brought a burnt offering and other sacrifices . . . in the presence of God.* Although it has been argued that the sacrificial ritual created a covenant relationship between the Midianites and the Israelites,[1] this suggestion goes beyond what the text clearly states. Jethro's words and actions, however, suggest that he embraces the Lord as his God. Some scholars argue that the expression "in the presence of God" places this event after the construction of the tabernacle, which becomes God's residence among the Israelites. However, it is more likely that God is perceived as being present when the sacrifices are offered to him (cf. 20:24).

18:13 *Moses took his seat to serve as judge.* It was customary for judges to be seated. Although God gives sample case laws in 21:1–22:20 as part of the Book of the Covenant, there is no need to assume, as some scholars argue, that the events described in this chapter occurred chronologically after the ratification of the Sinai covenant.[2] It seems likely that the Israelite community already had some system of law, possibly going back to the time of Abraham (cf. Gen. 26:5). Moreover, Moses appears to consult God for guidance in difficult cases.

18:17–23 *What you are doing is not good.* Jethro's lengthy speech offers wise and practical counsel to Moses. Although he is an outsider, Jethro mentions God frequently, and his comment in verse 23 indicates that he has no desire to usurp God's authority. Without undermining Moses's position as leader of the Israelites, Jethro advocates the appointment of additional "judges" (v. 22). He emphasizes in particular that these judges must be trustworthy and not open to bribery, a point reinforced later by God in the Book of the Covenant (cf. 23:8). Yet the creation of an accessible and trustworthy judiciary is not enough to establish justice within a community. There must also be a process of education involving the whole population (cf. v. 20). Interestingly, God incorporates into the Sinai covenant illustrative case laws (21:1–22:20) that will instruct the Israelites in matters of justice and righteousness.

18:24–26 *Moses listened to his father-in-law and did everything he said.* At the outset of the Exodus story, Moses was challenged by a defiant Israelite with the words "Who made you ruler and judge over us?" (2:14). Fittingly, years later, with God's approval, Moses now appoints others to help him fulfill this role.

Theological Insights

Moses's testimony about God's rescue of the Israelites from Egyptian control draws from Jethro a very positive response. No doubt Moses describes to him the substance of all that is recorded in Exodus 5–17, highlighting God's role in bringing the Israelites safely to Horeb. God's ability to rescue Moses and the Israelites from Pharaoh and the Egyptian army highlights his role as Savior.

If the first half of chapter 18 emphasizes God's power to save, the second half highlights his ability as Divine King to govern the Israelites by ensuring justice for the people in their disputes with one another. While the judicial process involves delegation, the ultimate authority in settling disagreements and quarrels is God. As verses 16 and 19 reveal, Moses consults the Lord in order to know how best to resolve every dispute. In comprehending God's nature it is important never to lose sight of his roles as Savior and Judge. Both aspects should inform our understanding of who God is; we should not emphasize one at the expense of the other.

Teaching the Text

The contents of Exodus 18 provide an opportunity to look back on all that God has done for the Israelites in bringing them to Horeb and to look forward to how God will govern the Israelites in order to create harmony within their community. As the hinge within the book of Exodus, chapter 18 reminds us of the importance of ensuring that God's role as Savior is not separated from his role as King. Both aspects of God's nature need to be emphasized, for they have an important bearing on how we should approach the issue of discipleship. In the same way, Christians need to appreciate how Jesus is both Savior and King.

Telling others about what God has done. Moses's testimony persuades Jethro to proclaim that there is no God like the Lord, who alone has the power to rescue Moses and the Israelites from the military might of Egypt. As an outside observer, Jethro recognizes the significance of what has occurred and praises the Lord for having rescued the Israelites from oppression in Egypt. His response is all the more remarkable because he is a Midianite priest. As witnesses to an even greater event, the apostles are commissioned by Jesus to testify to God's power in raising him from the dead. Repeatedly throughout the book of Acts, the testimony of Jesus's followers is vital in bringing others to a personal knowledge of God.

Recognizing our own shortcomings. While Moses's testimony has a profound effect on Jethro, Exodus 18 reminds us that even the greatest of leaders may not always see their own limitations. Concerned for the well-being of the Israelites, Moses is so preoccupied with addressing their needs that he is unable to appreciate the importance of delegating responsibilities to others. Although Moses acts out of concern for the well-being of others and not merely to sustain his own position as leader of the people, his best intentions are inadequate. Thankfully, Moses is gracious enough to accept Jethro's advice, which is offered with the recognition that it must be approved by God.

Sharing responsibilities with others. Looking on, Jethro quickly recognizes the challenge facing Moses and the strain that this is placing on him. Jethro's advice is timely and needed. With good sense, he highlights the importance of delegation, recognizing the benefits that may come from doing this. In doing so, he also underlines the importance of ensuring that those who are given responsibilities are suitably qualified to undertake them. This may involve creating structures that have different levels of responsibility. This passage is a reminder that God does not expect one individual to do all the work but readily approves when tasks are allocated to those appropriately qualified to undertake them.

Illustrating the Text

Testimony is a powerful tool for leading people to Jesus.

Applying the Text: Use this point as a chance to walk your people through the process of forming their own testimony. Inspire them to *always* be ready to share their story with another person. It can powerfully encourage believers and impact lost people. Consider teaching this simple way to form a testimony: BC † AD.

The format for this testimony is simple. "BC" describes our life before Christ. Identify a specific issue, behavioral pattern, or internal struggle that was part of your life before you met Jesus. The cross (†) briefly, but clearly, provides the basic message of the gospel—our guilt, Jesus's free sacrifice, and our confession of faith. "AD" describes how Christ is bringing transformation to the area we identified from our "BC" life.

Another way to modify this is by simply describing how we have seen the Lord come into an area of struggle in our present Christian life. For example, *I've always struggled with anxiety about the "What ifs . . ." of life. Recently, the Lord helped me see that this fear is rooted in a failure to trust him. I've been realizing it is crazy to doubt! If God sent his own Son to die for me, then surely he's going to take care of me. I still struggle, but I've had a lot more peace as I keep reminding myself of this truth. Even better, I can actually feel God helping me remember to trust him.*

Cooperation is important for success.

Science: The Scottish biologist and pharmacologist Sir Alexander Fleming is rightly credited with discovering in 1928 the antibiotic, or bacteria killer, penicillin. Subsequent research revealed that penicillin would destroy the bacteria that cause scarlet fever, pneumonia, meningitis, and diphtheria. However, Fleming struggled to find a way to isolate the antibiotic agent and in the end abandoned his attempts to mass-produce penicillin. Soon afterward, during World War II, Howard Florey and Ernst Boris Chain succeeded in producing penicillin in large quantities. The contributions of all three men were recognized in 1945 when they shared the Nobel Prize for their work on penicillin. Their efforts are a reminder of the importance of cooperation for the common good. No one of us is as smart as all of us together.

God's church is built not by one individual but by many people working together.

Art: The art world goes through phases. At times, art can confound those of us who are "less sensitive" to the complexities expressed in forms that only other artists can understand. Consider French artist Alphonse Allais, critically acclaimed for his poetry, painting, and musical composition. His most famous works in each arena were bound by one common feature—extreme minimalism. For instance, his *Funeral March for the Obsequies of a Deaf Man* was a musical score with nine measures but no notes. His painting *Première communion de jeunes filles chlorotiques par un temps de neige* (First communion of anemic young girls in the snow) was a single, unmarked sheet of white paper. He pioneered a form of poetry in which every line was homophonous (i.e., each word pronounced the same).

For most of us, what makes good art is not undifferentiated sameness. It takes contrast and complement to make something worth reading, hearing, or seeing (think *Starry Night* by van Gogh). In the same way, the beauty of the church is best expressed when many people are being used by God, performing service according to their gifts.

A Holy Nation for a Holy God

Big Idea

Celebrate the privilege of being in a covenant relationship with a most awesome and holy God.

Key Themes

- God conditionally promises the Israelites that they will fulfill both royal and priestly functions.
- Israel becoming a holy nation is linked to God's dwelling among them.
- The theophany at Sinai highlights the awesome holiness of God and prepares for the making of the covenant.

Understanding the Text

The Text in Context

At the start of chapter 19 a new and important stage begins in the Exodus narrative, leading to the establishment of a special covenant relationship between God and the Israelites. Arriving at Mount Sinai on the third new moon after their hurried departure from Egypt, the Israelites will remain camped at this location for ten months. Chapter 19 introduces the covenant by announcing God's gracious proposal to the Israelites (19:4–6) and their initial preparations in order for the covenant to be ratified, which happens in chapter 24. The ratification of the covenant at Mount Sinai transforms the Israelites from being oppressed slaves of the king of Egypt to being exalted servants of the King of kings.

The events at Mount Sinai are recorded in considerable detail, running from Exodus 19 to Numbers 10. This is an important period in the life of the Israelites in establishing them as God's special nation. This marks the climax of their redemption from slavery and anticipates their entry into the land of Canaan. The events at Mount Sinai, the mountain of God, anticipate and prepare for life at the mountain of God in the promised land (cf. 15:17).

The Covenant Obligations

With the arrival of the Israelites at Mount Sinai, the scene is set for the making of the covenant that will enable the Israelites to experience God's presence among them. The covenant requires the Israelites to fulfill certain obligations in order to enjoy the benefits of their special relationship with God. The obligations given by God to the Israelites consist of two distinctive documents: the Ten Commandments, or Decalogue (20:1–17), and the Book of the Covenant (20:22–23:33). The name of the former comes in 34:28, and the name of the latter comes in 24:7.

Historical and Cultural Background

The covenant made between God and the Israelites has features that resemble ancient Near Eastern vassal treaties, especially those of the second millennium BC. Such treaties formalized a special relationship between two parties, one strong and one weak. The treaty set out lists of obligations that the suzerain demanded of the vassal. These normally fell into two parts: general and detailed. This structure is reflected in the Ten Commandments (20:1–17) and the Book of the Covenant (20:22–23:33). The Israelites would have easily understood the vassal nature of the covenant that God was inviting them to accept at Mount Sinai. The book of Deuteronomy, which involves renewing the Sinai covenant, provides the closest literary parallels between a biblical covenant and an ancient Near Eastern vassal treaty.

Interpretive Insights

19:1–2 *On the first day of the third month.* Since the Hebrew term for "month" means "new moon," the Israelites arrive at Mount Sinai some seventy days, or two and a half months, after the Passover. As God has previously announced (3:12), Moses returns to the location where he encountered God in the burning bush (3:1–6).

19:3 *Moses went up to God.* The text contrasts Moses ascending to meet God with the Israelites remaining camped at the foot of the mountain. At this stage Moses alone meets the Lord, who remains at a distance from the Israelites.

19:4 *how I carried you on eagles' wings.* God is often pictured sheltering his people under his wings (Pss. 17:8; 36:7; 57:1; 61:4; 63:7; 91:4), but the image here is of God transporting the Israelites safely to Mount Sinai.

19:5 *obey me fully and keep my covenant . . . you will be my treasured possession.* By describing the covenant as "my covenant," God indicates that he alone determines the conditions. This is not, as some scholars suggest, a reference to a previously existing covenant.[1] After reminding the Israelites of what he has already done for them, God graciously invites them to become his "treasured possession." The Hebrew term for "treasured possession" is used elsewhere in the Old Testament to describe treasure prized by a king (1 Chron. 29:3; Eccles. 2:8). Unlike Pharaoh, God does not impose his authority on the Israelites against their wishes. The people are at liberty to reject God's invitation, for it requires exclusive loyalty; they must be prepared to obey God fully. While this is a demanding requirement, these former slaves are promised a wonderful prospect.

19:6 *you will be for me a kingdom of priests and a holy nation.* By entering into this unique covenant relationship with God, the Israelites are promised that they will benefit from an exceptional status compared with other nations. The expression "kingdom of priests" implies that the Israelites will have access to God as priests and rule as royalty. Underlying this idea is the restoration of the status enjoyed by Adam and Eve prior to their expulsion from the Garden of Eden. In Eden they experienced as priests the privilege of having immediate access to God's presence (Gen. 3:8); in this context priests are those who may approach God and serve him directly. At creation, they received from God authority to rule over the earth as his vice-regents (Gen. 1:26–30). Through disobedience Adam and Eve forfeited these privileges for both themselves and their descendants.

Now, by obeying God, the Israelites are granted the possibility of fulfilling God's original purpose for humanity. As a "holy nation" they will experience the privilege of having God dwell among them. This exclusive outcome will distinguish the Israelites from every other nation. However, it is conditional on the willingness of the people to observe everything God tells them, for the Lord says, "If you obey me fully . . . , then . . ." (19:5). Unfortunately, the story of Israel's future history reveals that, due to recurring disobedience, they never fully become all that God promises.

19:7–9 *Moses went back . . . "We will do everything the Lord has said."* Having received God's instructions, Moses returns to the people, who respond unanimously to God's proposal. Their positive reaction, which is reaffirmed in 24:3, 7, does not prevent them from soon afterward disobediently worshiping the golden calf (32:1–8).

19:10–13 *Go to the people and consecrate them today and tomorrow.* Since the covenant will create a unique relationship between God and the Israelites, it is essential that the people should be holy in order to experience God's presence among them. God instructs Moses to sanctify the people in preparation for their encounter with him.

19:14–15 *he consecrated them, and they washed their clothes.* The Hebrew word translated "consecrated" has the sense "make holy/sanctify." Within the Old Testament, the process of consecration is regularly associated with cleansing, not undertaking certain activities, and the offering of sacrifices. In chapter 19 cleansing and abstinence from sexual intimacy prepare the Israelites for God's coming. Later, in chapter 24, they will offer sacrifices to complete their consecration. Only then will the Israelites be permitted to ascend the mountain.

19:16–19 *Mount Sinai was covered with smoke, because the LORD descended on it in fire.* Previously, God revealed himself to Moses as fire in a burning bush (3:2); on this occasion his appearance will be much more dramatic. As God approaches the mountain, an ever-increasing fanfare announces his arrival. Fire and smoke surround the top of the mountain, as a thick cloud conceals the divine glory from the Israelites. Although some writers have speculated that the present account reflects volcanic activity,[2] the details of the description preclude this possibility. The phenomena on the mountain underline the uniqueness of this occasion. The theophany at Mount Sinai stands apart from other revelations of God's glory in the Old Testament.

19:20–25 *The LORD descended to the top of Mount Sinai.* Whereas verses 16–19 describe the natural phenomena associated with God's coming, the dialogue in verses 20–25 underlines the holiness of God's nature, an aspect that is not immediately visible. God's instructions to Moses reinforce what was previously said in verses 12–13. Even those Israelites who might have been considered holier than others, the priests, are warned not to ascend the mountain. Since the Levitical priesthood is not instituted until after the construction of the tabernacle (cf. Lev. 8), the priests mentioned here are probably elders drawn from all the tribes.

Theological Insights

God's ambition for the Israelites is that they should become a "kingdom of priests and a holy nation" (19:6). Although this is not fully realized in the Old Testament period, it remains central to the fulfillment of his redemptive plan. For this reason, the apostle Peter writes to Christian believers, echoing Exodus 19, "But you are a chosen people, a royal priesthood, a holy nation, God's special possession, that you may declare the praises of him who called you out of darkness into his wonderful light" (1 Pet. 2:9).

A striking feature of the theophany at Sinai is the trembling of the mountain. This clearly emphasizes the all-powerful nature of the Lord. Observing this, the writer of Hebrews draws an important contrast between Mount Sinai and "Mount Zion, . . . the city of the living God, the heavenly Jerusalem" (Heb. 12:22). Whereas the quaking of Mount Sinai underscores the temporary nature of this world, the new Jerusalem, which has yet to come, can never be shaken and so will remain forever: "Therefore, since we are receiving a kingdom that cannot be shaken, let us be thankful, and so worship

God acceptably with reverence and awe, for our 'God is a consuming fire'"
(Heb. 12:28–29; cf. Deut. 4:24).

Teaching the Text

The content of Exodus 19 provides an opportunity to reflect on three aspects
of God's nature and activity. Firstly, sinful people cannot enter the divine
presence without first being made holy. Secondly, in spite of Adam and Eve's
betrayal of God, he remains committed to bringing to fruition his creation
plan for the earth and humanity. Thirdly, throughout the process of salvation,
God always takes the initiative.

God alone is holy. Holiness is not an easy concept to grasp or communicate to
others. People today tend to associate it with "holy men" who belong to Eastern
religions. For this reason, it is important to appreciate the biblical descriptions
of God that provide an insight into his holy nature. According to the Bible, God
alone is innately holy. Consequently, holiness is associated with God's perfection and purity. To be holy is to be whole, complete, perfect in every aspect.

Only those who are made holy may approach God. While the concept of
holiness is developed more fully in the book of Leviticus, we are introduced
to it in Exodus. We meet it first in chapter 3 at the burning bush, where Moses
stands on holy ground. Once again at Mount Sinai in chapter 19 the whole
mountain becomes holy due to God's presence. By emphasizing the holiness
of God and the need for the Israelites to remain at a distance, the present
chapter graphically illustrates the gulf that exists between a holy God and
sinful people. As Exodus 19 illustrates, only those who are holy may safely
come near to God. To approach the Lord without being consecrated results
in death. Thankfully, Christians "have been made holy through the sacrifice
of the body of Jesus Christ once for all" (Heb. 10:10), are sanctified by the
indwelling of the Holy Spirit (Rom. 15:16; 1 Cor. 6:19), and are disciplined
by the Father "in order that we may share in his holiness" (Heb. 12:10).

From the perspective of the whole Bible, the book of Exodus provides a
paradigm for understanding the process of divine salvation. In the light of
this, God's desire for the Israelites to become a royal priesthood and holy nation also lies at the heart of the new covenant instituted by Jesus Christ (cf.
1 Pet. 2:9). Through Christ's sacrificial death, believers are given both a royal
and a priestly status. This reflects God's original purpose for people, whom
he created to rule over the earth as his vice-regents and to enjoy an intimate
fellowship with their Creator. As Christians we may rejoice in having this
special status (1 Pet. 2:9).

God graciously initiates the process of salvation. The Sinai covenant is a
further display of divine grace. Having already redeemed the Israelites from

slavery and ransomed them from death at the Passover, the Lord graciously invites them to embrace him as their sole sovereign. The special covenant about to be sealed is a gift from God. The new covenant is also a gift of grace and not something merited by first being obedient to God.

Illustrating the Text

Sinful people cannot enter the presence of a holy God.

Science: Severe combined immunodeficiency (SCID) is a genetic disorder that attacks the immune system. Those born with this malady are extremely sensitive to infectious disease. One sufferer, David Vetter (1971–84), spent his twelve years of life in a sterile plastic chamber. He was famously dubbed the "Bubble Boy" by the media. Any contact with germs would mean certain death for David. Eventually, after receiving a bone marrow transplant from his sister, he died. Her marrow had contained traces of a dormant virus that quickly induced cancer throughout David's body.[3]

Much as sufferers of SCID cannot tolerate any infection, God cannot tolerate unrighteousness. Not even a trace. But unlike those who suffer from SCID, God's intolerance of unrighteousness is not dangerous for him. It is anyone who brings sin into God's holy presence that, absent the covering of Christ, is subject to dire consequences.

Despite humanity's betrayal, God is committed to redeeming and dwelling with us.

History: Rome did not take kindly to rebels. Israel did not take well to occupation. These two nations were not wired to do well together. In AD 70, this led to the destruction of the Jerusalem temple by Roman armies. An even more brutal enforcement of Roman hegemony occurred during the Bar Kokhba revolt of the 130s. Bar Kokhba, thought by many Jews to be the Messiah, raised an army in rebellion against Rome. Emperor Hadrian responded. According to the Roman historian Dio Cassius, 580,000 Jews were killed in Judea. Fifty fortified towns and 985 villages were leveled. The empire sent a clear message: "Resistance is futile."

What a contrast with how our God responds to our rebellion! In the face of our indifference, he reaches out in love. Under the blows of the whip and the piercing of the nails, he cries, "Forgive!" Our God, the King of kings and Lord of lords, showed his greatness in this: while we were still sinners, he entered this world to die for us so that we might live with him.

A Radical Mission Statement for a Holy Nation

Big Idea

The demands of holy living are much more exacting and far reaching than we often assume.

Key Themes

- The Ten Commandments are not "laws," as many people think, but broad principles that point toward perfection.
- People are perversely inclined to believe in alternative deities and misrepresent the true nature of the Lord.
- Our sinful nature destructively distorts how we relate to other people as we make ourselves the center of existence.

Understanding the Text

The Text in Context

Standing at the foot of Mount Sinai, the Israelites have witnessed the dramatic arrival of the Lord. After Moses descends to them, a voice sounds from the mountain summit. In awe the Israelites listen as God speaks to them. Very deliberately the Lord chooses to address each Israelite in person—the "you" in verses 1–17 is always singular—setting out the obligations that will form the basis of the covenant about to be sealed. These "ten words," a title given later in 34:28 (see, e.g., CEB), encapsulate how the Israelites are to live as God's holy nation. These ten major principles are meant to shape the behavior of all the Israelites who witness the theophany at Mount Sinai.

The "ten words" have a unique status within the book of Exodus, for they alone are proclaimed directly by God to the Israelites. Everything else that God says is mediated through Moses to the people (cf. 20:19). The special status of the Ten Commandments is confirmed by the fact that they alone are inscribed on stone tablets by the "finger of God" (31:18) and recorded twice within the Pentateuch (cf. Deut. 5:6–21).

Interpretive Insights

20:1 *God spoke all these words.* Prior to this occasion, the Lord has always communicated his message to the Israelites through Moses. By speaking directly to the people, God underlines the importance of these covenant obligations. The Ten Commandments stand apart from everything else that God communicates to the Israelites.

20:2 *I am the* LORD *your God.* Although it is not immediately apparent in English Bibles, this expression in Hebrew forms a very distinctive introduction to the Ten Commandments. At the heart of the covenant is the establishment of a unique relationship between God and the Israelites. God identifies himself as the one who has already delivered the Israelites from bondage in Egypt. In the light of his prior actions God sets before the people these covenant obligations.

20:3 *You shall have no other gods before me.* God demands the exclusive obedience of each Israelite. The Israelites are to acknowledge the Lord as the one and only God. In the ancient world, where polytheism was the norm, this emphasis on one God is radically different. The expression "before me" does not imply order of priority. Rather, it means that the Israelites are not to place images of other gods in the Lord's presence. This was the custom of other people (cf. 1 Sam. 5:2–7). Importantly, the prohibition against other gods is expressed as broadly as possible and not limited merely to worshiping or bowing down before them.

20:4–6 *You shall not make for yourself an image.* The use of images was important to ancient worshipers because they believed that the deity was present in the image. An image provided immediate access to the god. By banning the making of images, the Lord indicates that his presence will not be experienced in this way. Rather, as the rest of Exodus reveals, God will reside among the Israelites in the tabernacle. It is this covenant obligation that the Israelites break when they make the golden calf (32:1–8).

20:7 *You shall not misuse the name of the* LORD *your God.* This commandment covers more than blasphemy or foul language. It prohibits any use of the divine name that would detract from how God is perceived. The Israelites must exercise extreme caution when talking about God or invoking his name, especially when using God's name in order to promote their own agenda.

20:8–11 *Remember the Sabbath day by keeping it holy.* The concept of the seventh day as a time of rest is unique to Israel in the ancient Near East. Through the giving of manna in the wilderness, God has already introduced to the Israelites the concept of a day of rest prior to their arrival at Mount

Sinai (16:1–36). The Sabbath takes on a special significance, because it is the sign of the Sinai covenant (31:12–17; 35:1–4).

20:12 *Honor your father and your mother.* Expressed positively, this commandment highlights the special status of parents. To "honor" means more than "obey"; it is to prize highly. Within the tribal structure of ancient Israel, parents exercised an important role in ensuring a stable society.

20:13 *You shall not murder.* The Hebrew verb *ratsah* is one of several verbs used to describe killing. It denotes the taking of human life and is broader than "murder." This commandment underlines that no one may take a human life without divine approval.

20:14 *You shall not commit adultery.* At the heart of this commandment is the issue of faithfulness in relationships, more so than sexual promiscuity, although the two are closely related. Marriage represents the most intimate human relationship possible. If an individual cannot be faithful to a marriage partner, he or she is unlikely to be faithful in other relationships.

20:15 *You shall not steal.* The Israelites were expected to respect the possessions of other people. This commandment reacts against the human propensity to be greedy.

20:16 *You shall not give false testimony against your neighbor.* The terminology used here associates this commandment with the judicial system. A fair trial depends on truthful witnesses.

20:17 *You shall not covet your neighbor's house.* In this context, the Hebrew word for "house" means "household" and embraces everything that a person might have. (In Deut. 5:21 "house" is used to refer to the physical property of a neighbor.) Although the commandment refers to the neighbor's wife, she is not presented here as his property. All the commandments address both men and women as individuals. In this instance, for simplicity, the commandment is presented from a male perspective. It is expected that a woman would automatically understand the commandment from a female perspective. By addressing the issue of coveting, this commandment indicates that thoughts matter as much as actions.

Theological Insights

Although the Ten Commandments are primarily a concise and selective list of obligations that the Israelites must fulfill, they provide an important insight into the nature of God. As the Creator of the universe Yahweh alone is the ultimate authority, determining the moral standards by which every creature will be judged. The Ten Commandments underline God's uniqueness as the supreme moral authority over all creation. As such, he rightly expects the exclusive obedience of those he has created and redeemed. Describing himself as a "jealous God" (20:5), he cannot but be angry when people give their

Understanding the Ten Commandments

As a short summary of the hallmarks of a holy society, the Ten Commandments address the most important elements of human existence. Adherence to these principles would transform any society for the better. Very obviously, they cover our relationship with God and other people. Each commandment is expressed using language that is deliberately broad. For example, "honor your father and mother" covers more and demands more than "obey your father and mother." The Ten Commandments are broad principles, and they need to be read and understood as such.

The Sinai covenant is based on the underlying assumption that the Israelites will fulfill the covenant obligations out of love for God. They do not keep the commandments in order to merit the love of God. God has already shown his love for them by delivering them from slavery in Egypt. This pattern is reflected in the words of Jesus: "If you love me, keep my commands" (John 14:15).

God's speech to the Israelites is a concise summary of what he wants them to be. It is like a constitution or mission statement, setting out what is expected of those who wish to serve the Lord as their sole God. Since the Ten Commandments are an integral component of the Sinai covenant, Christians, under the new covenant, are not directly required to keep them. This explains in part why Christians are no longer bound to keep the Sabbath (that is, the seventh day of the week) as a day of rest. Nevertheless, the Ten Commandments remain an authoritative guide to the kind of behavior that pleases God. We can learn much by pondering them.

It is not uncommon to find that the Ten Commandments are viewed as divine laws. However, they lack the precision necessary to be considered laws. We misunderstand them if we view them as distinguishing between what is legal and what is illegal. Too often discussion of the commandments centers on where the line is to be drawn between what is acceptable to God and what is not. Such an approach, however, reduces to a minimum what God expects from us. This explains why Jesus rejected the interpretation of the Ten Commandments promoted by other religious leaders in his day. Based on a correct understanding of the commandments, Jesus affirms that the statement "You shall not murder" must not be restricted to the act of killing. As a signpost pointing to holy behavior, the commandment also prohibits us from hating another person (cf. Matt. 5:21–22). Understood like this, the Ten Commandments present a very radical description of what God desires from us. As signposts to perfection they remind us that we should strive toward being perfect (Matt. 5:48), which requires us to love sincerely and wholeheartedly God and other people (Matt. 22:37–40). With good reason the Ten Commandments have been called a charter for our relationship with God and others.

worship to a created object rather than the Creator of all things. To worship an inferior, substitute god is to deny the incomparable supremacy of the Lord.

Teaching the Text

When we teach the Ten Commandments to a modern audience, it is important to set them in the context of the covenant being ratified between God and the Israelites. These are the principal obligations that the Israelites must obey in order to maintain their special relationship with God. As such they convey something of the expectations that God places on the Israelites. While these apply directly to the ancient Israelites, they can be instructive to modern readers, even if they are not considered to be directly binding today. (Although the issue is debated, the Sabbath, as a sign of the Sinai covenant, need not be viewed as universally binding for all time.)

Moreover, it is important to appreciate that each commandment expresses a broad principle. This influences significantly how each statement should be interpreted and explained. We are here dealing with not "laws" but "moral principles" (see the sidebar). This means, as illustrated by Jesus in Matthew 5, that the commandments are not simply intended to distinguish what is legal and illegal, but rather they are pointers toward the moral perfection that God desires.

Appropriately, given their purpose, the Ten Commandments focus initially on the divine-human relationship. The opening commandments highlight the importance of giving exclusive loyalty to God. This needs to be worked out practically in various ways that include how we worship him and honor him as our God in all that we do. The first four commandments provide an opportunity to consider from different perspectives the importance of giving God his rightful place as the sovereign Lord of all creation.

As the Ten Commandments illustrate, our commitment to God should influence how we relate to other people. In a highly selective way, commandments five through ten address different aspects of life, establishing moral values that promote a wholesome society in which every individual is given due respect.

As the summary of the values that God desires to see reflected in the life of each person, the Ten Commandments are likely to highlight our many failings. When carefully explained to others, they will not only describe how a healthy society may be formed, but they will also highlight the extent to which people fall short of God's requirements. While society at large tends to dismiss human shortcomings, because everyone sins, it is important for Christians to highlight, with due humility, the extent of all our failings. This provides the platform on which we may then proclaim the good news of forgiveness and redemption that comes through Jesus Christ.

Illustrating the Text

The Ten Commandments must be set in the context of the covenant between God and the Israelites.

Human Experience: Share a personal experience of having signed a contract (e.g., purchasing a car or a home, or even making a credit/debit card purchase) and explain the nature and terms of the relationship it initiated. It represents an agreement between two parties. Often, on larger purchases, we are committing ourselves to paying off a debt. The legal agreement sets the terms of payment. The Ten Commandments came within the context of an agreement, with God drawing a people to himself and establishing the terms of their life together.

Each commandment articulates a broad moral principle, not a narrow legal statute.

Story: This is the Tale of the Wise Mother: There was a mother who had four energetic boys. They were good-hearted lads who could turn a frown into a smile in a heartbeat. They were also rambunctious boys who could turn a neat room into a whirlwind in a wink. The wise mother, upon seeing a room so overturned, would scold her sons. She would follow them, pointing out each and every toy that needed to be picked up. She soon learned that she would just as soon pick up the toys herself as watch them slowly follow her each and every instruction. So the wise mother did something very wise indeed. She went to the store, bought a timer, came home, and set it for fifteen minutes. She turned to her sons and said, "This room must be picked up and put right in fifteen minutes or no pizza and movie tonight." It worked. The end.

The moral of the tale: Communicating broad principles can be more effective than attempting to address every behavioral scenario. The principles, applied according to the intent of the authority figure, will be worked out in countless ways.

Our commitment to God should impact how we relate to others.

Props: For this illustration, you will need a clear glass container filled with hot water and a tea bag. In front of the audience, place the tea bag into the hot water. Just as the tea permeates the entire glass of water, slowly transforming color, flavor, scent, and its very nature (i.e., it is no longer just hot water), our lives should be permeated by our relationship with God. No part should remain unaffected, including our relationships with others.

The Wide-Ranging Implications of Serving the Living God

Big Idea

Serving God impacts every area of life, from how we worship him to how we treat those around us.

Key Themes

- A reverent fear of God is a helpful and necessary motivation for holy living.
- God alone determines how he should be worshiped and where we should encounter him.
- Since slaves have rights that ought to be respected by their masters, the Divine Master will never take advantage of those who commit their lives to him.

Understanding the Text

The Text in Context

Together with the Ten Commandments, the Book of the Covenant records the terms of the covenant that the Lord wishes to make with the Israelites. Exodus 20:18–21 forms an important bridge between the Ten Commandments and the Book of the Covenant. Not only do verses 18–21 separate these two sets of obligations, but importantly they explain why only the Ten Commandments are spoken directly by God to the Israelites. Due to the people's fear, the Book of the Covenant is mediated through Moses.

Exodus 20:22–26 contains instructions that concern how the Israelites may encounter God in the future. (1) They are reminded that God does not manifest his presence through idols of gold or silver; rather, he will draw near to bless the Israelites when they offer sacrifices to atone for their sin. Unfortunately, as the incident involving the golden calf reveals, the Israelites quickly disregard this prohibition against making idols (32:1–8). (2) The instructions concerning the building of an altar and the making of sacrifices are immediately relevant for the ratification of the covenant (24:4–8). God leaves the people in no doubt about how they should worship him.

Exodus 21:1–11 forms the opening section of a long list of illustrative case laws that eventually concludes in 22:20. This material falls into four distinctive sections, with 21:2–11 functioning as a prologue. The main section of case laws (21:18–22:17) is framed by two shorter sections (21:12–17 and 22:18–20) that have their own distinctive format. Intentionally, regulations concerning slaves are placed at the beginning, recalling the Israelites' own experience as slaves in Egypt. By stating that no Hebrew should be enslaved for more than seven years, these regulations indirectly justify God's release of the Israelites after decades of slavery in Egypt.

Outline/Structure

The Book of the Covenant is less well known than the Ten Commandments. It extends from Exodus 20:22 to 23:33 and consists of a number of distinctive sections:

20:22–26	Instructions concerning the making of cultic objects
21:1–22:20	Legal judgments
22:21–23:9	Moral precepts
23:10–19	Instructions concerning the Sabbath and religious festivals
23:20–33	Promises and warning concerning the land of Canaan

In order for us to understand fully the nature of the covenant relationship being established between God and the Israelites, it is important to appreciate how each section contributes to the obligations placed on the Israelites.

Historical and Cultural Background

The Book of the Covenant is a complex document. Scholars have been especially interested in comparing its contents with various ancient Near Eastern law collections, the most famous of these being the Code of Hammurabi (ca. 1750 BC). While there is no evidence of direct borrowing, many of the case laws in Exodus 21:1–22:20 resemble laws found in the Code of Hammurabi and other law collections. Detailed comparison gives an insight into how the biblical material sometimes promotes values that differ from those found in other cultures. (See the "Additional Insights" following this unit.)

Interpretive Insights

20:20–21 *God has come to test you.* In this context, the Hebrew verb rendered "test" probably has the sense of "train." This is perhaps what is meant in 15:25 and 16:4, where the verb "test" also occurs, as God uses the wilderness trek to train the Israelites to trust and obey him.

20:23 *Do not make any gods . . . gods of silver or gods of gold.* The covenant at Sinai demands exclusive allegiance from the Israelites to the Lord. They are to give no place to other gods. Within the polytheistic culture of the ancient Near East, exclusive allegiance to one deity is largely unique. Although non-Israelites might favor a particular deity, they recognized the existence of other gods. In marked contrast, the Israelites must view other gods as nonentities. Idols of silver or gold were an important aspect of ancient Near Eastern religions. It was commonly believed that the deity manifested his or her presence through the image. When worshipers stood or bowed before an image, they were in the presence of their god. For the Israelites, the divine presence is to be associated with the tabernacle, in which God will reside. Ironically, the prohibition against making "gods of gold" will be the first to be broken by the Israelites (32:1–8).

20:24 *an altar of earth . . . sacrifice on it your burnt offerings and fellowship offerings.* The altar mentioned here is to be distinguished from the bronze altar associated with the tabernacle (27:1–8). This earthen altar would enable the Israelites to sacrifice burnt offerings and fellowship offerings. This verse provides the first reference to fellowship offerings in the Old Testament. This is no coincidence, because the covenant at Mount Sinai establishes an intimate relationship between God and the Israelites. Fellowship offerings involve shared meals and emphasize peace between God and his worshipers. These instructions for the construction of an altar and the sacrificing of burnt offerings and fellowship offerings will be implemented initially in Exodus 24, in order for the covenant to be sealed.

20:25–26 *If you make an altar of stones for me.* To ensure that the altar is not defiled the Israelites must avoid (1) building it with tools that may have been used for killing and (2) appearing naked before God. Religious rituals that involved naked participants appear to have been quite widespread in the ancient Near East.

21:2–4 *If you buy a Hebrew servant.* The Hebrew word translated "servant" may also mean "slave." Exodus 21:2–11 addresses different situations involving the release and nonrelease of Hebrew slaves. The designation "Hebrew" indicates that these regulations address debt slavery that arises due to poverty. Debt slavery provided some security to those who did not have any other means of support. As slaves they were ensured food and shelter. Whereas the main regulation regarding a male slave sanctions his release in the seventh year, this may be modified under certain circumstances. In the case of the female slave (see 21:7–11), the underlying expectation is that she will be married to either the master or his son. Because marriage brings her into a permanent relationship, she does not go free like the male slave.

The Bible and Slavery

It is sometimes stated that the Bible condones slavery, and the opening verses of Exodus 21 would appear to support such a claim. Yet the prominence given to the issue of slavery in this passage is oddly striking, especially given the broader context within which these verses occur. The book of Exodus narrates how God compassionately rescues the Israelites from harsh slavery in Egypt. Against such a background it is, therefore, somewhat surprising that the Book of the Covenant should contain regulations governing slavery. To understand why this is so, an important factor needs to be appreciated. It is widely accepted that this passage refers to debt slavery that occurs due to economic hardship. In such circumstances an individual might choose to become an indentured servant to secure food, clothing, and accommodation. In return, the indentured servant is expected to work for a period of time, normally a maximum of seven years, according to the regulations in this passage.

This kind of slavery needs to be carefully distinguished from other forms that force people into permanent servitude against their will, often involving considerable hardship and suffering. In marked contrast, properly regulated, indentured slavery offers security to those who find themselves destitute for whatever reason. As the present passage underlines, such an arrangement is normally meant to be temporary in nature. However, if an indentured servant loves his master, he may voluntarily ask to continue this arrangement beyond seven years. This suggests that such debt slavery need not necessarily involve the cruel exploitation of an individual. Rather, in the absence of alternative welfare options, indentured service may have provided a welcome relief for people in exceptional poverty.

21:5–6 *I love my master and my wife and children.* The provision of a wife for the slave will require the master to pay a betrothal present to the prospective bride's father. Such a gift might be equivalent to seven years' labor (Gen. 29:18).

21:7 *If a man sells his daughter as a servant.* In extreme circumstances of poverty, a father could sell his daughter as a debt slave, on the understanding that she might possibly become the wife of either the master or his son. This arrangement not only provided financial help for the family but guaranteed a secure future for the daughter. There is no evidence to suggest that the daughter was sold into slavery against her will. Since she is not strictly her master's property, if he becomes dissatisfied with her prior to marriage, he is not at liberty to sell her to anyone else, apart from back to her family.

21:9–11 *If he selects her for his son . . . food, clothing and marital rights.* If the girl is sold into slavery with the understanding that she will become a wife to the master's son, she is to be treated like a daughter. This legislation looks to protect the woman from exploitation. As verses 10–11 highlight, the female servant must not be ill treated. Her owner has an obligation to provide her with food and clothing and perhaps "marital rights." The Hebrew term translated "marital rights" occurs only here in the Old Testament and may possibly denote "oil/ointment" rather than "marital rights." Although the NIV translation assumes that the slave girl is married in verses 10–11, this may not be the case. It is possible that the girl may serve as a servant for several years before being married to the master or his son.

Theological Insights

Through the making of the covenant, God asks the Israelites to submit to his lordship for life. In doing so, they are to imitate the Hebrew slave who, motivated by love for his master, renounces his right to go free after seven years. Additionally, it is implicit in the regulations concerning the female slave that even slaves have specific rights that must be met at all times. As their master, God commits himself to caring for and providing for the needs of the Israelites. They can rest assured that God will not abandon or mistreat them.

Teaching the Text

Exodus 20:18–21 separates the Book of the Covenant from the Ten Commandments, explaining the Israelites' reluctance to have God speak to them. This short section provides an excellent opportunity to reflect on the spiritual barrier that exists between God and sinful people, and partially explains why God speaks to us through other people, rather than directly himself. In addition, these verses highlight the importance of having a healthy fear of God that comes from perceiving something of the awe of his majesty, glory, and holiness.

As the story of the exodus reminds us, the call to serve God is part of a liberating experience. Yet discovering true freedom involves much more than merely being freed from bondage; it also entails a willing commitment to serve God unconditionally. The thought of being a servant or slave, even to God, is not a popular one. Yet it lies at the very heart of being a Christian. With good reason Jesus teaches us to pray, "Our father, . . . your will be done." If we say this with any real conviction, it means that we are putting God's will before our own.

God calls us, first and foremost, not to serve but to be servants (cf. Matt. 20:28). An important distinction exists here. "To serve" is not the same as "being a servant." If I merely serve, I decide when and how. If I am a "servant," all personal choice is gone. Someone else gives the orders. Even a king can claim to serve others. But there is a world of difference between serving as a king and being a servant.

If, as Christians, we are to make a greater impact on our friends and neighbors, we must rediscover the importance of being called by God to serve those around us. In a world dominated by selfishness, it is not easy to be a servant to others. Yet this is the kind of commitment that Christ demands of me. With good reason he says: "Whoever wants to be my disciple must deny themselves and take up their cross and follow me" (Mark 8:34). Each day I need to put to death my self-centeredness and enthrone Christ as my king. Only then can I truly become the servant of others.

In the light of the popular cry for individual freedom, the call to be a servant seems strangely out of key. Yet it is only as we give ourselves in love to God, and through him to others, that we will find true personal liberty.

Illustrating the Text

A healthy fear of God comes from encountering the awe of his majesty, glory, and holiness.

Poetry: **"Holy Sonnet 15," by John Donne.** Donne writes:

> Wilt thou love God, as he thee? Then digest,
> My soul, this wholesome meditation,
> How God the Spirit, by angels waited on
> In heaven, doth make his Temple in thy breast.[1]

These tightly packed four lines encourage us to meditate on a stunning reality: the God who is surrounded by thousands of angels desires to dwell in us. This truth should move us to love God more even as we are overwhelmed by the reality of God's holiness. A true fear of the Lord is a healthy mixture of overwhelming awe, deep love, and desire to serve the God who dwells with us.

True freedom entails a willing commitment to serve God unconditionally.

Bible: **Philippians 2:6–8.** In Philippians 2, Paul holds up Jesus's humble obedience as an example for believers to emulate. The very Son of God chose not to assert his rightful privileges but made himself a servant, even submitting to death. This is the "mind" of Christ.

In a world of self-promotion, it is not easy to be a servant.

Popular Culture: The last decade has seen a revolution in social interaction. The introduction of "social networking" internet sites like Facebook and Twitter has grown exponentially. From 2005 to 2006, usage among young adults jumped from 9 percent to 49 percent. Today, 74 percent of adults who use the internet are using social networking sites.[2]

So much of the online, social-networking culture can cultivate an attitude of self-promotion. We are encouraged constantly to share the good, downplay the difficult. We check how many "likes" our posts receive. One cannot help but wonder what kind of community this virtual world is creating.

In marked contrast to the self-promoting culture of social media, we are called to be servants. That does not mean taking a "selfie" in the midst of serving, posting it on Facebook, and making a clever, self-effacing-yet-self-promoting quip (e.g., "Helping others 'cuz that's how I roll!"). True serving means getting our hands dirty in the everyday and loving by living for others.

The Book of the Covenant and Ancient Near Eastern Law Collections

The contents of the Book of the Covenant in Exodus 21–23 have come under intense scrutiny due to the discovery in the twentieth century of seven ancient Near Eastern law collections, all recorded in cuneiform script.[1] Various studies have explored the similarities and differences between these law codes and the Book of the Covenant.[2]

Table 1. Ancient Near Eastern Law Codes

Name of Law Code	Date
Ur-Nammu	ca. 2100–2050 BC
Lipit-Ishtar	ca. 1934–1924 BC
Eshnunna	ca. 1800 BC
Hammurabi	ca. 1792–1750 BC
Hittite Laws	ca. 1650–1100 BC
Middle Assyrian Laws	ca. 1075 BC
Neo-Babylonian Laws	ca. 700 BC

The most famous of these law codes is the Code of Hammurabi, which was recovered in AD 1901. This collection of 282 laws is named after the Babylonian king responsible for having it drafted and dates from about 1750 BC. Of the 282 laws listed in the Code of Hammurabi, about 70 may be viewed as addressing issues similar to those found in Exodus 21:1–22:18 (see table 2), although the degree of similarity is sometimes open to debate.

Table 2. Similar Laws in Exodus and the Code of Hammurabi

Exodus	Code of Hammurabi
21:2–7	117, 118 (119?, 175?)
21:10–11	148–49
21:12–14	207?
21:15	192–93?, 195
21:16	14?
21:18–19	206
21:20–21	208?
21:22	209–14
21:23–27	196–201

Exodus	Code of Hammurabi
21:28–32	250–52
21:37 + 22:3b–4	253–65
22:2a	21?
22:5	57–58
22:7–9	120, 124–25
22:10–13	265–67
22:14–15	244–49

Note: The table is based on Wells, "The Covenant Code," 72–73; Wright, *Inventing God's Law*, 9; Levinson, "Is the Covenant Code an Exilic Composition?," 290; Van Seters, *Law Book for the Diaspora*, 97.

A few scholars have argued at length that the Book of the Covenant was composed by drawing on the Code of Hammurabi,[3] but the evidence is not compelling.[4] Some of the "judgments" in the Book of the Covenant have closer parallels in other law codes. This is most evident in the case of the goring ox that is described in Exodus 21:35. The closest parallel to this comes in the Code of Eshnunna (53).[5] This highlights the fact that there is much in the Book of the Covenant that reflects "general Mesopotamian thinking and common literary conventions. The same structure and sequence of the laws, the same expressions, idioms, and words, verbs and legal terms were all a shared lore all over the ANE along its 3000 years of history."[6] While there is clear evidence of shared ideas, this does not require the existence of a "common law."[7] People in one culture may have been influenced by neighboring cultures, without necessarily adopting every detail.

It is also evident that the Book of the Covenant can be directly compared with other ancient Near Eastern law collections only with great caution, for the Exodus judgments, which are considerably fewer in number, "compress multiple legal issues into a small number of complex, paradigmatic cases."[8] In addition, it must be remembered that the Book of the Covenant in its entirety is not designed to be a legal code, but is rather a covenant agreement, detailing various obligations that the Israelites are expected to fulfill. This "covenant" function has an important bearing on how we should understand the nature of all that is recorded in Exodus 21–23, much of which does not fall into the category of "laws." The "legal" material is limited to Exodus 21:1–22:18.

An Eye for an Eye

Big Idea

To live a godly life, it is important to know and embrace God's values.

Key Themes

- The principle of "moral symmetry" requires the punishment to be no more or no less than the misdeed deserves.
- In assessing the punishment for any misdeed, the wrongdoer's motivation should be an important consideration.
- A healthy society depends on families where parents are honored by their children.

Understanding the Text

The Text in Context

A major part of the Book of the Covenant consists of illustrative case laws that are designed to guide the Israelites in making appropriate rulings regarding offenses committed by individuals. These case laws are found in 21:12–22:20. This section is framed by laws that have a distinctive structure, listing offenses that merit capital punishment (21:12–17 and 22:18–20). The remaining material is formulated using a *protasis* that describes a particular circumstance and an *apodosis* that sets out the penalty that should be imposed. The case laws are organized into short sections containing primary and secondary laws. The primary laws describe an offense and the penalty that should be imposed (e.g., 21:28); the secondary laws consider circumstances that vary somewhat from the primary case law (e.g., 21:29–32). Together, the primary and secondary case laws illustrate different levels of punishment that should be applied.

The case laws are given in order of descending importance, beginning with the most serious offenses. This is partially reflected in the punishments associated with each misdemeanor. We move from offenses that merit the death penalty to those that require financial compensation. Almost all the offenses listed in 21:12–36 involve physical injury, mainly to people. The next section of case laws, in 22:1–17, chiefly concerns offenses involving property. In God's value system people matter more than property.

The interpretation of particular case laws is often fraught with difficulty, due to the concise manner in which they are stated. It seems likely that they were not produced by lawyers for lawyers, and this needs to be kept in mind when interpreting the details.

Historical and Cultural Background

As noted in the "Additional Insights" following the unit on 20:18–21:11, some parallels exist between the laws in Exodus and those found in ancient Near Eastern legal collections. However, the biblical laws, unlike those of other ancient societies, place a much greater value on human life vis-à-vis property. Unlike other law collections, the biblical laws do not reinforce the existence of different social classes. Rather, they address the needs of a mainly egalitarian society.

Interpretive Insights

21:12–14 *Anyone who strikes a person . . . if it is not done intentionally.* An important distinction is drawn in verses 12–14 between premeditated killing and accidental manslaughter. Without undermining the value of human life, the provision of asylum ensures that someone who has not plotted to murder another person is not executed if manslaughter occurs.

21:15 *Anyone who attacks their father or mother.* As reflected in the Ten Commandments, God gives parents authority over their children. Parents must be respected even by adult children. It is especially noteworthy that in ancient Israel, a mother enjoys the same status as a father. This indicates that Israelite society was not as patriarchal as some scholars suggest.

21:16 *Anyone who kidnaps someone.* Respect for human life, including individual freedom, is one of the central values reflected in the case laws. No one has the right to take control of the life of another individual. To do so is to forfeit one's own life.

21:17 *Anyone who curses their father or mother.* The Hebrew verb translated "curses" denotes more than verbal imprecations. It conveys the sense of "disregarding, making light of, showing a lack of respect." It is the antonym of "honor" in 20:12.

21:18–19 *If people quarrel.* Whereas verse 12 addresses the situation of a fatal blow, these verses consider the appropriate punishment when someone is injured in a fight. The penalty requires the guilty party to compensate the victim for loss of earnings, ensuring that the victim is restored to full health again.

21:20–21 *Anyone who beats their male or female slave.* These case laws concern injury inflicted by a master on a slave. The law accepts that it may be necessary on some occasions for a master to discipline a slave. If, however, the punishment results in the slave's death, the master shall be punished. This highlights that in ancient Israel slaves were not viewed simply as the property of their masters. This outlook contrasts sharply with what is known of other ancient societies where slaves had few, if any, rights.

21:22–25 *If people are fighting and hit a pregnant woman and she gives birth prematurely.* The case laws in these verses have been the subject of extensive discussion and debate. The NIV reading "gives birth prematurely" is preferable to "miscarries" (cf. RSV; NRSV). Verse 22 assumes that there is no serious injury to either mother or child, but nevertheless a fine is imposed for the distress caused. Verses 23–25 set out what should happen if there is injury. The wording of these verses suggests that this was a commonly understood formula. It states that the punishment should be equivalent to the harm caused, restricting how much retribution might be demanded. This is often referred to as the *lex talionis*, "the law of retribution." Unfortunately, the concept of "an eye for an eye" is frequently misunderstood by people today, who consider it to be a primitive and barbaric form of justice. However, there is little evidence to suggest that the *lex talionis* involving bodily mutilation was applied literally within ancient Israel. This is apparent from what is said in the immediately surrounding case laws. In 21:18–19 the penalty for injuring another person is financial compensation, rather than physical punishment. Similarly, in 21:26–27 the slave's freedom is the compensation that the owner must make for knocking out an eye or a tooth.

21:26–27 *An owner who hits a male or female slave in the eye.* In ancient Israel, slaves enjoyed some protection under the law. This is rarely the case in other ancient Near Eastern cultures, where slaves were viewed as the property of their owners.

The Ten Commandments and the Book of the Covenant

In teaching this section of Exodus, it is important to explain the relationship between the Ten Commandments and the Book of the Covenant. Whereas the former are a very succinct summary of the broad principles that are intended to shape the community life of the Israelites as a holy nation, the Book of the Covenant not only fleshes out in a variety of ways how these principles should impact everyday living, but it also addresses other issues that are of importance for the future harmony of Israelite society. Unlike the Ten Commandments, the Book of the Covenant contains a number of distinctive sections that differ noticeably in both subject matter and style of content. Each section needs to be interpreted in a manner appropriate to its content. Taken together, these different parts reveal what God expects of the Israelites within the covenant relationship.

21:28 *If a bull gores a man or woman to death.* The laws move from injuries caused by people to injuries caused by animals. The primary case law sets out the appropriate penalty for the death of a person attacked by a bull. In this instance the animal's owner is not considered to be negligent. Nevertheless, the bull is put to death because it forfeits its own life by taking the life of another. The death of the bull is a distinctive feature of the biblical laws when compared with similar ancient Near Eastern laws. This underlines the special value that is placed on human life by God.

21:29–32 *If, however, the bull has had the habit of goring.* This secondary case law introduces the issue of negligence by the owner. He has failed to take appropriate action to protect others from his animal. By doing so, he forfeits his life. However, because this is not a premeditated killing, the owner is permitted to ransom his life by making a payment to the victim's family. Verse 31 indicates that the same penalty should apply regardless of the age or gender of the victim. Possibly, this is also intended to be a polemic against the practice of vicarious punishment that was sometimes adopted in other cultures, where the death of a son or daughter would be punished by the death of the guilty party's son or daughter.

21:33–34 *If anyone uncovers a pit or digs one . . . and an ox or a donkey falls into it.* From injuries to people, we move to injuries to animals caused by human negligence. Appropriate compensation is required from the party responsible.

21:35–36 *If anyone's bull injures someone else's bull . . . the bull had the habit of goring.* In the first instance neither owner is viewed as being negligent, and both parties share the cost of the loss. In the second instance, the negligent owner must bear a greater cost.

Theological Insights

The case laws in this passage indirectly provide an important insight into God's nature. At the heart of divine justice is the concept of "moral symmetry": the punishment must match the offense, being no more or no less than the offense requires. As the ultimate arbiter of justice, God demands equity when punishments are being imposed. However, such equity must be achieved in a way that is as humane as possible, avoiding physical assault and mutilation by substituting other appropriate means of restitution to those who have been wronged.

In addition, these case laws also reveal something of God's moral standards, indicating how God prioritizes the order of moral values. Thus, for example, in every circumstance the protection of human life is placed above the protection of property. In God's scale of values no person is more important than another, and every person is more important than any material object.

Teaching the Text

Every society requires laws to regulate human behavior. Laws, however, are much more than a collection of dos and don'ts. They enshrine the value system of a society. In these verses God uses selected examples to teach the values that he wishes to see embraced.

When we teach this passage, the repeated references to the death penalty in verses 12–17 require careful exposition. The principle of "a life for a life" is clearly applied in verse 12. However, it is important to note the qualification that comes in verses 13–14. A very clear distinction is drawn here between murder and manslaughter. Anyone who usurps the place of God by intentionally taking away the life of another forfeits his or her right to life. Regarding the complex issue of capital punishment, Christians should actively ensure that no one is unjustly executed.

By instituting the concept of asylum, God ensures that no one should be punished without having a proper trial. Christians ought to be active in promoting judicial systems that ensure a fair and impartial trial for those accused of serious offenses. No matter how heinous the crime, personal vengeance should not usurp the rule of law.

While these case laws demonstrate the principle of "moral symmetry," certain values underpin the judgments listed here. This is most apparent in the two cases involving parents in verses 15 and 17. People who attack or curse one of their parents commit a capital offense. Such actions are placed on a par with murder. This scale of values comes also in the Ten Commandments, where the requirement to honor parents is placed before the prohibition against killing (20:12–13). As Christians we should be ever careful to ensure that our words and actions do not undermine the authority that God gives to parents.

In God's eyes, respect for parents is a vital ingredient for creating a holy nation. How individuals behave within their family environment will be mirrored in their behavior outside the family. If respect for parental authority is missing, there will be no respect for other types of authority (Deut. 21:18–21). This, however, does not necessarily mean that Christians should automatically acquiesce to those in positions of power when their actions run counter to God's values. Nevertheless, respect for those in authority should influence the way in which Christians respond.

Illustrating the Text

Laws enshrine the value system of a society.

Law: Throughout America's history, a regard for the Sabbath has led many states to pass laws that, in a post-Christian culture, may now seem silly. These so-called blue laws can range from prohibiting the sale of alcohol to regulating how and when people may eat candy on a Sunday. For example, Wisconsinites from Winona Lake are prohibited from eating ice cream at a counter on Sundays. Some states have outlawed marbles and yo-yos on Sundays too.[1] These laws, still on the books, are an anachronism, enshrining values that have long passed away in American society.

A vast number of years separates us from Israel and the cultural realities their laws address. For that reason, some of these laws might seem strange, yet each of the laws we encounter in this text challenges us to think carefully about what God values. And God's values never go out of date.

Murder is a grave crime against God's handiwork.

Props: When we intentionally take a life, we are not only acting against the victim; we are acting against God, destroying God's own handiwork. To illustrate this point, consider displaying, then "destroying" a valuable work of art or object. One example would be to display a poster of a famous work of art that you have personally appreciated. Talk about its significance. Then dramatically brandish a permanent marker or a can of spray paint and strike a red X through the work or draw spectacles and a mustache on the face. This illustration will depend on startling the congregation with an act that appears to destroy something precious. Any time a human life is taken, one of God's precious works of art has been destroyed.

Parental authority is God given and must be honored.

News Story: In a litigious society, it is easy to find stories that are outrageous, humorous, or just plain silly. But the story of twenty-one-year-old Caitlyn Ricci and her biological parents is strikingly sad. In November 2014, a judge responded to Caitlyn's lawsuit against her long-divorced parents, Michael Ricci and Maura McGarvey, ordering them to pay $16,000 per year for her college tuition. There are, of course, conflicting stories. Caitlyn's mom claims her daughter moved out as a final act of defiance. Caitlyn says she was kicked out. Whatever truth lies behind the story, we have a clear breakdown in the parent-child relationship. In God's design plan, children are called to honor the parents who raise them, not take them to court.[2]

God's Property Values

Big Idea

Depriving others of what rightfully belongs to them may take many forms, all of which require appropriate restitution.

Key Themes

- Each person has a responsibility to ensure that they do not cause others financial loss, either deliberately or through negligence.
- When loss occurs, those responsible should make appropriate restitution, depending on the nature of the offense and the loss inflicted on others.

Understanding the Text

The Text in Context

This passage continues the series of case laws that begins in Exodus 21. A wide range of different scenarios is considered, from deliberate theft through injury to an animal that has been hired for agricultural work. The formal structure of primary and secondary laws continues, but the subject matter moves from issues concerning death and injury (21:18–36) to the misappropriation of property belonging to another (22:1–17). The case laws are brought to a conclusion with three laws that carry the death penalty (22:18–20). These latter laws form a frame with 21:12–17. The case laws, which are mainly set out in descending order of severity, are an integral part of the Book of the Covenant, illustrating the moral values that should regulate the behavior of the Israelites.

Historical and Cultural Background

As noted in the previous units and in the "Additonal Insights" following the unit on 20:18–21:11, the case laws recorded in the Book of the Covenant address issues that are also found in various ancient Near Eastern collections from the third and second millennia BC. Not surprisingly, laws concerning the misappropriation of property feature prominently in these law collections. In contrast to other ancient Near Eastern law collections, the biblical laws never view theft or misappropriation of property as a capital crime.

Interpretive Insights

22:1 *Whoever steals an ox or a sheep and slaughters it or sells it.* Farm animals were vital sources of income for Israelite families. For this reason, laws concerning their misappropriation head the list of rulings concerning theft. With good reason, the thief is required to pay back either fivefold or fourfold. Greater value is placed on an ox because it could be used for plowing. In this initial law particular attention is given to the fact that the thief has slaughtered or sold the stolen animal in order to conceal his illegal activity (cf. 22:4).

22:2–3a *If a thief is caught breaking in at night.* The preceding law indicates that, if caught, the thief must make financial restitution. The thief does not pay with their life, as occasionally happened in other ancient Near Eastern cultures. What happens, however, if the thief is killed in the process of stealing? Two scenarios are envisaged, with different outcomes. If the thief is killed at night, no action is taken against the householder. In marked contrast, if the killing occurs during the day, the householder is held responsible. The distinction between night and day probably rests on the expectation that the house owner should be able to ascertain correctly the intention of the burglar during the day. In the dark it would be difficult to know the intention of the one breaking in, who could be there to kill, not merely to steal. These laws indicate that every life is of value, even that of a thief. The act of stealing does not merit capital punishment.

22:3b–4 *Anyone who steals must certainly make restitution.* Verse 3b recognizes that theft may be motivated by poverty. When an impoverished thief is caught, they are to be sold as a slave, if necessary, to pay the penalty for the crime. Verse 4 modifies verse 1 by stating that if the animal is found alive in the possession of the thief, the thief makes twofold restitution. In this instance, in contrast to verse 1, the thief has not yet taken any action to conceal their wrongdoing. Given the ability of animals to stray, the provision of a lesser penalty in these circumstances may be designed to ensure that an innocent party found in possession of another's animal is not penalized unduly.

22:5–6 *If anyone grazes their livestock in a field or vineyard.* Whereas the opening laws address deliberate theft, verses 5–6 concern the destruction of crops through negligence. Since this is not taken to be a deliberate act of destruction resulting in the loss of property, the level of punishment is reduced, with the offender making full restitution to the victim for the actual loss that has occurred.

If a fire breaks out and spreads into thornbushes. This is a second instance of negligence leading to the destruction of another's property. Verses 5–6 are linked not only by addressing similar situations but also by a wordplay in Hebrew involving the verb *ba'ar*, which has the sense of "consume" ("grazes" and "they graze," 22:4; "started" the fire, 22:5).

22:7–15 *If anyone gives a neighbor silver or goods for safekeeping.* The laws in this section address a variety of situations that involve property or animals entrusted by one party to another. Covering a range of scenarios, various punishments are outlined, depending on the nature of the loss that occurs and reflecting the degree of culpability on the part of the guilty party.

22:16–17 *If a man seduces a virgin . . . he must pay the bride-price.* This law regarding the seduction of an unmarried girl may initially appear out of place after a series of laws dealing with misappropriation of property. However, this is a further example of something that falls under the broad umbrella of "theft." In this instance, the financial loss centers on the "bride-price" (a better term might be "betrothal gift"). Normally, a husband-to-be would give a monetary gift to his future father-in-law as part of a larger financial arrangement that looked to secure the well-being of the girl. If no betrothal gift was made, the girl might lack future financial security. While this law addresses potential financial loss, it also has the added consequence of discouraging premarital sex. Virginity was an important issue in Israelite marriage arrangements (cf. Deut. 22:13–29). The loss of it could lower the value of what might be expected as a betrothal gift.

22:18 *Do not allow a sorceress to live.* This is the first of three laws that address behavior that merits capital punishment. The first concerns activity associated with the occult. The Hebrew term used here to denote a "sorceress" is the feminine form of a noun used earlier in Exodus for the "sorcerers" who served Pharaoh (7:11). As is evident from what these "sorcerers" did, those who practice sorcery seek to manipulate the powers of nature in order to influence situations. To do this, they may rely on the use of spells, incantations, or other rituals. Such behavior is strongly condemned in the Old Testament (e.g., Lev. 19:26, 31; Deut. 18:9–14), for it runs counter to serving the Lord alone, the fundamental obligation of the covenant relationship.

22:19 *Anyone who has sexual relations with an animal.* Having intercourse with an animal may have been a feature of animal cults and fertility worship. Such activity transgresses the creation boundaries established by God.

22:20 *Whoever sacrifices to any god.* The exclusive nature of their covenant relationship with the Lord prohibits the Israelites from worshiping other gods. Those who sacrifice to other gods are especially condemned, because participating in sacrifices was perceived as forming a bond of intimacy with the deity.

Theological Insights

Two important concepts underlie the case laws in verses 1–17. Firstly, these laws emphasize the responsibility that individuals must exercise regarding the possessions of others. Actions, intentional or otherwise, that deprive others of what is rightfully theirs are wrong in God's eyes. Secondly, those who are responsible for causing another person financial loss must make appropriate restitution. The nature of the restitution should reflect the circumstances surrounding the loss, taking into account factors such as intention and negligence. These case laws give an important insight into the nature of divine justice and help us to understand something of God's nature. From the punishments that he imposes, we are enabled to see something of the values by which God himself lives.

Importantly, these case laws reveal that God is passionate about justice, seeking to ensure that each party in a dispute is treated equitably when every factor is taken into account. In the complexities of life this is often difficult to achieve, yet in God's eyes every punishment should be no more or no less than the wrongdoing demands. In the light of these case laws, we can be confident that God will be scrupulously fair in dispensing justice. Furthermore, God is concerned that in the process of punishing someone who has acted inappropriately, either by design or by accident, due attention should be given to the importance of reconciling opposing parties in a dispute. Each side should sense that the outcome is appropriate, paving the way for a return to normal relations. Reconciliation lies at the heart of God's nature.

Teaching the Text

The practicalities of everyday living create many situations where human behavior, either intentionally or accidentally, results in individuals suffering loss involving possessions. Verses 1–17 cover a wide range of offenses involving possessions and financial loss. These reveal something of how people lived over three thousand years ago. In spite of the cultural and historical gap between then and now, two important principles, evident in this passage, should govern our attitude and actions regarding "theft."

First, these regulations underline that everyone must act with responsibility to protect what belongs to others. Anyone causing financial loss, either deliberately or through negligence, must bear the cost of doing so. This places an onus on each of us to consider carefully how we handle the property of others, be they our employer, neighbor, or friend. We are all under an obligation to ensure that our actions do not cause financial loss for others. We must be careful that greed, jealousy, or laziness does not influence our behavior. In all our dealings, we should ensure that we do not cause harm by depriving other people financially. Slogans like "buyer beware" have no place in God's kingdom.

Second, these verses highlight the importance of making restitution to those who suffer loss as a result of theft, misappropriation, or negligence. At one level, this functions as a deterrent against taking or destroying the property of others. Anyone who deliberately sets out to steal from another deserves to be punished severely. This should act as a deterrent against greed. More important, it compensates the victim for the wrong done against him or her. Different levels of restitution exist, depending on the seriousness of the offense and the culpability of the offender. By making the guilty party compensate the victim directly, these regulations seek to reconcile the parties involved. Theft causes emotional scars that need to be healed.

While theft is a crime deserving of punishment, we should ensure that the level of punishment is appropriate to the nature of the misdeed. In this connection, those who seek to conceal their nefarious activity deserve to be punished more severely. Not only should a fine be a deterrent, but it should also compensate the victim, providing a means by which the two parties may be reconciled to each other. As the New Testament example of Zacchaeus reveals, making restitution to those we have wronged is an important sign of having a right relationship with Jesus (Luke 19:1–9).

Illustrating the Text

We must ensure that our actions do not cause others to suffer financial loss.

News Story: Ebony Weatherspoon learned an important lesson the hard way. One day, sitting at work, she posted a comment to her Facebook page: "Only 7½ more hours of ignorance. TGIF." When the comment was discovered, Weatherspoon was brought before her superior and fired for making the negative post during work hours.[1] It was an example of what some call "time theft"—misappropriating company time. Though she sought to have her firing reversed, the right of the employer to terminate her was upheld in court. Though the lines of what is protected and what is unprotected speech are still being drawn, one principle is clear: employees are not allowed to damage their companies.

Economics: In our age of digital files and easy access to the internet, unlawful sharing of video or audio content has become commonplace. It may be as simple as downloading the tracks from a friend's audio CD to your own computer or MP3 player instead of buying the disc yourself. *And who is really being hurt?* many think. *The performer has millions of dollars and won't miss the ten bucks I would spend.* But beyond the ethical aspects of the decision to steal material, there are broad economic aspects that affect a wide range of people from retail employees on up to movie or record producers and performers. DVDs often begin with an apt warning: "Piracy is not a victimless crime." Christians should rethink the decision to illegally download or stream a song or movie that they haven't paid for.

Restitution can be expensive when we fail to protect what belongs to others.

News Story: On April 20, 2010, an explosion on the Deepwater Horizon oil rig in the Gulf of Mexico caused the deaths of eleven people and injured many others. The subsequent oil spill, the largest at sea in the history of the petroleum industry, impacted the lives of many others, as the marine environment was polluted with over 200 million US gallons of crude oil. The extent of the damage done is still being assessed, but it has already cost BP over $42 billion in payments to compensate those who have suffered loss.[2] While the scale of such restitution is difficult to imagine, it illustrates well the biblical concept of restitution found in this passage of Exodus. Those responsible through neglect for depriving others of their livelihood are required to make good the loss.

True reconciliation is the ultimate aim of the regulations against theft.

Statistics: At the end of 2013, there were estimated to be 1,574,700 prisoners in state and federal correctional facilities in the United States.[3] That number represents almost 0.5 percent of the US population. And it represents the highest incarceration rate in the world by far. Based on 2010 statistics, the United States incarcerated people at a rate of about 716 per 100,000 residents. The next-closest incarceration rates in the world were Cuba, with a rate of 510 per 100,0000, and Rwanda, with a rate of 492 per 100,000.[4] Clearly our society has focused on punitive justice, doing time if you do the crime. But Prison Fellowship's Centre for Justice and Reconciliation is seeking to promote a different kind of justice process, one that looks a lot like biblical justice. In this model, the focus is not on mere punishment but on genuine restoration of community. One example of how this can work is related by Greg Vaughn. Around a circle of conversation, he was brought face-to-face with some boys who stole a golf cart from his workplace. Both the perpetrators and the victims were able to speak about the situation and what it meant for them. The boys heard how their actions affected others and apologized for what they had done. And the participants worked out a plan for the boys to volunteer along with some members of the company and fulfill other obligations to make reparation for the theft.[5]

Religion That God Our Father Accepts as Pure and Faultless

Big Idea

Holy living that is pleasing to God should have as its priorities care for the vulnerable and justice for everyone.

Key Themes

- God demands that the Israelites demonstrate practical compassion toward the weak and marginal members of society.
- Respect for God must lie at the very heart of everything the Israelites do.
- The Israelites must do everything possible, including overcoming personal prejudice, in order to ensure impartiality within their legal system.

Understanding the Text

The Text in Context

To understand fully the covenant obligations that God places on the Israelites at Mount Sinai, it is important to recognize that the material in the Book of the Covenant is not homogeneous. It falls into different sections, and each contributes something distinctive. Every part is important, but perhaps none more so than the present section, for here we see the holiness of God linked closely to the concepts of compassion and justice.

This passage forms a unique section within the covenant obligations that are given by God to the Israelites. The statements made here are expressed in a style that differs from that used in 21:2–22:20. No longer do we have case laws that describe a particular misdeed followed by an appropriate punishment. This distinctive section records an uncompromising list of moral exhortations or precepts. The change in style accompanies a change in content, as three different areas of life are addressed. Exodus 22:21–27 emphasizes the necessity of being compassionate toward the most vulnerable members of society. Exodus 22:28–31 focuses primarily on the Israelites' relationship to God. Exodus 23:1–9 is concerned with ensuring impartiality within the judicial system, in order to create a just society. Structurally, three ideas are set side by side in 22:21–23:9: compassion, God, justice. This arrangement is hardly coincidental given the larger narrative within the book of Exodus, which describes God's compassionate concern for the unjustly exploited Israelites. This larger context is underlined by the opening and closing verses of this passage (22:21; 23:9), which remind the Israelites of their oppression in Egypt.

Historical and Cultural Background

Over the last century or so, a variety of law collections and numerous other texts have been discovered by archaeologists, shedding new light on different ancient Near Eastern cultures (see the "Additional Insights" section following the unit on 20:18–21:11). While these law collections emphasize the importance of protecting the widows and the fatherless, the protection given to foreigners in the Book of the Covenant is unique. Throughout the ancient world, resident aliens were especially vulnerable to exploitation, as the Israelites' own experience in Egypt bears testimony.

Interpretive Insights

22:21 *Do not mistreat or oppress a foreigner.* In the listing of those who are not to be exploited, priority is given to foreign or migrant workers and residents. The Hebrew term *ger* denotes someone from another place and culture who takes up residence in a different country. In Genesis, Abraham is a *ger* within the land of Canaan, having left his family and homeland in northern Mesopotamia. Although the Israelites lived in Egypt for centuries, they were still considered to be foreigners. As such, they were vulnerable to exploitation and oppression, as the early chapters of Exodus reveal. In the light of their own experience, the Israelites must not oppress foreign residents, a point reinforced by the repetition of this instruction in 23:9.

22:22–24 *Do not take advantage of the widow or the fatherless.* Alongside foreign residents, widows and fatherless children could easily find themselves in a situation of hardship. The story of Naomi in the book of Ruth illustrates well the plight of a widow in the ancient world.

22:25–27 *If you lend money . . . who is needy.* Although verse 25 is often interpreted as a universal ban against lending at interest, the prohibition may be limited to charging interest from the poor, who are forced through poverty to borrow from others. This focus on the poor is clearly the case in verses 26–27, where the borrower has only one cloak with which to keep warm at night. God demands that the Israelites exhibit compassion in caring for the destitute and less fortunate.

22:28 *Do not blaspheme God.* The Hebrew verb translated here as "blaspheme" denotes more than verbal curses against God. It also covers activities such as disregarding him, dishonoring him, or treating him with contempt. It is the antonym of the verb translated "honor" in 20:12.

22:29–30 *Do not hold back offerings . . . give me the firstborn.* Showing respect to God requires the Israelites to be generous toward him. The mention of firstborn recalls the Passover, when God ransomed from death all the firstborn males and required the Israelites to give their firstborn to God (13:11–16).

22:31 *You are to be my holy people. So do not eat the meat . . . torn by wild beasts.* At the heart of the covenant is God's desire for the Israelites to become a holy nation. Much more of what this will require is set out in the book of Leviticus, where special instructions are given regarding "clean" and "unclean" foods (Lev. 11). Underlying the prohibition about eating the meat of an animal killed by a predator is the idea that holiness is associated with "life" and uncleanness with "death." In this instance, the meat is ritually "unclean" and must not be eaten.

23:1 *Do not spread false reports.* This is the first in a series of precepts that seek to ensure a fair and just legal system. In ancient Israel, there were no professional lawyers or judges. Local elders would normally oversee lawsuits. For a just settlement to be achieved, truthfulness on the part of witnesses was essential.

23:2–3 *Do not follow the crowd.* The Hebrew word translated "crowd" could also be rendered "majority" or "mighty." A witness must tell the truth and not be unduly influenced by either social pressure or a powerful lobby. When giving testimony, a witness must be totally impartial and must not favor the poor out of compassion for them.

23:4–5 *If you come across your enemy's ox or donkey.* Although verses 4–5 appear to disrupt this collection of moral precepts relating to justice, they highlight well the issue of impartiality. The Israelites are to help those whom they might consider enemies. Here the Old Testament affirms the concept of loving one's enemy (cf. Matt. 5:44; Luke 6:27).

23:6–7 *Do not deny justice to your poor people in their lawsuits.* The theme of impartiality continues with the demand that those who are poor, and therefore unlikely to have influence within society, should not be discriminated against in the legal process.

23:8 *Do not accept a bribe.* The Hebrew term translated "bribe" could denote an ordinary gift, not necessarily one given in secret to buy a favor. No one is to accept any kind of gift that might influence their role as a witness or judge. Throughout verses 1–8 there is a strong concern to ensure that the judicial process is not corrupted in any way.

23:9 *Do not oppress a foreigner.* While this verse echoes 22:21, in this context it may refer especially to how foreigners are treated in legal disputes.

Theological Insights

While most of the material in the first half of the Book of the Covenant (21:2–22:20) resembles detailed legislation that might be used in a court setting, 22:21–23:9 comprises moral precepts. Through these God requires the Israelites to adopt a standard of behavior that goes well beyond what may be enforced by civil or religious legislation. Holy living cannot be created through laws alone. God's moral standards are exceptionally high and very demanding. To live a holy life requires more than keeping on the right side of a line that distinguishes between what is legal and what is illegal. The moral precepts set out in this passage point to perfection as the goal. For this reason there are close parallels between what is said here and Jesus's teaching in the Sermon on the Mount in Matthew 5. To be perfect demands much more than merely not breaking the letter, or even the spirit, of the law.

To be a holy nation, the Israelites must adopt a caring attitude toward the weakest members of their society. Attention is drawn to those who are especially open to exploitation: resident foreigners, widows, fatherless children, and the poor. In requiring the Israelites to care for those who are vulnerable, God reminds them of their own experiences in Egypt. Compassion must also be shown to those who may be viewed as enemies (23:4–5). Jesus's command to "love your enemies, do good to them, and lend to them without expecting to get anything back" (Luke 6:35) echoes God's instructions to the Israelites. Through being compassionate the Israelites reflect God's holy nature (Exod. 22:27).

Compassion for the weak and concern for justice are necessary components of holy living. Compassion and justice are integral to the very nature of God himself, and they are recurrent themes throughout the book of Exodus. Divine compassion and justice lead to the rescue of the Israelites from harsh exploitation in Egypt. In the light of God's actions and instructions, every Christian should prioritize caring for the less fortunate members of the community and ensuring equity and impartiality within the legal system.

At the heart of the Sinai covenant is God's desire to create a holy nation. The contents of the Book of the Covenant provide an insight into the kind of society that God wishes to have. In the light of 22:21–23:9, it is worth recalling that two closely related measures of the quality of any society are (1) its concern for its weak and marginalized members and (2) the fairness of its judicial system. With good reason, this passage has much to teach us on how best to create and ensure a healthy society.

Teaching the Text

This section of the Book of the Covenant divides into three parts, with precepts that draw attention to the holiness of God in 22:28–31 being surrounded by others that emphasize the importance of caring for the vulnerable members of society and ensuring justice for all people regardless of their status within the community. In the teaching of this passage, it is important to emphasize the priority that God gives to these issues.

Compassion for the weak. There is often an unfortunate tendency to consider migrant workers, widows, fatherless children, and the poor as less important than others, but this is not how God views them. With good reason, the book of James states, "Religion that God our Father accepts as pure and faultless is this: to look after orphans and widows in their distress and to keep oneself from being polluted by the world" (1:27). True religion that is pleasing to God will exhibit genuine compassion for the most needy members of society, regardless of their ethnic background. God's heart goes out to those in greatest need, and he utters a chilling warning to those who might take advantage of women or children who have no male to defend them (Exod. 22:22–24).

Impartial treatment of others. God addresses the issue of human prejudice, especially as it impacts the legal system. For justice to be done, everyone from judge to witness must set aside inappropriate antagonistic feelings toward others. Witnesses must not favor either the rich or the poor, and their testimony must not be influenced by either public opinion or secretive bribery. Since we may be blind to prejudices that are deep-seated in us, we need to take to heart the words of Jesus: "But love your enemies, do good to them, and lend to them without expecting to get anything back. Then your reward will be great, and you will be children of the Most High, because he is kind to the ungrateful and wicked" (Luke 6:35).

Honoring God. Sandwiched between the moral exhortations concerning compassion and justice are a few precepts that address attitudes and actions concerning God. Motivation to care for the vulnerable and to resist the temptation of prejudice comes from an appreciation of how we are recipients of God's grace. Since God has embraced us in spite of our enmity toward him, we must be willing to love our enemies. Without a true sense of our indebtedness to God, we will struggle to care for the less fortunate and to overcome our ingrained dislike of others.

Being generous to the poor and impartial in how we treat others are not actions that can be imposed on people through legislation. It is not illegal to charge interest or turn away from helping an enemy in trouble, but doing these things runs counter to being truly righteous. In teaching this passage, we should emphasize that holy living demands more than merely a scrupulous commitment to obeying the law. It is not enough to achieve legal righteousness, if that is even possible. God sets the bar much higher. It is no less than what Jesus states, "Be perfect, therefore, as your heavenly Father is perfect" (Matt. 5:48).

Illustrating the Text

Religion pleasing to God exhibits compassion for the needy, regardless of their ethnicity.

Human Experience: Everywhere throughout history we see that humans are clannish creatures. We tend to gather ourselves together in groups. These groups are formed for mutual provision and defense. They are often hard to penetrate, and we know who "belongs" and who doesn't. This pattern is repeated on elementary school playgrounds and geopolitical stages around the world. Examples from the news abound, such as the denial by the government of Myanmar of the legitimacy of the Rohingya as an ethnic group and as legitimate residents of that country, subjecting them to possible expulsion and ill treatment. God calls us to remember that justice and compassion should be meted out not to preferred insiders but to everyone equally. This is an important potential for witness, especially in a culture that often weighs justice for others against self-interest, whether it is in regard to personal or national involvement and whether it relates to immigrants at home or oppressive situations abroad.

God's heart goes out to the needy, and he warns those who exploit the defenseless.

Bible: **Amos 5.** The Prophets contain many clear statements of God's ringing condemnation of economic exploitation. One such example is the Lord's denunciation of Israel through the prophet Amos.

> There are those who hate the one who upholds justice in court
> and detest the one who tells the truth.
>
> You levy a straw tax on the poor
> and impose a tax on their grain.
> Therefore, though you have built stone mansions,
> you will not live in them;
> though you have planted lush vineyards,
> you will not drink their wine.
> For I know how many are your offenses
> and how great your sins. (Amos 5:10–12)

The overall context should be kept in mind: Amos proclaims that God's universal justice will one day reign.

Justice requires impartiality.

History: Throughout Western history, stretching back to the Greeks, the idea of justice has often been personified as a woman. Typically, she is holding a scale in her hand. Over time, she has also been depicted holding a sword in her right hand. The scale indicate the merits of one's case—the evidence must be weighed. The sword indicates both reason—which must be employed—and power to punish the guilty. Over time a third element has been added—the blindfold. This third feature indicates impartiality. True justice cannot be rendered based on the identity of the accused or the accuser. True justice must be rendered based on the merits of the case.

Making Time for God

Big Idea

We all need to work into the rhythm of life time that we devote to drawing near to God.

Key Themes

- The Old Testament sabbatical rest anticipates the greater rest that comes through Christ's defeat of evil in the world.
- Out of thankfulness Christians should willingly give of their time and wealth to God.

Understanding the Text

The Text in Context

The Book of the Covenant consists of various sections. After listing moral precepts that the Israelites must obey (22:21–23:9), God instructs them regarding the ordering of their time for rest and worship (23:10–19). This latter section falls into two distinctive parts, separated by verse 13. Verses 10–12 pick up on the concept of the Sabbath and the motif of rest. While the content of verses 10–12 is distinctive, a concern for the poor and the foreigner links these verses with the preceding passage. Verses 14–19 contain instructions concerning three pilgrimage festivals that the Israelites must celebrate annually. Verse 15 focuses on the Festival of Unleavened Bread, recalling the Israelites' deliverance from Egypt at the Passover. All of the material in this section anticipates the future settlement of the Israelites in the land of Canaan.

Outline/Structure

This passage is carefully structured through the repetition of the numbers six (vv. 10, 12) and three (vv. 14, 17). The number six links together verses 10–11 and 12, which emphasize rest in the seventh year and on the seventh day, respectively. This recalls how the keeping of the Sabbath is one of the Ten Commandments. Verses 14–19 consist of two parallel panels that focus on the celebration of the Festivals of Unleavened Bread, Harvest, and Ingathering. While these three festivals are clearly named in verses 15–16, the instructions in verses 18–19 are probably best interpreted as also relating to these festivals. Binding together the materials in verses 10–12 and 14–19, verse 13 highlights the importance of obeying the Lord, the fundamental principle on which the entire covenant depends.

Historical and Cultural Background

The three festivals are discussed in chronological order. The Festival of Unleavened Bread comes in the first month of the calendar year. This seven-day festival is celebrated in the springtime. The next two festivals are connected with harvest; the first of these comes in the late spring, with the other taking place in the early fall. The climate of Israel favors an agricultural cycle that begins in the fall with plowing for the planting of cereal crops. These are then harvested in the late spring.

Interpretive Insights

23:10–11 *during the seventh year let the land lie unplowed and unused.* Every seventh year the agricultural land is to lie fallow. How this worked in practice is not clear, and it is possible that it was never fully implemented. Did a system of rotation operate, whereby one-seventh of the agricultural land was rested each year? Or was all the land rested in the same year? The latter policy would require the Israelites to trust God for a sufficient harvest in preceding years to feed them during the sabbatical year. Either way, God is concerned that the poor and wild animals should not suffer hardship but have access to any food that might grow on the fallow land.

23:12 *on the seventh day do not work . . . may rest . . . be refreshed.* The associated concepts of rest and refreshment lie at the heart of the Sabbath, as highlighted in 20:8–11. God's passionate concern for slaves and migrant workers is evident. They in particular are listed, not forgetting farm animals, as deserving of rest. The close association of the Sabbath with rest is noteworthy in the light of God's deliverance of the Israelites from harsh slavery in Egypt. The motif of rest also figures prominently in the book of Joshua, linked to the Israelites' obtaining both security and a bountiful provision of food in the promised land.

23:13 *do everything I have said to you. Do not invoke the names of other gods.* The covenant requires the Israelites to give their exclusive allegiance to the Lord. In the polytheistic world of antiquity, the expectation that the Israelites should be monotheistic is radically different.

23:14 *Three times a year you are to celebrate a festival to me.* Fuller details regarding these three festivals are found elsewhere in the Pentateuch (Lev. 23:4–43; Deut. 16:1–17). They are pilgrimage feasts, requiring the Israelite men to travel to a central location, in later times the Jerusalem temple. These festivals will celebrate both God's intervention in Egypt on behalf of the Israelites and his provision of fertile territory in the land of Canaan.

23:15 *Celebrate the Festival of Unleavened Bread.* Fuller instructions regarding this festival come in 13:3–10, where God commands an annual commemoration of the Passover. The eating of unleavened bread distinguishes this festival from other occasions, recalling how the hasty departure of the Israelites from Egypt prevented them from baking and eating bread made with yeast (12:39). The month of Aviv comes in the spring (March–April); in the postexilic period the name Aviv is replaced by Nisan. Unlike the other festivals, Unleavened Bread is not associated with the harvest. The name Aviv denotes "green grain" and refers to barley that is not yet ready to harvest (cf. 9:31).

23:16 *Celebrate the Festival of Harvest.* This festival is also known as the Festival of Weeks because it comes seven weeks after the Passover (Exod. 34:22; Deut. 16:9–12), and it is later referred to as Pentecost (meaning "fiftieth"), seven weeks being approximately fifty days. The main crops harvested in the late spring are barley and wheat.

Celebrate the Festival of Ingathering. This festival marks the end of the agricultural year, when other crops, such as grapes and olives, have been harvested. It is also known as the Festival of Tabernacles, or Booths, because it commemorates the Israelites' trek through the wilderness when they lived in tents.

23:17 *Three times a year all the men are to appear before the Sovereign* LORD. Perhaps for pragmatic reasons only the men are required to make the pilgrimage to the central sanctuary, where the festivals are celebrated. Women are not prohibited from attending, but mandatory attendance would prove exceptionally difficult for those who might be pregnant or have small children.

23:18 *Do not offer the blood of a sacrifice to me along with anything containing yeast.* The mention of yeast provides an important clue for understanding the context of this instruction. It refers to the Passover. This is confirmed by a parallel instruction in 34:25, which specifically mentions the Passover festival.

23:19 *Bring the best of the firstfruits.* This instruction fits well with the Festival of Harvest.

Do not cook a young goat in its mother's milk. Scholars have debated at length the significance of this particular prohibition.[1] Although links have been claimed by scholars in the past, there is no evidence to connect this instruction with Canaanite rituals. Possibly this prohibition is graphically worded to ensure moderation in eating during the Festival of Ingathering by symbolically reminding the Israelites that the source of life (i.e., milk) should not be associated with death (i.e., the killing of the young goat). Overindulgence at the festival might have involved cooking young goats that were born close to the time of the festival. Perhaps as late as the first century AD, this prohibition became the basis of the Jewish custom of not eating meat and dairy produce at the same meal.

Theological Insights

Two related reasons for worshiping the Lord permeate this passage: the Israelites' deliverance from slavery in Egypt and the divine provision of a land "flowing with milk and honey" (3:8). In different ways these represent a reversal of the tragic consequences that proceeded from Adam and Eve's rebellion against God in the Garden of Eden.

The concept of the Sabbath has a unique place within the Sinai covenant. It is designated as the sign of the covenant that is established between the Lord and the Israelites (Exod. 31:13–17). For this reason, to disregard the Sabbath was equivalent to rejecting God; anyone who broke the Sabbath was severely punished (Num. 15:32–36).

The commemoration of the Passover through the Festival of Unleavened Bread underlines the significance of God's deliverance of the firstborn males from death and anticipates a greater Passover fulfilled in Jesus Christ. The two harvest festivals are intended to remind the people of God's role in providing for their prosperity within the land. Out of thankfulness, they were not to appear empty handed before God at the central sanctuary.

Teaching the Text

After exhorting the Israelites to be compassionate and impartial in their treatment of other people, God stresses that their commitment to him should influence their use of time in a variety of ways. This remains true for Christians, even if we are no longer bound by the same precise instructions that God gave as part of the Sinai covenant. From this passage, three features are worth highlighting.

Time for worship. The Israelites are to set aside regular periods of time for worship in order to thank God for all that he has given so generously to them. Likewise, Christians should ensure that they reserve time of both quality and quantity for worshiping God. While God does not impose pilgrimage festivals on Christians, nevertheless there is an expectation that Christians will adopt a pattern of living that will enhance their relationship with God. Understandably, a routine that involves regular meeting with other believers is most likely to strengthen an individual's spiritual life (cf. Heb. 10:25). In addition to weekly worship activities, time should also be made to participate in additional God-centered activities.

Time for rest. Symbolizing God's rescue of the Israelites from toil and bondage in Egypt, the seventh year and the seventh day were to be occasions of rest from labor. These times were also intended for the good of other people, especially the poor, slaves, and resident foreigners. Even animals, both domestic and wild, were to benefit. Christians should be to the fore in advocating labor systems that ensure workers are not exploited by having to work exceptionally long hours for little reward. This should be especially so when multinational companies make use of cheap labor to enhance their own profits. By their words and actions Christians should be active supporters of organizations that foster fair trade.

Time to anticipate. While the Old Testament concept of the Sabbath has practical implications that seek to transform the lives of ancient Israelites, the Sabbath concept has also a prophetic dimension. It points forward to a greater rest that will come when the world in rebellion against God is finally brought fully under his authority. When the prince of this world is overthrown, we shall enter fully into the rest achieved by Jesus Christ. In the meantime, we are exhorted by the author of Hebrews to "make every effort to enter that rest" (Heb. 4:11) by remaining obedient to God.

Illustrating the Text

Our use of the precious commodity of time should reflect our devotion to the Lord.

Bible: **The Parable of the Talents.** In Matthew 25:14–30, Jesus tells the parable of the talents. Often, this parable is applied to our use of treasure, talents, and abilities. What about life's most precious commodity—time? Every one of us has sixty minutes each hour, twenty-four hours each day. God has appointed each of us *stewards* of those hours. They belong not to us but to him. He allows us to invest them. One day, he will approach us and seek a return on his investments.

Christians should reserve time of both quality and quantity for worshiping God.

Church History: In 1647, the General Assembly of the Church of Scotland adopted a document called the Directory for Family Worship. This lesser-known work teaches that worship is not just a "Sunday thing." It should extend to the rest of our lives as well. One of the clauses states:

> It is most necessary, that everyone take part in private prayer and meditation. This practice brings benefits that are impossible to describe, and which are only fully appreciated by those who are most careful to put it into practice. This is the means whereby, in a special way, one communes with God, and is properly

prepared for the Christian life. Therefore it is necessary that pastors encourage everybody to this practice, morning and evening, and at other times as well. But it is also the duty of the head of every family, to take good care that both they themselves, and those in their care are diligent in this practice every day.[2]

The Sabbath calls us to live in light of God's future kingdom, a place of celebration.

Scenario: From the moment two people become engaged, they start planning their special day. But it is sometimes the case that brides have been "planning" their weddings since they were young. Grooms are sometimes less engaged in the process, but even the less enthusiastic participants usually have a good time meeting with caterers, tasting different dishes and deciding which will be most suited to the special day. All of the planning and preparation builds anticipation for the wedding day.

As believers, we are people of hope. We look forward to something that we do not have yet. But by God's grace, we are to sample and anticipate it. One day, we will be freed from sin and placed in a perfect world. Every time we turn from sin and embrace righteousness, we receive a foretaste of that perfect, eternal home and the everlasting wedding feast of the Lamb (Rev. 19:6–9).

You Cannot Serve God and . . .

Big Idea

Commitment to God can easily be undermined by the culture in which God's people are immersed.

Key Themes

- God rightly expects exclusive loyalty from his people.
- God's people should be ever alert to the insidious temptations that threaten to undermine their special relationship with God.
- God goes before his people, preparing the way and ensuring that they will enjoy their inheritance with him.

Understanding the Text

The Text in Context

Exodus 23:20–33 brings to a conclusion the Book of the Covenant, which details the obligations that God expects the Israelites to keep as their contribution to the covenant relationship. This section of God's speech differs noticeably from those that have preceded it. It has a much more personal tone, marked by the frequent use of "I" and "you." In these verses, God promises to assist the Israelites as they settle in the land of Canaan, driving out those who might oppose them. In return, the Israelites are encouraged to remain faithful to God. They are especially warned against making alliances with those already living in Canaan. Their relationship with the Lord must take precedence over every other relationship.

Historical and Cultural Background

Two features in particular distinguish Canaanite religion from that of Israelites committed to worshiping the Lord only. Firstly, Canaanite religion was polytheistic in nature. Among the various gods worshiped by the Canaanites, the Old Testament mentions Baal, Asherah, and Molek. Secondly, Canaanite religion involved fertility-cult practices. Rituals involving both men and women in sacred prostitution were sometimes practiced (Deut. 23:18–19; Hosea 4:14).

Interpretive Insights

23:20–22 *I am sending an angel ahead of you.* These verses are dominated by the angel that God promises to send before the Israelites. The identity of this angel has prompted much discussion. The angel's role suggests that he is more than merely a messenger sent by God. The close correlation between the angel and God strongly suggests that the two are to be equated. In particular, it is implied that the angel has the authority to forgive sin. In the light of other passages within the book of Exodus, it seems likely that the angel is a manifestation of God himself. We see this at the initial commissioning of Moses, when God appears as "flames of fire." In one sense the flame of fire is God, and yet God is much more than the flame of fire. To draw out this distinction, the narrative uses the expression "angel of the LORD" (Exod. 3:2; cf. Gen. 16:7–13).

to bring you to the place I have prepared. God promises to bring the Israelites "to the place I have prepared." While this could be simply a reference to the land of Canaan, it seems more likely that "the place" denotes a sacred location, such as a temple. This makes good sense in the light of 15:17, which speaks of the Israelites residing in the land close to God's sanctuary. To this end, the construction of the tabernacle anticipates God living among the Israelites as together they journey to their destination.

I will be an enemy to your enemies. God promises this on the condition that the Israelites will be fully obedient to him. Although the land of Canaan is already inhabited by various nations, they will be removed, but only if the Israelites obey God. This reflects a consistent theme in the Old Testament, whereby obedience guarantees tenure of the land, but disobedience results in exile. We witness this first when Adam and Eve are expelled from the Garden of Eden. Later, the Israelites themselves will be exiled from the land, when first the northern kingdom and then later the southern kingdom are attacked by the Assyrians and Babylonians, respectively. While this passage may imply that God favors the Israelites more than any other nation, the demands of the covenant relationship will weigh heavily on them. Their failure to be faithful to God will result in punishment.

23:24 *Do not bow down before their gods . . . You must demolish them.* Since the Sinai covenant requires the Israelites to be loyal exclusively to God, they must not worship other deities. To facilitate this, they are to destroy anything associated with pagan worship. While God's instructions are unambiguous, the Israelites do not appear to have implemented this requirement. The Old Testament itself, as well as archaeological evidence, suggests that unorthodox religious practices existed throughout the pre-exilic period.

23:25–26 *Worship the* LORD *your God, and his blessing will be on your food and water.* God will reward the Israelites for their loyalty to him. Unfortunately, the subsequent story of Israel reveals that the Israelites are prone to go after other deities. As the book of Judges records, the repeated disobedience of the Israelites prevents them from enjoying a peaceful and prosperous existence in the promised land (cf. Judg. 2:10–3:6).

23:27–30 *I will send my terror ahead of you . . . I will send the hornet.* Although the Israelites will face opposition, God states that he will overcome their enemies. In these verses, the emphasis is on driving out the present inhabitants of Canaan, rather than exterminating them. By promising to send "my terror" and "the hornet"[1] ahead of the Israelites, God emphasizes that he will take the lead in securing possession of the land (cf. Josh. 24:11–13).

23:31 *I will establish your borders from the Red Sea to the Mediterranean Sea.* Similar border descriptions are given in Genesis 15:18; Numbers 34:3–15; Deuteronomy 11:24; and Joshua 1:4. Israel's territory extended to these boundaries only for a short period during the reigns of David and Solomon. As the larger Old Testament narrative underlines, the ongoing apostasy of the Israelites is a constant barrier to the fulfillment of God's promises.

23:32–33 *Do not make a covenant . . . with their gods. Do not let them live in your land.* This prohibition is a natural corollary of the covenant being ratified at Mount Sinai. God expects the wholehearted commitment of the Israelites to him alone. As God justifiably warns, the worship of other gods will be a snare to the Israelites. To foster this exclusive loyalty to the Lord, the Israelites must not permit those who worship other gods to live within the land of Canaan. As the first of the Ten Commandments affirms, the Israelites are to have no other gods (20:3).

Theological Insights

The final part of the Book of the Covenant underlines the reciprocal nature of the agreement being made at Mount Sinai between God and the Israelites. With the Lord's support, the future of the Israelites is secure; God promises to overcome all their enemies. Yet this will depend on the Israelites obeying God. Throughout the Bible obedience is never a prerequisite for entering into a special relationship with God. Yet it is an essential requirement for maintaining a healthy relationship with God. No one can truly claim to love God and yet not obey him. Highlighting this principle, Jesus reminds his disciples, "If you love me, keep my commands" (John 14:15).

The temptation to worship other gods is very insidious. The Israelites lived in a world dominated by polytheism. To be monotheists, the Israelites had to swim against the current of popular thought. Moreover, there was little room for compromise, because the worldviews of polytheism and monotheism cannot be reconciled to each other. They are diametrically opposed, with one affirming what the other rejects.

Teaching the Text

In a modern Western culture that aggressively promotes multiculturalism and pluralism, and vociferously condemns those who practice ethnic cleansing, the present passage makes for uncomfortable reading. There is little sense here of tolerating those who have different religious beliefs. On the contrary, they are to be driven out in case they should contaminate the religious thinking and practices of the Israelites. How should a modern-day Christian respond to this exclusive attitude? Do not all faiths ultimately lead to the same God? Can Christians be confident that their beliefs are right and everyone else is wrong? These are difficult questions to address in a postmodern world, where many reject the idea of absolute truth.

Warnings about false religions. These verses caution against the insidious nature of religious thinking that is based on gods invented by people. As the products of the human mind, false gods cannot claim absolute authority. Yet, the God of the exodus and the Sinai covenant is no construction of the human imagination. He alone is the sovereign Lord of creation, the one and only God, who has brought everything into being. As the ultimate source of all truth, he views the worship of other gods as an act of betrayal, fueled by ignorance, at the very least, or arrogant rebellion, at the most. Since the inherent inclination of people is to worship anything and everything but the sovereign Lord, this passage is a sober reminder of why humanity is alienated from God. To enjoy a special relationship with God, the Israelites must be truly countercultural, a challenging task in a world that bears enmity toward God and where all kinds of other gods are offered as false substitutes.

Summons to exclusive commitment. As Christians we must always be vigilant that our attitudes and actions do not lead us to compromise our commitment to God. As regards our allegiance to him it must be "God alone," not "God and . . ." Yet we must also be on our guard that we do not make loyalty to God an excuse for sinful intransigence in our dealings with others. As Jesus has taught us, we are to love our enemies and pray for those who persecute us. Yet like Jesus, we must do nothing to compromise our sole allegiance to God.

Reassurances that God goes ahead of us. In Exodus 23:20–33 the NIV translation repeats the phrase "ahead of you" several times as God reassures the Israelites that he will go before them. In the light of this promise, the Israelites need not fear the nations already living in Canaan. Looking to the future, God consistently emphasizes that he will bring the Israelites safely into the land promised to the patriarchs. In a similar fashion, Jesus reassures his disciples that he is going before them in order to prepare a place for them in his Father's house (John 14:1–3). In his absence, Jesus promises "the Spirit of truth," the Holy Spirit, whom the Father will send to teach the disciples all things and remind them of everything Jesus said (John 14:17, 26). As Christians, we may face the future with confidence because we know that God goes ahead of us.

Illustrating the Text

God views idolatry as an act of betrayal, like spiritual adultery.

Popular Culture: When the gossip magazine covers are not emblazoned with the latest diet or tips for hooking up, they frequently post news about the latest celebrity breakup. It is fascinating to see how even our "anything-goes" culture can still manage a modicum of moral outrage when spouses cheat on each other. If the fallen culture of Hollywood can see the problem with adultery, why can't God's people? When we turn from him toward idols, we act like a cheating spouse.

In a world filled with idols, Christians must be countercultural.

News Story: The beaches of Southern California are usually packed with people wanting to catch a few rays, play volleyball, or ride some waves. Those with experience know the danger of being caught in a riptide. When trapped in one of these, people can be swept out to sea, despite their greatest effort. On September 16, 2014, just such an event took place. In one day, nearly two hundred people had to be rescued by lifeguards.[2]

As believers, if we simply "go with the flow," we are going to be moving in the wrong direction. We must actively stand against the tide of our culture if we are going to live for the Lord. Only dead fish go with the flow.

Other loyalties must never be allowed to undermine our loyalty to God.

Human Experience: In a world where we are constantly bombarded with requests to give our loyalty to someone or something, it is easy for our commitment to God to be compromised. When advertisers tempt us to adopt a particular brand of food or clothing, we may not sense that there is anything amiss in giving our loyalty to one product rather than another. But what happens when we are asked to support a particular political party or advocacy group? Do we risk the danger of compromising our loyalty to God by placing our trust in humans? And how should we respond when the demands of nationalism are placed on a par with our commitment to God? Regrettably, the church has not always stood apart from human governments but has allowed itself to be compromised. The history of the Protestant Church in Germany during the 1930s is a vivid reminder of how easily Christians can be lulled into giving support to a political regime that espouses non-Christian values.

History: Visitors to Edinburgh, the capital of Scotland, may be surprised to discover that one of the city's tourist attractions is a commemorative statue devoted to a dog. Known as Greyfriars Bobby, this Skye terrier became famous in the nineteenth century for spending fourteen years guarding the grave of its owner. According to tradition, it belonged to John Gray, a night watchman, who was buried in the graveyard at Greyfrairs Kirk in the Old Town of Edinburgh. When Bobby eventually died, he too was buried in the graveyard, not far from the grave of his owner. Like many dogs, he displayed a loyalty to his owner that can challenge all of us about the depth of our commitment to our Lord and Savior.

Christians can face the future with confidence, knowing that God goes ahead of us.

Sports: When climbing a high peak, novice climbers gain confidence and security by being linked by a line to those with more experience. They know that the guide, who goes before them, can pick the best route. If they slip, they will be kept safe because they are connected to others. Our Lord has gone before us and prepared not only our final destination but the path that will lead us there.

Feasting in God's Presence

Big Idea

Access to God's presence depends on the establishment of a special relationship with him.

Key Themes

- Atonement and sanctification are fundamental to creating a covenant relationship with God.
- While the covenant relationship is initiated by God's grace and not human obedience, the covenant itself requires ongoing obedience to God.

Understanding the Text

The Text in Context

Chapter 24 describes the sealing of the covenant between God and the Israelites. Having been invited to become God's special possession (19:5), and having received both the general obligations (20:1–17) and the detailed obligations (20:22–23:33), the Israelites unanimously affirm their willingness to accept the terms of God's covenant. After they do so, the agreement is sealed through a ritual that involves the offering of sacrifices and the sprinkling of blood. When this is completed, Moses and selected individuals are permitted by God to partially ascend the mountain, where they have the privilege of witnessing something of the divine glory. To celebrate their new relationship with God, the Israelite leaders feast in the holy presence of the Lord. The ratification of the covenant is highly significant, for it transforms the Israelites into a holy nation, preparing the way for God to come and dwell in their midst. To facilitate this, God invites Moses to ascend the mountain even farther, where he remains for forty days, during which time he receives instructions for the building of the tabernacle.

Historical and Cultural Background

The sealing of the covenant involves the sprinkling of blood on both the altar and the people. This takes on a special significance when compared with other rituals in the books of Exodus and Leviticus. Parallels exist between this passage and the description of how the Levitical priests are consecrated for service within the tabernacle (Exod. 29; Lev. 8). There are also similarities with Leviticus 14, which describes the process of reintegrating into the Israelite camp someone who has been designated unclean. Further links may be observed with the Passover ritual in Exodus 12. Common to all these occasions is the concept of consecration or sanctification, whereby those who are ritually unclean are made clean or holy. This process is essential if the Israelites are to become God's holy people. Confirmation of their new holy status comes through the ability of the Israelite leaders to ascend Mount Sinai in safety. Only after their consecration are they permitted to come close to God.

Interpretive Insights

24:1 *the* Lord *said to Moses.* The NIV translation adds "the Lord" to remind the reader of the speaker's identity. The Hebrew text simply says "he said to Moses." Unfortunately, the chapter division has the effect of implying that something new begins in Exodus 24. On the contrary, however, the opening two verses of the chapter are the concluding words of the divine speech that begins in 20:22 and continues throughout chapters 21–23. Whereas the rest of God's speech is directed to the Israelites as a whole, his final words are for Moses alone. These instructions relate to the final stage in the ratification of the covenant.

24:3–5 *Moses went and told the people all the* Lord's *words and laws.* Having been invited by the people to be their mediator with God (20:19), Moses now reports back. Some commentators interpret "the Lord's words" as a reference to the Ten Commandments, but it seems more likely that this denotes those sections of the Book of the Covenant that surround the case laws listed in 21:1–22:20. The people have already heard for themselves the Ten Commandments.

he sent young Israelite men, and they offered burnt offerings and . . . fellowship offerings. Those who offer burnt offerings and fellowship offerings are designated "young Israelite men." At this stage, Aaron and his sons have not yet been consecrated to serve as priests. Whereas the whole carcass of the "burnt offering" was placed on the altar and consumed by fire, only a part of the fellowship offering was burned on the altar. The remainder was eaten by the worshipers. This is the first mention of fellowship offerings being made in the Old Testament—a fitting introduction, because these offerings symbolize the existence of a harmonious relationship between God and those eating the sacrifice. For this reason the fellowship offering is sometimes known as the "peace offering" (cf. KJV; ESV). While the twelve pillars clearly represent the Israelites, the altar possibly represents God.

24:6–7 *Moses took half of the blood . . . and the other half he splashed against the altar.* As an obvious symbol of life, blood plays an important role in the sacrificial rituals. The shedding and sprinkling of blood are associated with paying a ransom and cleansing, respectively. Since the concepts of ransom and cleansing together constitute atonement, the burnt offerings atone for the sins of the Israelites.

24:8 *Moses then took the blood, sprinkled it on the people.* The sprinkling of blood on the people cleanses them from the defilement caused by sin (cf. 29:20–21). This is necessary in order to sanctify them as a holy nation.

24:9–11 *Moses and Aaron, Nadab and Abihu, and the seventy elders of Israel went up.* To confirm and celebrate the new relationship established between God and the Israelites, Moses and other influential leaders ascend Mount Sinai. They are rewarded with a remarkable vision of God, although the detailed description suggests that they merely see the area around his feet. Since Moses was previously warned that anyone ascending the mountain would be punished (19:21–22), verse 11 explicitly states that "God did not raise his hand against these leaders of the Israelites."

24:12 *I will give you the tablets of stone with the law.* After the formal sealing of the covenant, God promises to give Moses a set of stone tablets that will contain instructions for the Israelites. The Hebrew term translated "law" is the word *torah.* A more accurate rendering would be "teaching/instruction." Ironically, before Moses returns with these stone tablets, the people will have already disobeyed God.

24:13–14 *Aaron and Hur are with you.* Aaron and Hur are delegated the responsibility of governing the Israelite community.

24:15–18 *Moses went up . . . and the glory of the* LORD *settled on Mount Sinai.* Not only do these verses associate Moses with God's presence and glory, but by describing Moses's departure from the Israelite camp they set the scene for the illicit making of the golden calf (cf. 32:1).

Theological Insights

With the sealing of the covenant, the Israelites enter into a unique relationship with the Lord. In recognition of this, Moses and the seventy elders ascend Mount Sinai. Although they witness God's radiant glory, no attempt is made to give a full description; rather, we are only told briefly about the splendor of the ground beneath God's feet. This suggests that the leaders' vision of God is restricted. Consequently, there is no contradiction between what is said in verses 10–11 and 33:20, which affirms that no one can see God's face and live.

The opportunity given to the Israelite leaders foreshadows a greater time of feasting that will ultimately come through the redemptive activity of Jesus

Christ (Matt. 8:11). Christians anticipate this time of special communion when they participate in the Lord's Supper (Matt. 26:26–29).

Teaching the Text

Difficult as it may be to imagine, there will come a time when every sincere believer will see God in all his radiant splendor. The present chapter provides a glimpse of that time when we shall gather to feast in the presence of God (Matt. 8:11). The covenant-sealing ceremony also sheds light on the process by which we are prepared in order to come into the majestic presence of God. The ratification of the Sinai covenant parallels the making of the new covenant sealed by Christ's death. This passage reminds us of two core features of our Christian faith.

Our need of atonement and sanctification. Firstly, our relationship with God involves both atonement and sanctification. Like the Israelites at Mount Sinai, we too require the making of a sacrifice that will ransom us from the power of death and cleanse us of the defilement caused by our sins. These steps are essential components of atonement, but they also contribute toward being made holy. Only after being sprinkled with the sacrificial blood are the Israelites permitted to ascend the mountain closer to God's presence. We also need to be made holy, for "without holiness no one will see the Lord" (Heb. 12:14). While the Israelites sacrificed young bulls, as Christians we rely on the sacrifice of Jesus on the cross. With good reason, the author of Hebrews contrasts the "blood of goats and bulls" with the "blood of Christ," so that we might have our consciences cleansed "from acts that lead to death" and "serve the living God" (Heb. 9:13–14). In the light of this the author of Hebrews comments, "For this reason Christ is the mediator of a new covenant, that those who are called may receive the promised eternal inheritance" (Heb. 9:15). As the means by which the new covenant is sealed, the cross of Christ is central to our salvation. For this reason, we must rely solely and wholly on what Christ has done for us and not depend on anything that we may do to merit God's forgiveness. We should be ever thankful that Christ's suffering on our behalf prepares the way for us to enter safely into the glorious presence of God.

Obligations to be fulfilled. In Exodus 24 Moses sets before the Israelites the responsibilities that they must fulfill under the terms of the Sinai covenant. To underline the importance of these, Moses delivers them on two occasions, and on both occasions the people unanimously say that they will do everything the Lord has said (vv. 3, 7). Importantly, God does not ratify the covenant at Mount Sinai because of the past obedience of the Israelites. However, to enjoy the benefits of their newly established covenant relationship with God they must be fully obedient to him. Such obedience should flow out of love for God and thankfulness for his grace and mercy.

The situation under the new covenant is no different. We do not merit salvation through obedience to God, but obedience flows naturally when we trust Christ for our salvation. These two elements of Christian living should not be divorced. We are saved because of God's love for us, but this becomes the basis of our love for God. Love for God should lead to obedience (John 14:15).

In the light of God's love, demonstrated by Jesus's death on the cross, obedience to Christ must be the priority of each believer. With good reason we confess him to be both Savior (the one who saves us) and Lord (the one whom we obey). In doing so, we live as new-covenant people, anticipating Christ's return and the coming of the new Jerusalem, when we shall live in God's presence forever.

Illustrating the Text

Our relationship with God involves both atonement and sanctification.

Science: One of the concepts embraced by the Intelligent Design movement—which argues that life is best explained as the product of intelligent design—is called "irreducible complexity." In essence, this means that a working system will cease to have meaningful function if any of its parts are removed. Take, for instance, a mousetrap. As a system, it has a certain set of basic parts. If any one of them is subtracted, the mousetrap serves no purpose.

In understanding how our relationship with God is established in salvation, certain concepts *must* be present. The doctrines of atonement and sanctification cannot be removed, or the system ceases to function. Only atonement can cleanse our defilement. Only sanctification, becoming holy, can allow us to "see God." These two realities must be present, or we are left with a nonfunctional, imitation salvation—works righteousness or cheap grace.

The cross of Christ, by which the new covenant is sealed, is central to our salvation.

Literature: Imagine someone summarizing *The Lord of the Rings* without mentioning the Ring of Power. Or suppose a student turned in a paper on *The Grapes of Wrath* without including Tom Joad. Some stories simply can't be articulated in adequate or recognizable fashion without including key ideas. Anything less would be a betrayal or complete misunderstanding. This is true for the story of new-covenant redemption, which is held together by the cross of Jesus Christ.

We must rely solely on what Christ has done for us to merit God's forgiveness.

Object Lesson: The Golden Gate Bridge in San Francisco, California, spans the nearly nine-thousand-foot Golden Gate strait. Rising 746 feet above the water, the great bridge is a wonder to behold. Ten different contractors were involved in building the bridge. Eleven men were killed in construction accidents. A safety net, suspended under the bridge during construction, saved the lives of nineteen men who fell; those "lucky" enough to be caught by this net were inducted into the "Halfway-to-Hell Club." Approximately 600,000 rivets hold together each tower of the bridge, and the total cost for building such a construct today would run nearly $1.2 billion.[1]

When someone drives across the Golden Gate Bridge, they contribute *nothing* to the suspension of their vehicle above the Golden Gate strait. It is entirely the work of architects, ironworkers, and maintenance crews that makes the trip possible. In the same way, we contribute nothing to God's gracious act of salvation. Christ alone spans the chasm of sin and death that separates us from God.

We do not merit salvation through obedience; obedience flows naturally when we trust Christ for our salvation.

Nature: The delicious apples that grow on a tree do not cause the tree to grow, but a healthy, growing apple tree will certainly produce apples. Good works are the fruit of our salvation. They do not cause it, but if we really do know Christ, then obedience will follow.

Heaven and Earth United

Big Idea

God intends to dwell on the earth in a residence modeled on his heavenly sanctuary.

Key Themes

- The tabernacle and its furnishings are a vivid sign of the reality of God's presence among the Israelites.
- The lavish nature of the tabernacle and its furnishings is intended to honor God's majesty.
- The tabernacle provides a meeting point where people can come close to God.

Understanding the Text

The Text in Context

With the ratification of the covenant at Mount Sinai (Exod. 19–24), everything is set for God to come and dwell among the Israelites. However, before this can be accomplished, a suitable residence must be constructed. Of necessity, it must be portable, for the Israelites will journey away from Mount Sinai into the land of Canaan.

After summoning Moses up Mount Sinai (24:12–18), the Lord addresses him in a lengthy speech that is recorded in chapters 25–31. The first half of this speech contains instructions regarding the construction of the tabernacle and the main items of furniture (25:8–27:21). The second half concentrates on the appointment of the priests who will serve within the tabernacle and on the manufacture of their clothing and other items associated with their service (28:1–30:38). Finally, Exodus 31:1–18 contains (1) some final instructions from God regarding those who will oversee the construction of the tent and everything associated with it and (2) a reminder that the Israelites must observe the Sabbath, which is the sign of the Sinai covenant.

After a hiatus caused by the Israelites' worshiping the golden calf (Exod. 32–34), chapters 35–39 describe the fulfillment of God's instructions, leading to the setting up of the tabernacle (40:1–33), after which God comes to dwell in it (40:34–38). This brings the book of Exodus to a remarkable conclusion as the Lord for the first time takes up residence on the earth. By living in the midst of the Israelites he demonstrates the reality of the special covenant relationship ratified at Mount Sinai.

Interpretive Insights

25:2–7 *the offerings you are to receive from them: gold, silver . . . yarn and fine linen.* Although the Israelites were slaves in Egypt, they did not leave empty handed. As instructed by God (11:2; cf. 3:21–22), they received articles of silver and gold and clothing (12:35). The list of offerings covers everything needed to manufacture both the tabernacle and the items associated with it. Exodus 36:3–7 reveals that the Israelites gave generously.

25:8–9 *make a sanctuary for me, and I will dwell among them . . . Make this tabernacle.* The tent about to be constructed will function primarily as a divine residence. In these verses two different Hebrew words are used to denote the tent. The term *mishkan*, translated "tabernacle" in verse 9, denotes a place where someone lives; elsewhere it is used of human dwellings (e.g., Num. 16:24). In verse 8 the tent is called a *miqdash*, "sanctuary." This word is not used very often to describe the tabernacle (cf., e.g., Lev. 12:4; 16:33), but it underlines especially the holy nature of the tent in which God will dwell. Since God himself is innately holy, his presence sanctifies the tent. Only those who are holy, the priests, may enter the tent, and only the holiest priest, the high priest, may enter the Most Holy Place, the inner throne room of the tabernacle. According to verse 9, Moses sees either a construction plan or, perhaps more likely, the heavenly temple that is the basis on which the tabernacle is patterned (cf. Exod. 25:40; 26:30; 27:8). The tabernacle is a "copy and shadow of what is in heaven" (Heb. 8:5).

25:10–16 *make an ark of acacia wood.* As the first item listed, the ark is the most important. According to 1 Chronicles 28:2, this gold-covered chest is the footstool of God's heavenly throne (cf. Pss. 99:5; 132:7). The Lord is enthroned between the two cherubim that form part of the lid of the ark (cf. 1 Sam. 4:4; 2 Sam. 6:2). At this point heaven and earth are linked, with God seated in heaven and his feet resting on the earth. Of the different furnishings made for the tabernacle, only the ark is located in the innermost compartment, the Most Holy Place. As a chest, the ark stores a variety of items that are placed within it at different times. Because it houses the stone tablets containing the covenant obligation, the chest is sometimes called "the ark of the testimony" (e.g., Exod. 25:21–22; 26:33–34 ESV; NIV: "ark of the covenant law").

25:17–22 *Make an atonement cover of pure gold.* The lid of the ark, measuring about four feet by two feet, is made of pure gold. As the footstool of the heavenly throne, this is the appropriate location for Moses to receive God's instructions for the Israelites (v. 22). Moses probably stood in the Holy Place

Diagram of the Tabernacle

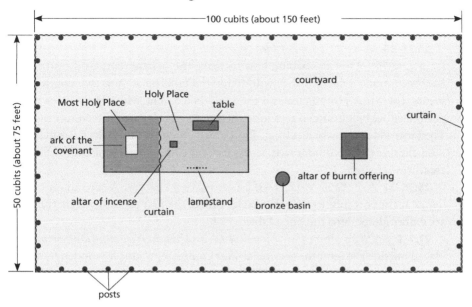

The following labels appear in the diagram:

- 100 cubits (about 150 feet)
- 50 cubits (about 75 feet)
- courtyard
- Holy Place
- Most Holy Place
- table
- curtain
- ark of the covenant
- altar of burnt offering
- altar of incense
- lampstand
- bronze basin
- curtain
- posts

when God addressed him through the curtain from the Most Holy Place (cf. 27:21). The Hebrew term *kapporet*, "atonement cover," is sometimes translated "mercy seat" (e.g., KJV; ESV). The concept of atonement involves both paying a ransom and cleansing. On the Day of Atonement, the high priest sprinkles blood on the lid of the ark to remove the defilement caused by the sins of the Israelites.

25:23–30 *Make a table of acacia wood . . . Put the bread of the Presence on this table.* The second item of furniture is a gold-plated table. This table is placed in the second compartment of the tabernacle, the Holy Place, which ordinary priests may access. The twelve loaves probably represent the twelve tribes (Lev. 24:5–8). By instructing the Israelites to place bread on this table "before me at all times" (v. 30), God makes the table a testimony to his presence within the tent.

25:31–40 *Make a lampstand of pure gold . . . shaped like almond flowers.* This is the second item of furniture in the Holy Place. Shaped to resemble an almond tree, the lampstand may symbolize the tree of life in the Garden of Eden. When lit, the lampstand indicates that God is resident in the tabernacle. All the furnishings in the tabernacle point to its function as a residence. The plentiful use of gold emphasizes the importance of the resident.

26:1–30 *Make the tabernacle with ten curtains.* The tent within which the Lord will dwell has an overall length of forty-five feet and is fifteen feet high and fifteen feet wide. Gold-plated wooden frames form a skeleton over which

155   Exodus 25:1–27:21

four layers of materials are placed. The use of gold and silver, together with richly embroidered fabrics, indicates that the occupant of this tent is someone exceptionally special. This is a tent worthy of a king.

26:31–35 *Make a curtain of blue, purple and scarlet yarn . . . with cherubim woven into it.* After describing how to make the ornate tent, God instructs Moses to make a curtain that will divide the tabernacle into two compartments: the Most Holy Place and the Holy Place. The Most Holy Place is a perfect cube, being fifteen feet long, fifteen feet wide, and fifteen feet high. The Holy Place is thirty feet long. The curtain, made of linen, is embroidered with cherubim, a reminder that access to God's presence is guarded by these creatures (cf. Gen. 3:24).

26:36–37 *For the entrance to the tent make a curtain.* A second curtain hangs at the entrance to the tabernacle. Unlike the first curtain, no cherubim are embroidered into the linen fabric.

27:1–8 *Build an altar of acacia wood . . . and overlay the altar with bronze.* Placed outside the tent, the sacrificial altar comprises a square wooden frame, overlaid with bronze. Measuring 7.5 feet square, and 4.5 feet high, the altar is used to roast animal sacrifices. Like the other furnishings associated with the tabernacle, the altar is designed to be portable. Its location outside the tent is a vivid reminder that people can approach God only after they have atoned for their sin.

27:9–19 *Make a courtyard for the tabernacle.* The tent is to be pitched within a rectangular courtyard, about 150 feet long and 75 feet wide, running east to west, surrounded by a curtain fence 7.5 feet high. On the eastern side, one of the shorter sides, there is an entrance protected by linen curtains.

27:20–21 *Command the Israelites to bring you clear oil . . . In the tent of meeting.* This oil fuels the lamps on the lampstand within the tabernacle. For the first time, the tabernacle is designated the "tent of meeting." This highlights one of the central functions that will take place within the tent. The necessity of this function is underlined by the fact that a temporary "tent of meeting" is used by Moses prior to the completion of the tabernacle (cf. 33:7–11).

Theological Insights

The tabernacle provides confirmation of the special relationship created between God and the Israelites through the ratification of the Sinai covenant. God makes practical arrangements in order to live with the Israelites within their camp. God's coming to dwell among the Israelites on earth is a significant new development in the history of salvation. For the first time God and people cohabit on the earth. This event recalls God's creation plan and anticipates its ultimate fulfillment in the new Jerusalem.

Teaching the Text

Three chapters of instructions for the construction of a tent and its furniture may not appear to be a promising source for rich theological teaching. Yet these chapters should not be dismissed too quickly, because they provide an opportunity to reflect on God's majesty and immanence. Additionally, they contribute in a significant way to the larger picture of God's redemptive plan, linking backward to the Garden of Eden and forward to the temple in Jerusalem, the church, and ultimately the new Jerusalem.

The construction of the tabernacle is important because it emphasizes the reality of God coming to dwell with the Israelites. It gives concrete expression to God's presence with his people, for the tent is constructed to be a portable royal residence. Everything intimates strongly that the tabernacle is no empty shrine but a dwelling for God's use. To underline its residential use, there is bread on a table, with a lampstand nearby providing light. Yet God is not confined to this tent, for it is linked to his heavenly residence. The ark of the covenant is the footstool of the heavenly throne. This is the first stage toward the kingdom of God being fully established on the earth, as the footstool of God's throne is placed within the Most Holy Place.

As a natural consequence of being God's earthly residence, the tent is also the place where God may be encountered most directly. Hence, the tabernacle is designated "the tent of meeting" (Exod. 27:21). Yet access to God is restricted to those who are holy, the priests, and even they cannot look directly on the Lord but must be shielded from his presence by a curtain. The author of Hebrews alludes to the function of the curtain when he links it with Jesus's body (Heb. 10:19–20; cf. John 1:14). As the curtain permitted the priests to come close to God, so Christ's body, in which all the fullness of deity dwells, enables ordinary people to encounter God close-up (cf. John 12:45; 14:9).

The temple was sacred space because God's presence was there in a unique way. In contrast, God is not in the church building in a unique way. Instead, he indwells his people. When we sing about "God being in this place" or refer to church as "God's house," it is important to understand the distinction. The temple was always the place of God's presence whether people were there or not. The church building is the place of God's presence only when his people are gathered there. The temple was holy because of God's presence. The church building has no holiness attached to it. The function of the temple was to provide a place of residence for God among his people; very little corporate worship took place there. The function of the church building is to provide a place for God's people to gather in corporate worship. Priests performed the rituals necessary to maintain the holiness required for God's presence. Pastors instruct and care for God's people.

Illustrating the Text

The tabernacle was the first stage in God's establishment of his residence with humanity on earth.

Science: For decades, dreamers have imagined what it would be like if humanity could leave Earth and colonize space. Like Eriksson and Columbus before them, these explorers want to establish a new beachhead for humanity. Mars One is an international organization that hopes to send its first unmanned mission to Mars in 2018. Following this initial foray, it hopes to build a human settlement on Mars beginning in 2024, sending crews of four colonists every two years. The only catch: the new colonists can never return to Earth.[1]

Whether or not this plan for Mars is realistic, the planners realistically understand that such a great undertaking begins with initial steps. It slowly builds and does not suddenly happen. If we look at God's great plan to re-establish his kingdom on rebel Earth, the tabernacle certainly represents a key beachhead.

As the curtain permitted priests to come close to God, so Jesus enables us to encounter God close-up.

History: Children of the 1970s and 1980s probably have some memory of Jacques Cousteau, the famous filmmaking French oceanographer. Cousteau allowed us to travel with him aboard the *Calypso* to exotic locales and visit underwater worlds that defied imagination. Capturing these places on film, he let us see something that most people will never have an opportunity to witness firsthand.

In a much more profound way, Jesus brings us face-to-face with the unseen, infinite, incomprehensible God. Unless God discloses himself, we have no hope of understanding the first thing about him. Jesus is the *perfect* image of this unseen God.

The church building is the place of God's presence only when his people are gathered there.

Church History: The Religious Society of Friends (Quakers) is a fellowship of Christians who take seriously the doctrine that the church is the *people* of God, not a building. Historically, they emphasized that the place of meeting was nowhere near as important as the people who met. So they would intentionally hold their meetings outside. When meeting in a building, they never referred to the place as a "church" but called it a "meeting house." Whether or not one agrees with everything in Quaker theology, this is certainly a laudable emphasis. Similarly, Irish Presbyterians historically referred to their place of worship as a "meeting house."

Serving in the Presence of God

Big Idea

Access to the Lord's presence is only for those who have been made holy as God is holy.

Key Themes

- To serve in the tabernacle the priests must be given a holy status.
- To be made holy requires sacrifices to atone for human wrongdoing.

Understanding the Text

The Text in Context

God's speech concerning the construction of the portable residence that he will occupy in the midst of the Israelite camp continues with instructions relating to those who will serve within the tabernacle. Chapter 28 describes the sacred garments that must be manufactured for the newly appointed priests to wear. Particular attention is given to the clothing of the high priest, which is intentionally made of materials that match those used for the construction of the tent. After this God gives instructions in chapter 29 for the formal procedure that will set Aaron and his sons apart from other Israelites, consecrating them for the duties associated with the tabernacle. By distinguishing those who serve in the tabernacle from others, God once more highlights the distinction that exists between his holy nature and the less-than-holy nature of people.

Interpretive Insights

28:1 *Have Aaron your brother brought to you from among the Israelites.* There is no indication prior to this in Exodus that Aaron and his sons are to be appointed priests to serve in the tabernacle. While the mention of priests in 19:22–24 suggests that some Israelites were recognized as such, the construction of the tabernacle creates an entirely new situation. For the first time God chooses to dwell among the Israelites. This new development brings with it the need to appoint personnel who will fulfill duties associated with the tabernacle.

28:2–5 *Make sacred garments for your brother Aaron to give him dignity and honor.* Aaron's priestly clothing will distinguish him from others. Aaron's close connection with the tabernacle is underlined by the use of materials identical to those used in constructing the tent. The high priest's attire consists of various items, details of which are given in verses 6–39.

28:6–8 *Make the ephod of gold.* The ephod is an ornate outer garment that covers the upper body.

28:9–14 *Take two onyx stones and engrave on them the names of the sons of Israel.* To symbolize Aaron's role as representative of the people, the names of the twelve "sons of Israel" are to be engraved on two onyx stones. Jacob's twelve sons (in order of birth) are Reuben, Simeon, Levi, Judah, Dan, Naphtali, Gad, Asher, Issachar, Zebulun, Joseph, and Benjamin. The tribe of Joseph is subdivided into the tribes of Ephraim and Manasseh, but these tribes are not specifically named on the onyx stones.

28:15–30 *Fashion a breastpiece for making decisions.* Some nine inches square, this item of clothing forms a pouch that rests on the high priest's chest. On the front of the pouch are four rows of precious stones, engraved with the names of Jacob's sons. As verse 29 indicates, the breastpiece is designed to be a "continuing memorial." Each time the high priest stands in God's presence, he bears on his chest the names of God's people. In addition, the pouch contains "the Urim and the Thummim" (v. 30), two items by which decisions relating to the Israelites may be made (cf. Num. 27:21; 1 Sam. 14:41–42). Although scholars have little idea about how the Urim and the Thummim worked, their use is clearly an important function linked to the breastpiece, as verse 15 implies.

28:31–35 *Make the robe of the ephod entirely of blue cloth.* This tunic covers most of the priest's body and is worn underneath the ephod and breastpiece.

28:36–39 *Make a plate of pure gold and engrave on it as on a seal:* HOLY TO THE LORD. The wording on the gold plate attached to the turban emphasizes Aaron's holy status. In order to communicate directly with God, Aaron must be holy. Only those who are holy may enter God's presence (Heb. 12:14).

28:40–41 *Make tunics, sashes and caps . . . anoint and ordain them. Consecrate them.* Suitable attire must be provided for the ordinary priests. Apart from clothing the priests, Moses must undertake three activities in order to set them apart to serve in the tabernacle. Detailed instructions for the anointing of the priests, filling their hands (ordaining?), and consecrating them are given in chapter 29.

28:42–43 *Make linen undergarments as a covering for the body.* To avoid accidental exposure, each priest must wear undergarments (cf. 20:26).

29:1–3 *to consecrate them . . . make round loaves without yeast.* To serve in the tabernacle, the priests must be holy. God instructs Moses regarding the process by which Aaron and his sons will be made holy. Central to this process is the offering of sacrifices. The use of unleavened bread recalls the Passover (12:8).

29:4–9 *wash them with water. Take the garments and dress Aaron.* The process of consecration begins with washing to symbolize cleansing from defilement. After this the priests are clothed.

29:10–14 *Bring the bull to the front of the tent of meeting . . . It is a sin offering.* The bull is slaughtered as a "sin offering" (or "purification offering") to cleanse the altar from defilement due to the wrongdoings of Aaron and his sons.

29:15–18 *Take one of the rams, and Aaron and his sons shall lay their hands on its head.* This ram is sacrificed as a whole burnt offering to atone, by paying a ransom, for the sins of Aaron and his sons.

29:19–21 *Take the other ram . . . he and his sons and their garments will be consecrated.* The ritual associated with the second ram involves the use of blood, firstly to "cleanse" Aaron and his sons, and then to consecrate them. This second stage uses blood that has been made holy by touching the altar. This two-stage process involving blood bestows on Aaron and his sons a holy status.

29:22–30 *the ram for the ordination . . . the perpetual share from the Israelites for Aaron and his sons.* The next stage in the process focuses on the provision of both bread and meat for the priests. Their allocation comes from the offerings that other Israelites will make (cf. Lev. 6:14–18; 7:6–10, 31–35). Although verse 22 speaks of the "ram for the ordination" (cf. v. 27), the Hebrew term translated "ordination" conveys the idea of "filling" and is linked to how Aaron and his sons' hands are filled by the portions that they receive from the sacrifices.

29:33–34 *eat these offerings by which atonement was made.* A further stage in the process of setting Aaron and his sons apart as priests involves their eating the sacrificial meat and bread. By doing so a bond is established between them and the sacrifice that atones for their sins. Because the sacrificial meat is holy, it must not be given to others. These instructions resemble those given in connection with the Passover (12:10).

29:35–37 *taking seven days to ordain them.* This phrase could also be translated, "seven days you shall fill their hands." While most English translations understand this as an idiom referring to "ordination," it could be taken more literally, referring to the giving of food to Aaron and his sons. Each day for seven days a bull is to be offered to purify the altar and consecrate it.

29:38–43 *offer on the altar regularly each day: two lambs a year old.* The appointment of the priests is a necessary step in order for the tabernacle to function as a meeting place, where the Israelites may encounter God and communicate with him. To ensure that regular contact between God and the Israelites is not disrupted, two lambs are sacrificed daily as whole burnt offerings to atone for the sins of the people.

29:44–46 *So I will consecrate the tent of meeting . . . Then I will dwell among the Israelites.* The making holy of the tent and those who will serve within it is a necessary preparation in order for God to come and dwell within the tabernacle. As these verses underline, God is the one who makes holy; human rituals cannot make anyone holy without God's active involvement.

Theological Insights

Prior to their betrayal of God in the Garden of Eden, Adam and Eve were naked (Gen. 2:25). After disobeying God, they perceived their nakedness and their need to be clothed, especially in God's presence (Gen. 3:10–11). In the light of this, the clothing of the high priest is highly symbolic because it enables him to stand before God without any sense of shame. Even so, Aaron must normally remain in the Holy Place, separated from God by an embroidered curtain. Unrestricted access into God's presence will require a high priest who is superior to Aaron. As the author of Hebrews points out, Jesus Christ by his sacrificial death achieves what the Aaronic high priest was unable to do; he opens the way into God's presence (Heb. 10:19–22).

Teaching the Text

The instructions regarding the consecration of the Aaronic priests provide an opportunity to reflect on the process established by God in order to consecrate people as holy, enabling them to have access to his presence.

The need to be holy, as God is holy, is a recurring motif within the book of Exodus. As far as the whole nation of Israel is concerned, both the Passover and the covenant-making ceremony involve rituals that are designed to consecrate the Israelites as holy. The consecration of the Aaronic priests provides a further illustration of how God makes people holy so that they may serve in his presence. Without the week-long sacrificial ritual Aaron could not wear on his forehead the gold plate with the inscription "HOLY TO THE LORD" (28:36).

The motif of holiness takes on special significance with the construction of the tabernacle, as God, the Holy One of Israel, comes to dwell with his people. While God draws close to the Israelites, the people as a whole lack the holiness necessary to come into God's presence. Consequently, God delegates to Aaron and his sons the responsibility of serving within the tabernacle. To fulfill this task they must be consecrated to ensure that they are holy.

The ritual that sets the priests apart provides insight into how God makes people holy. As the book of Leviticus confirms, the process of atonement involves both the payment of a ransom to avoid the penalty of death and the removal of defilement caused by sin. Additionally, the priests eat the meat of the sacrifice, an action that involves consuming something holy, for the sacrifice belongs to God. These different elements combine to make the priests holy. In a similar way, Christians become a royal priesthood through the sacrificial death of Christ (e.g., 1 Pet. 1:18–19).

Animal sacrifices, however, cannot imbue Aaron and his sons with sufficient holiness to enable them to enter freely into the Most Holy Place. In the outworking of God's redemptive plan, the tabernacle is a temporary measure, with access to God restricted. Nevertheless, the construction of the tabernacle foreshadows a future time when no barrier will exist between God and humanity (cf. Rev. 21–22).

Illustrating the Text

God makes people holy through the sacrificial death of Christ.

Comics: Many parents watch in amazement as their children are introduced, seemingly by osmosis, to the world of the comic-book superhero. Even if they have never read an issue or seen an episode of *X-Men* or *Wonder Woman*, kids seem to know everything about the characters. If left unchecked, this enthusiasm can lead to a next stage of obsession: costumes! Soon, parents are asked to help tie capes, fasten Velcro straps, and fashion masks, and children run around the home, leap from furniture, hold out their hands, and make *Zing-Zing-Zing-Zing* laser-beam sounds. Imagine a child's delight if they learned that they didn't need to settle for "dress up," that they could actually *gain* these superpowers.

As Christians, we are called to do more than just pretend we are like Jesus. Jesus actually sends his Spirit to live in us, setting us free from the tyranny of sin and death and empowering us to live lives that are continually being conformed more and more to the likeness of Christ (Col. 3:9–10).

The tabernacle was a temporary measure.

History: February 2012 marked an important milestone for New Orleans. Six years before, Hurricane Katrina had swept through the area, devastating the city when the levee system failed. People died. Homes were destroyed. Hopes were crushed. The Federal Emergency Management Agency (FEMA) provided trailers for residents as a temporary measure as houses were rebuilt. Those temporary shelters became home for many people over the next six years. In 2012, FEMA announced that the last trailer had departed.[1] Everyone now had a home.

As God rescues his people from the devastation of sin, he sets up temporary measures. The tabernacle was not God's final dwelling place with humanity. That is still to come!

One day, no barrier will exist between God and humanity.

Film: A familiar scene in many movies is the "prison visit." Typically, a wall of glass separates two people. To speak, they each hold a phone to their ear. Inevitably, one presses his or her hand to the glass and the other follows suit. Everything emphasizes the deep desire for contact that cannot be fulfilled, separation that cannot be overcome.

As believers, we have received a great inheritance. The Holy Spirit dwells in us, connecting us to God. Even so, the reality of sin still inhibits our intimacy with the Lord. One day, this barrier will melt away, and we will "know fully, even as [we are] fully known" (1 Cor. 13:13).

Gifted by God

Big Idea

God equips his servants through the Holy Spirit for the complex task of building his dwelling place on earth.

Key Themes

- The Holy Spirit empowers people to participate in the building of God's dwelling on earth.
- The concept of ransom is integral to restoring the broken relationship between God and humanity.

Understanding the Text

The Text in Context

The material in Exodus 30:1–31:18 forms the final part of God's speech to Moses. Up to this point God has given instructions for the construction of the tabernacle and its furniture and for the consecration of Aaron and his sons as priests. Instructions are now given for the manufacture of various other items associated with the tabernacle. These include an incense altar and a large bronze basin. Additionally, Moses is instructed to collect a ransom payment from all adult males. God also informs Moses that he has specially gifted Bezalel and Oholiab to oversee the manufacture of the tabernacle. Finally, God reminds Moses about the importance of observing the Sabbath, the sign of the Sinai covenant.

Interpretive Insights

30:1–5 *Make an altar of acacia wood for burning incense.* The gold-plated incense altar is located in the Holy Place, close to the curtain leading into the Most Holy Place. It resembles in shape the bronze altar that stands in front of the tent but is considerably smaller in size.

30:6 *before the atonement cover that is over the tablets of the covenant law.* The location of the atonement cover over the tablets of the "covenant law" (or "testimony") is significant. When blood is sprinkled on the lid, it atones for the sins of those who break the covenant obligations. On the Day of Atonement (cf. Lev. 16), the high priest ritually cleanses this altar using the blood of the purification offering. The Israelites' sins contaminate or defile the furnishings within the tabernacle. If God is to continue dwelling in the tent, this contamination needs to be removed. This ritual draws attention to the holiness of the tent.

30:7–10 *Aaron must burn fragrant incense on the altar every morning.* Used for burning incense, the altar produces a pleasant aroma within the tent. This is a further indicator that the tent is constantly occupied by the Lord, who appreciates the distinctive perfume.

30:12–16 *each one must pay the* LORD *a ransom for his life.* The tax imposed on adults, both male and female, provides all the silver necessary for the construction of the tabernacle (cf. 38:25–28). By emphasizing that every person, whether rich or poor, must contribute toward the ransom of his or her life, this instruction links the construction of the tabernacle with the concept of atonement. God's presence among the Israelites is dependent on their having atoned for their sin. By insisting that every person pay the same amount, regardless of the social status of the contributor, God's instructions indicate that every life is of equal worth. The census ensures that every adult is counted.

30:18–21 *Make a bronze basin, with its bronze stand, for washing.* Placed in the courtyard outside the tent, the basin provides a facility for the priests to wash before entering the Holy Place. It is a further reminder that only those who are ritually clean may come into God's presence.

30:23–33 *Make these into a sacred anointing oil . . . consecrate them so they will be most holy.* The process of making holy or consecrating the tabernacle, its furnishings, and its personnel involves the use of fragrant oil. By restricting the use of this oil to the tabernacle complex, God highlights the existence of an important difference between things that are holy and those that are common (cf. Lev. 10:10). This distinction permeates the instructions and regulations found in Leviticus and is meant to have a profound influence on how the Israelites view the world. This worldview in turn shapes their behavior, for they are to be holy as God is holy.

30:34–38 *make a fragrant blend of incense.* Following on from the anointing oil, God gives instructions for the manufacture of the incense that is to be burned on the altar within the Holy Place (cf. 30:1–10).

31:2–11 *filled him with the Spirit of God, with wisdom, with understanding, with knowledge.* Bezalel and Oholiab are equipped to oversee all the various tasks that need to be done to manufacture the tabernacle and its furnishings. The qualities of "wisdom," "understanding," and "knowledge" (v. 3; cf. 35:31) are later present in Huram, who oversees the construction of the temple in the time of Solomon (1 Kings 7:14). Importantly, all these qualities are elsewhere linked with God constructing the earth: "By wisdom the LORD laid the earth's foundations, by understanding he set the heavens in place; by his knowledge the watery depths were divided, and the clouds let drop the dew" (Prov. 3:19–20). These parallels between those responsible for constructing the tabernacle and temple and God creating the cosmos are noteworthy because the tabernacle and temple are considered to be models of the world. Elsewhere it is stated that wisdom, understanding, and knowledge are necessary for the successful building of a family home (Prov. 24:3–4). By linking the making of a family home with the construction of God's earthly dwelling place, these passages reinforce the Old Testament belief that God's ultimate purpose in creating the world is to dwell there with his people. According to Proverbs 2:6, the attributes of wisdom, knowledge, and understanding come from the Lord. Exodus 31:3 supports this claim by highlighting the role of the Holy Spirit in gifting Bezalel and Oholiab to supervise others as they work with metals, wood, cloth, and even perfume.

31:13–17 *observe my Sabbaths. This will be a sign between me and you.* Up to this point everything mentioned by God has related to the tabernacle and its personnel. Although the reference to observing the Sabbath may initially appear out of place at this point, the Sabbath, like the tabernacle, is concerned with the issue of holiness. The Sabbath is a sign so that the Israelites "may know that I am the LORD, who makes you holy" (v. 13). God's remarks ensure that those constructing the tabernacle are entitled to rest on the Sabbath. As the sign of a covenant, the Sabbath is like the rainbow (Gen. 9:12–13) and circumcision (Gen. 17:11).

31:18 *he gave him the two tablets of the covenant law.* The Hebrew text speaks of the two tablets of the "testimony," which the NIV translates as "covenant law." Testimony conveys the idea that the tablets will be a witness against the Israelites if they break the covenant obligations (i.e., the Ten Commandments). These obligations are not "laws" in the strictest sense but rather are broad principles. While we cannot be fully certain, on the basis of ancient Near Eastern practices it is likely that the two tablets are duplicates; each party to the covenant receives a copy of the obligations. The two tablets, inscribed by God, are stored inside the ark of the covenant (25:21). Often tablets were made of clay, but these are formed from stone, emphasizing the enduring nature of the covenant relationship initiated by God. According to 34:1 and 28, the tablets contain the Ten Commandments.

Theological Insights

The construction of a temporary, portable residence for God anticipates a time when God's holy presence will fill the whole earth. The tabernacle is viewed as a microcosm of the world, and the process by which it is constructed deliberately resembles how God created the cosmos. When centuries later the church replaces the Jerusalem temple as God's earthly residence, the apostle Paul sees his role as resembling that of Bezalel. Recognizing that he has been equipped by the Holy Spirit, Paul writes, "By the grace God has given me, I laid a foundation as a wise builder, and someone else is building on it" (1 Cor. 3:10). Every Christian is gifted by the grace of God to participate in building up God's temple, the church, although different grace-gifts may be allocated to different people (cf. Rom. 12:6–8; 1 Cor. 12:1–31; Eph. 4:11–13).

Teaching the Text

As God continues to instruct Moses concerning the tabernacle and issues associated with it, this section of Exodus highlights various concepts that may be used to explain helpfully two important topics.

God gifts people to be involved in the construction of his dwelling place. The detailed description of Bezalel and Oholiab draws attention to the manner in which God empowers individuals to participate in the construction of his earthly dwelling place. Through the presence of God's Spirit filling him, Bezalel is equipped by God to supervise others in the manufacture of the tabernacle. God gifts him with the qualities needed to undertake this work, ensuring that everything is done appropriately. In a similar fashion, the apostle Paul is gifted by the Holy Spirit to oversee the process of establishing the church as God's dwelling place (1 Cor. 3:10). Paul probably sees his apostolic role as paralleling that of Bezalel.

In doing so, Paul is conscious that others are also gifted by the grace of God to be coworkers in this process. Not everyone is gifted in the same way, because there are different grace-gifts. All grace-gifts, however, are needed in the task of building up the church as God's dwelling place.

The payment of a ransom is integral to restoring the broken relationship between God and humanity. The inclusion of instructions relating to the payment of a ransom as a memorial recalls how the paying of a ransom is a vital element in atoning for the sins of the Israelites. A ransom payment lies at the heart of the Passover, when the sacrificial animals die as substitutes for the firstborn male Israelites. However, as the author of Psalm 49 insightfully observes, human wealth cannot ransom an individual from the realm of the dead. Only God has the power to do this. The concept of ransom figures prominently in the New Testament explanation of Christ's death on the cross. As Jesus himself emphasizes to his disciples, he gives up "his life as a ransom for many" (Matt. 20:28; Mark 10:45; cf. 1 Tim. 2:5–6). Alluding to this, the apostle Peter writes, "For you know that it was not with perishable things such as silver or gold that you were redeemed from the empty way of life handed down to you from your ancestors, but with the precious blood of Christ, a lamb without blemish or defect" (1 Pet. 1:18–19).

Illustrating the Text

God empowers individuals to participate in building his home.

Human Experience: Many people can remember a time when a parent or grandparent taught them to perform a task around the home—changing the oil, painting the garage, baking bread, tending the garden, and so on. Share a time from your own memory, or share a time when you helped one of your children learn something new. Of course, when they do this, parents are probably taking more time to teach us to do something than if they did it themselves. But by allowing us to participate, they share themselves with us and allow us to take an important step in maturing. In much the same way, God has chosen to use us, his children, to shape his creation, salt our societies, and especially build his church in ways that, under his power and looking forward to God's ultimate fulfillment of his purposes, prepare for his arrival.

All grace-gifts are needed in building up the church as God's dwelling place.

Applying the Text: This section provides a perfect opportunity to teach about grace-gifts. Key New Testament texts (Rom. 12:3–8; 1 Cor. 12; Eph. 4:11–12; 1 Pet. 4:10–11) can help introduce the concept. Consider providing a practical way for people to discover their own gifts, such as distributing a printed grace-gifts inventory.[1] Of course, a full treatment of such an important teaching could not be incorporated into an illustration. However, if properly planned and implemented, this introductory teaching could easily be supplemented with other learning opportunities (e.g., adult education class, online resource, suggested reading list in the bulletin).

Human wealth cannot ransom us from death; only God has the power to do this.

Church History: Several factors influenced Martin Luther's formation as the great Protestant reformer. Certainly one of them was witnessing the terrible teaching of indulgences, typified by Johann Tetzel. This preacher of the Dominican order was made a commissioner for indulgences in Germany by Pope Leo X. In this capacity, Tetzel traveled through German villages, encouraging people to purchase indulgences, which were said to shorten one's time in purgatory. His sales pitch was said to be: "As soon as a coin in the coffer rings / the soul from purgatory springs." Luther, that preacher of justification by grace through faith alone, was understandably vexed. Only the ransom provided by Jesus Christ, the sinless and obedient God-man, can atone for sin.

The concept of ransom is prominent in the biblical explanation of Christ's death.

Theological Reference: It is important to distinguish a *biblical* understanding of ransom when articulating this perspective on the atonement. It would be a mistake, for instance, to follow in the footsteps of Origen (ca. AD 184–253), who posited that the ransom (mentioned in Mark 10:45) has been paid to the devil. As reflected in the exodus story, no ransom is paid to Pharaoh for the release of the Israelites. However, the firstborn Israelite males have to be ransomed from death. Through his death, Christ ransoms us from death.

Actions Have Consequences

Big Idea

The human tendency to pervert all that is good extends even to the worship of God.

Key Themes

- False religion may look deceptively similar to true religion, for it is typically modeled on the real thing.
- God will punish those who use religion to mask immoral activity.

Understanding the Text

The Text in Context

Chapters 25–31 concentrate on Moses receiving instructions for the manufacture of the tabernacle and the consecration of the Aaronic priesthood. All these instructions are designed to prepare the way for God to dwell in the midst of the Israelite camp. In the light of God's plan to live among the people, the events narrated at the start of chapter 32 are highly ironic, for the Israelites manufacture a golden calf, believing that God's presence will be manifest in it. Their actions demonstrate that they have not yet grasped clearly and fully who God is and how he is to be known. Moreover, by making an idol, they break one of the primary obligations of the covenant, thus endangering their special relationship with God. Everything that God has been working to achieve is placed in jeopardy by the seditious actions of the Israelites. In the light of this, chapters 32–34 provide an important insight into the multifaceted nature of God and how he deals with rebellious human nature.

Historical and Cultural Background

The use of idols was a major feature of ancient Near Eastern religions. At the heart of this practice was the belief that the image provided immediate access to the deity represented by it. Not only did the image resemble the deity, but more important, the deity was present in the idol. Against this background, the Israelites' request for an idol is motivated by a desire to guarantee God's presence with them. In doing so, they seek to manipulate God rather than obey him.

Interpretive Insights

32:1–3 *Come, make us gods who will go before us.* As indicated by the NIV text note, the Hebrew noun *'elohim*, "God/gods," may be understood as denoting either one deity or many. This issue reappears in 32:4, 8, and 23. In all four instances, *'elohim* comes in a quotation attributed to the Israelites. Although it has a plural ending, in the Old Testament *'elohim* normally denotes God in the singular. When *'elohim* refers to one God, associated verbs and pronouns are usually in the singular. While this appears to be grammatically incorrect, it is theologically accurate. Sometimes, however, *'elohim* refers to "gods." When this is so, the verbs or pronouns linked to *'elohim* are in the plural. Although this is grammatically correct, it is theologically inaccurate, for there is only one God. Taking this distinction into account, the Israelites' words imply that they speak of "gods," for the verbs associated with *'elohim* in 32:1, 4, 8, and 23 are in the plural. Yet it seems apparent from the context that they are not expecting Aaron to manufacture various "gods" for them. The people are clearly satisfied when Aaron produces one idol for them to worship. Their request for an idol, however, is incompatible with the worship of the Lord. By asking Aaron to make *'elohim*, the Israelites are acting as pagans. This explains the ambiguity surrounding their words. While readers of the Hebrew text will appreciate the dissonance of what the Israelites say, this is difficult to replicate in English translation.

32:4 *made it into an idol cast in the shape of a calf.* The translation "calf" may mislead readers into thinking that the image resembles a newborn animal. The Hebrew noun *'egel* denotes here a young, but probably fully grown, bull that could be up to three years old. Bulls are widely linked with ancient Near Eastern religious practices. Although some scholars have proposed that the golden bull was a pedestal or throne on which the Lord sat, the remarks of the Israelites strongly suggest that the bull itself is an idol representing the Lord.[1] The people desire more than a throne on which an invisible God might sit; they want to see their "god." By making an idol, Aaron disregards one of the core obligations of the Sinai covenant (20:4–6; cf. 20:23).

32:5–6 *he built an altar in front of the calf.* The activities described in these verses partially resemble the covenant-making ritual described in 24:4–11, with an altar being constructed and sacrifices offered on it. Aaron may have hoped that these religious activities would please God, but the reverse is true. The people's actions greatly anger the Lord.

32:7–10 *your people, whom you brought up out of Egypt.* By referring to the Israelites as "your people," God conveys his disdain for their behavior. Previously in Exodus, God frequently has spoken of them as "my people" (e.g., 3:7, 10; 5:1; 6:7; 7:4). By their actions they have shown their disdain for God's authority and alienated themselves from him.

32:11–13 *Why should the Egyptians say, "It was with evil intent that he brought them out . . . "?* Since God desires to make himself known through rescuing the Israelites from slavery (cf. 7:5; 9:14; 10:2), his destruction of them in the wilderness would negate what he has already done.

32:19–23 *he threw the tablets out of his hands.* Moses shares God's anger at the "idolatry" of the Israelites. By shattering the stone tablets inscribed with the covenant obligations, Moses dramatically shows that the covenant itself is broken. This is a telling action, for it signals the end of God's special relationship with the Israelites. While the covenant will subsequently be renewed in Exodus 34, this will occur only after the Israelites express remorse for what they have done and Moses intercedes on their behalf.

32:24 *I threw it into the fire, and out came this calf!* Aaron attempts to distance himself from all that has happened. Yet even if he felt pressured into obeying the people, he nevertheless has acted inappropriately.

32:25–29 *Moses saw that the people were running wild.* The people's idolatry causes them to cast off moral restraint. False worship and immorality are frequently linked. While Moses has previously mediated with the Lord to prevent the destruction of the whole nation (32:14), he now seeks to safeguard the Israelites' relationship with the Lord by preventing further immorality. The crisis causes Moses to take exceptional steps. His instructions in verse 27 imply that the Levites are to identify and punish systematically those who are unwilling to abandon their idolatry.

32:30–35 *You have committed a great sin . . . perhaps I can make atonement.* Although three thousand Israelites are killed, this cannot atone for the sins of their fellow Israelites. Conscious of the enormity of their wrongdoing, Moses returns to God to seek forgiveness. Yet even Moses's offer of his own life cannot atone for the people's disobedience to God. While the book of Exodus does not record how many died, 1 Corinthians 10:8 states that twenty-three thousand died on account of the golden bull; later at Baal Peor a further incident involving idolatry results in twenty-four thousand deaths (Num. 25:1–9). These are solemn reminders of the serious consequences of idolatry.

33:1–3 *Go up to the land flowing with milk and honey. But I will not go with you.* God reassures Moses that he will fulfill his promise to the patriarchs to give the land of Canaan to their descendants, but he indicates that he will not accompany Moses and the Israelites. As the events surrounding the golden bull demonstrate, God's presence with the Israelites will place them in danger due to their sinfulness. The reality of God's words is underlined by the many deaths that have already occurred at Mount Sinai.

33:4–6 *they began to mourn and no one put on any ornaments.* As an expression of their contrition the Israelites remove their jewelry. Ironically, they previously removed their rings to make the golden bull (32:2–3).

Theological Insights

God takes willful disobedience very seriously. In the main list of covenant obligations God prohibits the Israelites from making and worshiping idols (20:4–6). Yet they disregard this crucial requirement, in spite of having voluntarily committed themselves to obeying God completely. In the light of the newly formed covenant relationship, their actions may be compared to that of a bride committing adultery on her wedding day. While at first sight God's response may appear extreme, it is fully justified and no less than the Israelites deserve. Aware that they are a stiff-necked people, God rightly emphasizes that his continued presence with the Israelites will result in their destruction if they persist in disobeying him.

Teaching the Text

The contents of this passage provide an opportunity to explore a number of related issues concerning true and false worship. However, the events of Exodus 32–34 need to be read against the background of all that God has already done for the Israelites. Moved with compassion for the plight of the Israelites, God rescues them from oppression in Egypt. He then generously provides for them in the wilderness as they journey to Mount Sinai, supplying them with food and water. At Mount Sinai they are especially privileged by God when he invites them to become his "treasured possession" by establishing a unique covenant relationship with him (19:5). No other nation enjoys this privilege. In the light of everything that God does for the Israelites, their willful disobedience of him invites stern condemnation. After they have repeatedly promised to obey God totally (19:8 and 24:3, 7), their behavior is deeply offensive.

Counterfeit religion. Although God has prohibited the making and worshiping of idols, the Israelites mask their disobedience by undertaking activities that resemble true worship. Ironically, they even offer sacrifices intended to atone for human sin. Yet as God clearly indicates, their actions anger him, for counterfeit religious activities can never be a substitute for true devotion. Unfortunately, it is a recurring human propensity to turn from true worship to false religion (cf. Gal. 1:6–9).

Self-gratification masked by religion. The actions of the Israelites illustrate well how people manipulate religion to suit their own desires. They want God to be there for them on their own terms, not on those set by God. In doing so, they pervert the true worship of the Lord, substituting self-pleasing activities that become a source of human gratification. While it is not clear that the Israelites engaged in inappropriate sexual activity (cf. Num. 25:1–13), their exuberant feasting results in some of the people running wild and being out of control (Exod. 32:25).

God is not mocked. Few things can be more offensive to God than false worship. With good reason, the Bible condemns idolatry because it is a mockery of true worship. God's condemnation rightly rests on those who deliberately promote religious practices that do not reflect truly how God should be worshiped. The Israelites discover for themselves the fatal consequences of disregarding God's instructions.

Illustrating the Text

Counterfeit religious activities can never be a substitute for true devotion.

Cultural Institution: Since 1865, the US Department of the Treasury has been waging war against counterfeiters. It is aided in this effort by the Secret Service, which investigates reports of counterfeit currency. Perhaps the best protection has been continuously updating the way currency is produced, making it difficult for criminals to copy the design. The quality of paper, type of ink, specially designed borders and threads, and other key features of genuine currency have been part of the battle against those who would pass off a fake as the real thing. Those who know what to look for will easily spot when these marks of authenticity are missing. In terms of authentic worship, the touchstone of true devotion is a heart that genuinely fears the Lord. This mark of a believer cannot be faked.

Humans habitually turn from true worship to false religion.

Object Lesson: The piano is an amazing instrument. Eighty-eight keys. A more or less ornate housing and lid. Pedals to dampen or lengthen notes. Hammers and strings to produce notes. These are the basic parts. Interestingly, no matter how well made each part is, a piano will need regular tuning. This need for periodic maintenance is part and parcel of owning a piano, and every player knows what it is to sit down and realize it is time to call the tuner. As believers on this side of eternity, we need constant recalibration. Unless we actively retune our hearts, we will gradually slip into false religion rather than true worship.

God is deeply offended by false worship.

Props: For this illustration, you will need a volunteer. Explain that you are seeking someone with a refined sense of smell. Bring the person up and blindfold him or her. Have a set of scented candles prepared. Use three distinct, easily identifiable scents (e.g., apple, cinnamon, vanilla). For the last scent, hold up an offensive-smelling object or candle (e.g., a container of strong onions and tuna fish). Scripture often speaks of pure worship as a pleasing aroma to the Lord. False worship is a stench!

Food: One of the most unappealing experiences we have is sitting down to a favorite meal in our favorite restaurants only to discover there is a hair in our food. It makes us feel nauseous. It can even ruin our taste for the dish. God is nauseated by false worship.

God, Glory, and Goodness

Big Idea

Although God graciously forgives the sins of his people, they are still obliged to obey him fully.

Key Themes

- A key component of God's nature is his willingness to forgive those who rebel against him.
- No one should presume upon the forgiveness of God, for he is equally a God of justice.
- Those who experience the forgiveness of God are fully expected to serve him faithfully.

Understanding the Text

The Text in Context

Whereas 32:1–33:6 highlights the Israelites' disregard for the newly established covenant and the negative consequences that follow, 33:7–34:35 records how Moses plays a key role in restoring the broken relationship between God and the Israelites. While Moses's contribution is clearly important, this is not the decisive factor in terms of ensuring God's ongoing presence with the Israelites. Rather, as 34:6–7 highlights, God's willingness to travel onward with the Israelites is not determined by the people's contrition or Moses's mediation but rests in the very nature of God himself. It is the Lord's willingness to forgive that saves the covenant relationship.

Outline/Structure

This section of Exodus begins and ends with two short passages (33:7–11; 34:34–35) that interrupt the narrative describing the immediate consequences that follow the Israelites' worship of the golden calf. Marked off from the surrounding material by the distinctive form of the verbs used, 33:7–11 and 34:34–35 describe events that were regular occurrences. Both passages focus on Moses's relationship with the Lord, an important factor as regards healing the breach between God and the Israelites.

Interpretive Insights

33:7 *Moses used to take a tent*. This verse introduces a short section (vv. 7–11) that forms an interlude in the report of what occurred after the Israelites worshiped the golden bull. Verses 7–11 describe how Moses regularly has pitched a tent, possibly beginning shortly after the Israelites left Egypt, when God guided them using the "pillar of cloud." This special tent enables Moses to meet with God. For this reason, Moses designates it "the tent of meeting." The same title is later given to the tabernacle (e.g., Lev. 1:1), but the two tents need to be carefully distinguished. Whereas the initial "tent of meeting" is pitched outside the camp, the tabernacle is located at the center of the camp. While God resides in the tabernacle, he never enters the tent pitched outside the camp. After the tabernacle is manufactured and erected, the first "tent of meeting" becomes redundant. While some scholars suggest that Numbers 11:16–17, 24–26; 12:1–8 refer to the tent outside the camp, it is more likely that these verses refer to the tabernacle.

33:8–10 *Moses went into the tent, the pillar of cloud would come down . . . all stood and worshiped*. Moses enters the tent and stays inside it, but the pillar of cloud remains outside the tent. Recognizing that God comes to Moses as the pillar of cloud, the Israelites bow down in worship.

33:11 *The LORD would speak to Moses face to face, as one speaks to a friend*. This verse underlines Moses's special relationship with the Lord. Although they are separated by the fabric of the tent wall, God speaks directly to Moses. By emphasizing that God meets with Moses on a regular basis, verses 7–11 provide background information that has an important bearing on the conversation recorded in 33:12–34:3. Details of the conversation and especially Moses's desire to see God face-to-face are best understood in the light of God's regular encounters with Moses.

33:12–13 *"Lead these people," but you have not let me know whom you will send with me*. As described in 33:7–11, Moses speaks to the Lord at the "tent of meeting." Having been commissioned by God to lead the Israelites, Moses asks for help to do so. In particular, he raises the issue of God's presence with the people in the future.

33:14–17 *My Presence will go with you . . . I am pleased with you and I know you by name*. God assures Moses that he will accompany the Israelites. This reassurance rests on the fact that the Lord is pleased with Moses and knows him intimately, confirming what has been said in 33:7–11.

33:18–23 *Now show me your glory*. With boldness Moses requests to see God's glory. From God's reply in verses 19–20 we learn that his glory includes seeing his face, although undoubtedly it also includes the description of God's goodness given in 34:6–7. Previously, Moses and the leaders of the Israelites witnessed something of God's splendor, but they appear at most to have seen only his feet (24:9–10).

you cannot see my face, for no one may see me and live. Responding positively to Moses's requests, God promises to reveal something of his glory to Moses, but not his face. By stating that no one can see his face and live, God highlights the gulf that exists between him and sinful humanity. Even Moses, despite his intimate relationship with God, cannot look on the face of God without endangering his own life.

34:1–5 *Chisel out two stone tablets like the first ones.* By replacing the tablets shattered by Moses (32:19), God signals his willingness to reestablish the covenant relationship with the Israelites. Once more a boundary is placed around Mount Sinai that only Moses may cross (cf. 19:12–13, 23).

34:6–7 *The Lord, the Lord, the compassionate and gracious God.* As a concise description of God's nature, this comes with his full authority. This is God's assessment, not that of a human theologian. Consequently, this affirmation is often quoted or alluded to elsewhere in the Old Testament (e.g., Num. 14:18; Neh. 9:17; Pss. 86:15; 103:8; 145:8; Joel 2:13; Jon. 4:2; Nah. 1:3). Remarkably, God's description of himself holds in tension two contrasting aspects of his nature: his compassion and his justice. These features are especially relevant in the present context, reflecting God's treatment of the Israelites following their worship of the golden calf. There is both forgiveness and punishment. In the light of the Israelites making the golden calf, verses 6–7 echo what God has previously said in Exodus 20:4–6. Interestingly, the order of grace and punishment is reversed between the passages, indicating perhaps that the relationship between them is finely balanced, with neither of them taking priority over the other.

34:10–11 *I am making a covenant with you.* God renews the covenant just broken by the Israelites. The terms of the covenant will be written down by both God and Moses (see 34:27–28).

34:12–17 *Be careful not to make a treaty with those who live in the land.* The Hebrew word translated "treaty" here is the same word rendered "covenant" in 34:10. The warning against making a treaty with the inhabitants of Canaan recalls what is said in the final section of the Book of the Covenant (23:20–33). Once again, God emphasizes that the Israelites must not allow the religious practices of others to influence how they worship him. Unfortunately, this has already happened with the making of the golden bull. God is very conscious that the Israelites will be easily influenced by the religious ideas of others.

34:18–26 *Celebrate the Festival of Unleavened Bread.* The contents of these verses recall God's earlier instructions in the Book of the Covenant regarding the celebration of the three annual festivals.

34:29–35 *he was not aware that his face was radiant.* The light emanating from Moses's face is a visible sign to others of his intimate communion with God. It confirms that Moses has indeed encountered God. Whereas verses 29–33 report a one-off event, verses 34–35 describe regular occurrences. When Moses speaks with the veil removed, he speaks with divine authority and communicates God's message to the Israelites. The transformation of Moses's appearance due to his intimate contact with God provides the background for understanding Jesus's transfiguration (cf. Matt. 17:2; Mark 9:2–3; Luke 9:29).

Theological Insights

Of the many passages of Scripture that speak of the unmerited love of God, the present is one of the most striking. Here God himself highlights that he is "compassionate and gracious" (34:6), and he does so in the context of the Israelites willfully disobeying him. Since this description of God comes from his lips, it carries ultimate authority. Whatever else may be said about God's nature, his willingness to show mercy must always feature prominently.

Teaching the Text

The present passage provides an excellent opportunity to explore the relationship between divine grace and justice, especially as it relates to discipleship.

The grace of God is evident in salvation. As the book of Exodus clearly reveals, the Israelites do nothing to gain their release from slavery in Egypt. Their salvation is all of grace. It is God alone who saves them. And God's grace is all the more evident when the Israelites disobey him and commit idolatry by worshiping the golden bull. In these circumstances, they rightly deserve to be punished by God. Yet in spite of their willful disobedience, he shows mercy and forgives them. As he declares to Moses, he forgives "wickedness, rebellion and sin" (34:7).

God's grace is free but costs everything. Human obedience to God does not merit salvation, but it is an appropriate response to salvation already given. Divine forgiveness does not remove the obligation that people have to obey God fully. On the contrary, in Exodus 34 the Lord's pronouncement that he is a God of compassion and mercy is given in the context of the covenant obligations being reinstated. God announces his forgiving nature just prior to giving Moses a new set of stone tablets. The grace of God does not do away with the need for obedience. Rather, God expects those who have experienced his forgiveness to be all the more committed to obeying him.

Divine grace is not given automatically. While the grace of God is an amazing truth in the light of our inherent sinfulness, we must not arrogantly presume upon the mercy of God. The Lord's proclamation to Moses also features a reference to the punishment of those who sin persistently. While this may seem to contradict the concept of forgiveness, it is a solemn reminder that the grace of God does not automatically extend to everyone. Many Israelites were punished for their idolatry at Mount Sinai. And in the centuries that followed, God frequently found it necessary to rebuke and punish his people for disregarding the covenant obligations.

Illustrating the Text

Salvation is entirely a work of God's extravagant grace.

Everyday Experience: Many people have had the experience of applying for a home loan. The amount of paperwork is seemingly endless. Financial figures must be carefully assembled and amply documented. Once the extensive application is completed, it is vetted and analyzed by actuaries, and the bank's risk is carefully assessed. If approval is forthcoming, it is a carefully calculated approval, with a specific limit and terms. It is, if nothing else, a calculated decision based on your ability to pay. Much as the bank seeks to understand our financial situation fully, God knows all about us. But God's decisions are exceedingly unlike those of any bank. God's grace is not proportional to merit or demonstrated potential. God enlivens the dead and raises up the unworthy. And nothing we subsequently do can ever come close to repaying God for his grace and mercy. Divine forgiveness does not remove the obligation to obey God fully.

Sports: People often act as if rules are obstacles to fun. But in sports, rules are the guidelines that *make the fun happen*! Imagine what would happen if a basketball referee refused to blow his whistle when a player took five steps without dribbling the ball. Would the game be any fun if a player was allowed to tackle an opponent heading in for a layup? What would happen if one team put eleven players on the court? Soon, it would no longer be a game of basketball, would it?

As Christians, we believe that obedience is not "I've got to" but "I get to." If we really understand the Lord, we know that his will is *good* for us. Obedience allows us to live in the joy of our salvation.

God's grace is free, but it costs everything.

Quote: *The Cost of Discipleship*, by Dietrich Bonhoeffer. Bonhoeffer, a German theologian, warns against the danger of offering people cheap grace:

Cheap grace is not the kind of forgiveness of sin which frees us from the toils of sin. Cheap grace is the grace we bestow on ourselves.

Cheap grace is the preaching of forgiveness without requiring repentance, baptism without church discipline, Communion without confession, absolution without personal confession. Cheap grace is grace without discipleship, grace without the cross, grace without Jesus Christ, living and incarnate.[1]

We must beware of presuming upon God's mercy.

Quote: Johann Heinrich Heine was a German poet born into a Jewish family in 1797. From 1831 until his death in 1856 he lived in Paris, where he was an influential figure on the literary scene. The story is told that when asked on his deathbed if God would forgive him, he said, "Of course God will forgive me; that's his job." A careful reading of Exodus 32–34 reveals that we should not presume upon the grace of God, for not every Israelite was forgiven.

God in Our Midst

Big Idea

God invites and equips his people to build his dwelling place on the earth.

Key Themes

- God's plans for Israel prompt the people to be generous, giving of their possessions, time, and skills.
- God's presence within the tabernacle is an important step toward his glorious presence filling the whole earth.

Understanding the Text

The Text in Context

These chapters bring the book of Exodus to an important climax with the Lord coming in all his glory to inhabit the tabernacle in the midst of the Israelite camp. The whole of Exodus has been moving toward this remarkable event. To achieve this, the Israelites have committed to becoming a holy nation through the covenant at Mount Sinai. This builds on the Passover ritual, by which the Israelites are ransomed from death and sanctified, necessary preparation for fellowship with God.

With the renewal of the covenant relationship between God and the Israelites following the making of the golden bull, the construction of the tabernacle can begin. Moses communicates the Lord's instructions to the people. He starts by listing the materials needed and by identifying those chosen by God to oversee the task. Each item is manufactured according to God's instructions. When everything has been made, Moses inspects all the items to ensure that they meet God's specifications. God then instructs Moses regarding the erection of the tabernacle and its consecration. Obeying God's instructions, Moses erects the tent and places all the furnishings in their proper location. Finally, the glory of the Lord fills the tabernacle. God now dwells with the Israelites, making them unique among all the nations of the world.

Outline/Structure

Much of the material concerning the construction of the tabernacle and its furnishings in chapters 35–39 resembles closely God's instructions in chapters 25–30 (see table 1). The detailed repetition is intentional, confirming that the Israelites construct the tabernacle exactly as God has instructed. One difference is the order in which the items are presented. Whereas the instructions list the tabernacle furniture before the tent, in the reporting of their manufacture the tent is listed before everything else, with the clothing of the priests coming last.

Table 1. Order of Instructions and Construction of the Tabernacle and Furnishings

Instructions	Construction
Ark (25:10–14, 17–20)	Tent (36:8–38)
Table (25:23–29)	Ark (37:1–9)
Lampstand (25:31–39)	Table (37:10–16)
Tent (26:1–11, 14–29, 31–32, 36–37)	Lampstand (37:17–24)
Bronze altar (27:1–8)	Incense altar (37:25–28)
Courtyard screen (27:9–19)	Anointing oil (37:29)
Ephod (28:6–12)	Bronze altar (38:1–7)
Breastpiece (28:15–28)	Bronze basin (38:8)
Robe (28:31–34)	Courtyard screen (38:9–20)
Gold plate (28:36–37)	Ephod (39:2–7)
Tunic, turban, sash (28:39–40)	Breastpiece (39:8–21)
Incense altar (30:1–10)	Robe (39:22–26)
Bronze basin (30:18)	Tunic, turban, sash (39:27–29)
Anointing oil (30:25)	Gold plate (39:30–31)

Interpretive Insights

35:4–9 *From what you have, take an offering for the* Lord. The list of materials covers everything necessary for the construction of the tabernacle, its furnishings, and associated items.

35:10–19 *All who are skilled among you are to come.* As well as donating material possessions, those Israelites with expertise and skills are challenged to offer their time and abilities to God. Everyone is encouraged to play a part in making the tabernacle.

35:30–36:7 *the* Lord *has chosen Bezalel son of Uri . . . and Oholiab son of Ahisamak.* Moses recognizes the special role to be undertaken by Bezalel and Oholiab. See the comments on 31:2–11. The generosity of the people is such that they have to be "restrained from bringing more" (36:6).

36:8–38 *All those who were skilled among the workers made the tabernacle.* The first item to be manufactured is the tent. As with all the items mentioned in chapters 36–39, the description of how the tent is made follows closely the instructions given earlier by God to Moses (see table 1).

37:1–9 *Bezalel made the ark of acacia wood.* Bezalel takes special responsibility for making the ark that is to be placed inside the Most Holy Place. This is the only item constructed by him alone.

37:10–38:20 *They made the table of acacia wood.* Skilled workers manufacture the table, lampstand, incense altar, bronze altar, basin, and courtyard screen. These items are listed in order of descending importance, moving from the Most Holy Place to the tabernacle courtyard.

38:21–31 *These are the amounts of the materials used for the tabernacle.* A summary is provided, quantifying the materials used in the construction of the tabernacle and its furnishings. Approximately one ton of gold, four tons of silver, and two and a half tons of bronze are used. While these are significant quantities, they are not unusual when compared with similar ancient Near Eastern constructions. The quantity of silver used is in keeping with the "atonement money" mentioned in 30:11–16. Each of the 603,550 adults was required to give half a shekel. This makes a total of 301,775 shekels. One hundred talents is equivalent to 300,000 shekels. (For more on the total number of adults, see comments on 12:37.)

39:1–32 *They also made sacred garments for Aaron, as the LORD commanded Moses.* The statement "as the LORD commanded Moses" recurs as a concluding remark for the items of clothing (vv. 7, 21, 26, 29, 31), emphasizing that everything has been done as the Lord instructed. This point is reinforced by the general statement made in verse 32 regarding "all the work on the tabernacle."

39:33–43 *Then they brought the tabernacle to Moses.* Verses 33–41 list all the items associated with the tabernacle. When Moses inspects these, he confirms that they have been made as "the LORD had commanded," a point emphasized by the repetition of this phrase in verses 42 and 43 (cf. 39:32).

40:1–8 *Set up the tabernacle, the tent of meeting.* With everything manufactured, God instructs Moses regarding the erection (40:2–8) and consecration (40: 9–11) of the tabernacle and the consecration of the Aaronic priests (40:12–15). Here the emphasis is placed on what Moses must do, in contrast to the activities of the Israelites in manufacturing the tent (cf. 39:32 and 40:16).

40:9–11 *Take the anointing oil . . . consecrate it and all its furnishings, and it will be holy.* Moses is delegated the task of consecrating the tabernacle and everything associated with it. Once again the holy nature of the tabernacle is emphasized. To become God's dwelling place on earth, the tent must be made holy.

40:12–15 *Bring Aaron and his sons . . . anoint him and consecrate him.* Those serving in the tabernacle must also be consecrated. Fuller instructions for this process are given in Exodus 29. Leviticus 8 describes the fulfillment of these instructions.

40:16–33 *Moses did everything just as the* LORD *commanded him*. As the Israelites were faithful in constructing everything as "the LORD commanded" (cf. 39:32), so Moses also complies fully with the Lord's instructions. This is confirmed not only by the summary statement made in verse 16 but through the repetition of the phrase "as the LORD commanded him" in verses 19, 21, 23, 25, 27, 29, 32. Interestingly, the description of what Moses does includes activities that are not specifically mentioned in 40:2–15. This would suggest that the report of God's speech in 40:2–15 conveys only part of what God said.

So the tabernacle was set up on the first day of the first month in the second year. The erection of the tabernacle takes place "on the first day of the first month." The timing is hardly coincidental. God's coming to dwell among the Israelites is an important landmark in the history of the Israelites. It marks a new beginning and appropriately happens on the first day of a new year.

40:34–38 *the cloud covered the tent of meeting, and the glory of the* LORD *filled the tabernacle*. This brings the book of Exodus to a remarkable climax. Having rescued the Israelites from slavery in Egypt and having guided them through the wilderness to Mount Sinai, God now comes to dwell among them. The significance of this event cannot be overstated. It represents a major new development in God's plan of redemption, as he comes to reside on earth with his people.

As elsewhere in Exodus, God's presence is marked by a cloud that glows with fire at night (13:21–22; 14:24; cf. 14:19–20; 16:10; 19:9, 16, 18; 24:15–17, 18; 33:9–10; 34:5). God's glory, which is associated with the cloud that signals the divine presence in 16:10 and 24:16–17, comes to fill the tabernacle. When the tabernacle is later replaced by the temple constructed by Solomon in Jerusalem, God's glory also comes to fill it (1 Kings 8:10–11).

Moses could not enter the tent . . . the glory of the LORD *filled the tabernacle*. Although God's arrival among the Israelites is an important new development, the people are not able to have unhindered access to God's presence. Due to God's presence in the tabernacle, Moses cannot enter it. A barrier still exists between God and the Israelites that will be removed only when Jesus Christ is crucified (Matt. 27:51; Mark 15:38; Luke 23:45).

Theological Insights

The second half of Exodus is dominated by the report of the construction of the tabernacle and items associated with it. This eventually results in the Lord coming to dwell in the midst of the Israelite camp. God's willingness to take up residence among the Israelites brings the book of Exodus to an important climax. This event is highly significant in the light of God's plan not only for

Israel but for all of humanity. From the outset of creation it was God's intention that the earth would be his dwelling place, shared with human beings and other creatures. Unfortunately, the actions of Adam and Eve in the Garden of Eden complicated the fulfillment of God's plan, requiring God to redeem the whole of creation from the grip of evil. The deliverance of the Israelites from slavery in Egypt foreshadows a greater salvation that will come through Jesus Christ. While the exodus from Egypt enables the Israelites to construct an earthly residence for God, this merely foreshadows something greater in the future. Subsequently, the tabernacle will be replaced by the Jerusalem temple, which in turn will give way to the church as God's dwelling place on earth. As God's presence filled the tabernacle and temple, so through the Holy Spirit at Pentecost God comes to dwell within the church, an ever-growing temple.

Teaching the Text

In teaching this section of Exodus it is important to explain that much of the material in 35:1–40:38 duplicates what has already been covered in chapters 25–30 (as illustrated in table 1). This repetition is intended to demonstrate that the Israelites obey in every respect God's instructions for the manufacture of the tabernacle and all the items associated with it. To avoid repeating unnecessarily what has already been taught on the basis of Exodus 25–30, the following topics offer something new.

God's desire to dwell with the Israelites requires them to be generous, giving of their possessions, time, and skills. While God graciously initiates the building project, the Israelites themselves must undertake the task of manufacturing everything. This provides them with an opportunity to show their gratitude to God for all that he has already done for them. As 38:21–31 reveals, they generously contribute all the raw materials needed for the tabernacle. Additionally, those involved will enjoy a deep sense of satisfaction through having constructed a royal residence for God. In a similar way, the apostle Paul encourages Christian believers at Corinth to be wholeheartedly committed to building the church, God's new temple (1 Cor. 3:12–13).

God's presence among the Israelites foreshadows his glorious presence filling the whole earth. As the footstool of the divine throne is placed within the Most Holy Place and God subsequently comes to reside within the tabernacle, heaven and earth are linked. This is an important step toward God's kingdom being established on the earth. However, the extension of God's reign throughout the world will proceed slowly. While the coming of Jesus Christ marks a major new development in the process of expanding God's kingdom, only with the future return of Jesus and the creation of a new earth will God's glory fill the whole world.

Illustrating the Text

We are called to invest our time and treasure in building up the church.

Scenario: Imagine being the "lucky" person who has invested a fortune in the last generation of the horse-drawn plow industry. They would probably be the best, most technically advanced plows. They would be impressive in every detail and built on the wisdom of several millennia. But it would be a terrible investment in a product headed for museums, not modern farms. In the end, we would regret our investment.

We are tempted to invest our time and treasure in many things that will not last. In the end, these investments will leave us feeling dissatisfied and disenchanted. In contrast, investing our lives in building God's house allows the joy of investing in something of eternal worth.

God's vision is to establish his kingdom on earth.

Music: If you have ever been to a symphony, you probably know the moments of anticipation: The musicians have taken their places. For a few minutes, everything seems like barely controlled chaos. Timpani players turn tuning bolts. Violinists squeak their way into harmony. Horns blat. Clarinets run scales. The concertmaster leads a brief tune, but this too usually devolves into a cacophony of sound. Then the conductor mounts the stage and taps the music stand, and all grows still. A moment later, with a sweep of the hand, the conductor leads the orchestra into a landscape of beautiful song.

Our world is a cacophony of sounds, disparate and often dissonant strains, like many musicians working in isolation from and often even against one another. But fragments of the themes of the coming symphony, signs of God's coming reign, can also be heard. And we look ahead to that day when all things will operate in perfect submission to our Conductor. God's kingdom will be fully realized, and all things will be unified under Christ. And the beautiful sound, the grace-filled rhythm of life, will last forever.

God's kingdom expands slowly.

Bible: The Parable of the Growing Seed. In Mark 4:26–29, Jesus tells of a farmer who scatters seed and then does very little else. He sleeps. He wakes. He repeats the pattern. The plants grow, "though he does not know how." The kingdom of God is not something we can create. We sow the Word. We cultivate the field. Only the King can bring the growth.

Only Jesus's return will usher in the full realization of God's kingdom on earth.

Cultural Institution: Describe all that goes into a wedding day. People usually decorate, setting up candles and spreading out flower arrangements. Musicians arrive and prepare their instruments. The wedding party readies itself. The guests arrive and sign their names in a book. Ushers walk people down the aisle. Eventually all is set. But the wedding does not *really* start until the bride and groom come together.

In this world, the church can give witness to the reality of the kingdom—God dwells in our midst. When the world sees us, it should know that something eternal is touching space-time and something new is coming. Our presence should create anticipation, but the fullness of the kingdom will never be ushered in through human efforts. We are waiting for Jesus, the Bridegroom of the church. When he returns, the glory of God will come and the true celebrations begin.

Notes

Introduction to Exodus

1. For a survey of how modern scholarship has given priority to exploring the supposed sources underlying the books of Genesis to Deuteronomy, see Alexander, *From Paradise*, 3–110.

2. Dever ("Archaeological Evidence," 81) writes, "Not only is there no archaeological evidence for an exodus, there is no need to posit such an event. We can account for Israelite origins, historically and archaeologically, without presuming any Egyptian background." Cf. Grabbe, *Israel in Transition*, 2:90–94.

3. Scholars who support the historicity of the exodus generally opt for either a fifteenth- or thirteenth-century BC date for the event. A fifteenth-century date is supported by Bimson, *Redating*; Wood, "Rise and Fall." A thirteenth-century date is favored by Kitchen, *On the Reliability*; Hoffmeier, "Biblical Date."

Exodus 1:1–22

1. See Jacob, *Second Book*, 18; Houtman, *Exodus*, 1:252; Propp, *Exodus 1–18*, 137.

2. E.g. Houtman, *Exodus*, 1:257–58.

3. "History," Corrie ten Boom House Foundation, http://www.corrietenboom.com/old/history.htm.

4. "Four Members of Pocatello Family Found Dead in Home," KTVB, February 24, 2014, http://www.ktvb.com/story/news/local/2014/07/02/12094611/.

5. Julie Makinen, "Tiananmen Square Mystery: Who Was 'Tank Man'?," *Los Angeles Times*, June 4, 2014, http://www.latimes.com/world/asia/la-fg-china-tiananmen-square-tank-man-20140603-story.html.

Exodus 2:1–25

1. Bietak, "Perunefer," 15–17. Cf. Bietak, *Avaris*; Hoffmeier, *Israel in Egypt*.

Exodus 3:1–22

1. Fretheim, "Yahweh"; Davies, "Divine Name in Exodus."

2. See Roberts, "Hand of Yahweh," 247; Hoffmeier, "Arm of God"; Kitchen, *On the Reliability*, 253–54.

Exodus 4:1–31

1. The verb *sam*, "to place" or "to put," is used twice in this verse after the interrogative "who." The form of the verb switches from perfect to imperfect. This leaves open the possibility that the verb should be understood as a permissive imperfect with the sense, "Who may make . . ." See Gesenius, *Gesenius' Hebrew Grammar*, §107s; Williams, *Hebrew Syntax*, 71.

2. David Garrison, *A Wind in the House of Islam: How God Is Drawing Muslims around the World to Faith in Jesus Christ* (Monument, CO: WIGTake Resources, 2014), 243.

3. The Global Slavery Index website, accessed October 30, 2015, http://www.globalslaveryindex.org.

Exodus 5:1–6:9

1. See, for example, Seitz, "Call of Moses."

2. See Andersen, *Sentence in Biblical Hebrew*, 102; Garrett, *Rethinking Genesis*, 21n24; Niehaus, *God at Sinai*, 188n11.

Exodus 6:10–8:19

1. See Heidel, *Babylonian Genesis*, 106; Cassuto, *Book of Exodus*, 94; Larsson, *Bound for Freedom*, 54–55; Galpaz-Feller, "Hidden and Revealed."

2. Wells, "Exodus," 195–96.

3. See Keener, *Miracles*.

4. Quoted in Salmon, "Religion and Science," 176.

5. Jacalyn Duffin, "Can a Scientist Believe in Miracles?," Religion and Ethics, BBC, February 14, 2014, http://www.bbc.co.uk/religion/0/24660240.

Exodus 8:20–10:29

1. For fuller information, see Zevit, "Three Ways"; Hoffmeier, "Egypt, Plagues in," 376; Kitchen, *On the Reliability*, 253.

2. This idea was initially advocated by Hort, "Plagues of Egypt"; cf. Humphreys, *Miracles of Exodus*; Sivertsen, *Parting of the Sea*. The case against such proposals is strong; see, for example, Kitchen, *On the Reliability*, 250–51; Stuart, *Exodus*, 191–94.

3. R. C. Sproul, *Chosen by God*, rev. ed. (Wheaton, IL: Tyndale, 1986), 16–17.

Exodus 12:31–13:16

1. For a variety of approaches to this issue, see Fouts, "Hyperbolic Interpretation"; Humphreys, "Number of People"; McEntire, "Response"; Humphreys, "Further Appraisal"; Milgrom, "Decoding"; Rendsburg, "Additional Note"; Fouts, "Numbers, Large Numbers"; Waite, "Census of Israelite Men." As regards the lists in Numbers 1 and 26, although these are generally taken to list only men, the possibility that the census includes women should not be dismissed. The noun *tsaba'* (Num. 1:3, 20, 22, 24, 26, 28, 30, 32, 34, 36, 38, 40, 42, 45, 52) may refer to war, but it is also used to denote cultic service (e.g., Num. 4:23; cf. Exod. 38:8; 1 Sam. 2:22). The fact that the census in Num. 1 involves "all the congregation of the people of Israel" (Num. 1:2 ESV; cf. 26:2) suggests that women are included. The expression "every male" in Num. 1:2, 20, 22 (ESV), may indicate that tribal allegiance was determined by a father's identity and not a mother's; contrast Num. 3:22, 28, 34, where "names" is omitted.

2. Although it is widely accepted that the census in Numbers 1 lists the men of military age, it may be that it lists all Israelite adults who might be expected to make an atonement payment.

3. For a fuller discussion, see Wenham, "Large Numbers."

4. Charles C. Ryrie writes, "Propitiation means the turning away of wrath by an offering. In relation to soteriology, propitiation means placating or satisfying the wrath of God by the atoning sacrifice of Christ." *Basic Theology: A Popular Systematic Guide to Understanding Biblical Truth* (Chicago: Moody, 1999), 339.

Exodus 13:17–14:31

1. Among the advocates of this approach are Cross, "Song of the Sea"; Day, *God's Conflict*; Batto, *Slaying the Dragon*.

Exodus 15:1–21

1. Various scholars favor interpreting v. 13 as referring to Mount Sinai: e.g., Cassuto, *Book of Exodus*, 176; Jacob, *Second Book*, 421; Davies, "Theology of Exodus," 147; Hamilton, *Exodus*, 232. Stuart takes it as referring to the promised land (*Exodus*, 356n92). Childs suggests that it may refer to the "whole land of Canaan . . . or simply Zion" (*Book of Exodus*, 243).

2. Charles Spurgeon, "Knowledge. Worship. Gratitude," Sermon 1763, Spurgeon Archive, http://www.spurgeon.org/sermons/1763.htm.

Exodus 15:22–16:36

1. Among the scholars who view the manna as a purely natural phenomenon, see Noth, *Exodus*, 132; Fretheim, *Exodus*, 182; Propp, *Exodus 1–18*, 599–600.

2. Molière, *The Miser*, act 3, scene 1.

3. Heidelberg Catechism, question and answer 125.

4. Suzanne S. Brown, "Consumers Spend $330 Million on Halloween Pet Costumes," *Denver Post*, October 23, 2013, http://www.denverpost.com/lifestyles/ci_24373408/consumers-spend-310-million-halloween-pet-costumes.

Exodus 17:1–16

1. E.g., Propp, *Exodus 1–18*, 50.

2. Keil and Delitzsch, *Pentateuch (Exodus–Leviticus)*, 89–90; Jacob, *Second Book*, 1060–63.

3. For differing interpretations of the "hand," see Houtman, *Exodus*, 2:388; Stuart, *Exodus*, 401; Gispen, *Exodus*, 171; Durham, *Exodus*, 233–34.

Exodus 18:1–27

1. Fensham, "Did a Treaty"; cf. Cody, "Exodus 18:12"; Avishur, "Treaty Terminology"; Lerner, "Redefining התלאה."

2. Those who argue that chapter 18 is chronologically misplaced and was included here for theological reasons include Hyatt, *Exodus*, 186–87; Sarna, *Exodus*, 71–72; Carpenter, "Exodus 18," 107; Motyer, *Message of Exodus*, 185.

Exodus 19:1–25

1. E.g., Fretheim, *Exodus*, 211; Jacob, *Second Book*, 527; Motyer, *Message of Exodus*, 196.

2. See, for example, Dozeman, *God on the Mountain*, 25–27, 47–49, 101–3; Kuntz, *Self-Revelation of God*, 72–100; Newman, *People of the Covenant*, 39–51; Noth, *Exodus*, 159.

3. "The Boy in the Bubble: David's Death," *American Experience*, pbs.org, created March 6, 2006, http://www.pbs.org/wgbh/amex/bubble/peopleevents/e_death.html.

Exodus 20:18–21:11

1. "Holy Sonnet 15," in *Poems of John Donne*, ed. E. K. Chambers (New York: Charles Scribner's Sons, 1896), 1:165.
2. "Social Networking Fact Sheet," Pew Research Center, http://www.pewinternet.org/fact-sheets/social-networking-fact-sheet/.

Additional Insights, pp. 114–15

1. English translations are available in Roth, *Law Collections*; Hoffner, *Laws of the Hittites*.
2. E.g., Boecker, *Administration of Justice*, 135–75; David, "Codex Hammurabi"; Paul, *Book of the Covenant*, 43–105; Finkelstein, "Ox That Gored"; Westbrook, "Biblical and Cuneiform Law Codes"; Driver and Miles, *Babylonian Laws*; Malul, *Comparative Method*.
3. Wright has argued at length that the Book of the Covenant is directly dependent upon the Laws of Hammurabi, contending that the former was composed during the period 740–640 BC as "a creative academic work, by and large a unitary composition, whose goal is mainly ideological, to stand as a symbolic counterstatement to the Assyrian hegemony prevailing at the time of its composition" (*Inventing God's Law*, 346; cf. Wright, "Laws of Hammurabi"). However, Wright's approach has been severely criticized by scholars familiar with ancient Near Eastern legal codes (e.g., Westbrook, "Laws of Biblical Israel," 107–9; Wells, "Covenant Code"; Malul, review of *Inventing God's Law*; Wells, review of *Inventing God's Law*). Van Seters argues that the Book of the Covenant draws on the Laws of Hammurabi and other law codes, as well as the Deuteronomic Law Code and the Holiness Code, but locates the time of composition in the sixth century BC during the period of the exile in Babylon (*Law Book*, 172–75; for a critique, see Otto, review of *Law Book*; Levinson, "Covenant Code"; see also the counterresponse of Van Seters, "Revision").
4. Wells ("Covenant Code") offers a helpful analysis, highlighting for some of the judgments differing degrees of similarity between the Book of the Covenant and the Laws of Hammurabi.
5. Westbrook, "Laws of Biblical Israel," 107.
6. Malul, review of *Inventing God's Law*, 158.
7. As Jackson, *Comparison*, has shown.
8. Propp, *Exodus 19–40*, 222.

Exodus 21:12–36

1. Stephanie Morrow, "Top Craziest Laws Still on the Books," *LegalZoom*, October 2009, https://www.legalzoom.com/articles/top-craziest-laws-still-on-the-books.
2. Rheana Murray, "Parents Ordered to Pay Estranged Daughter's College Tuition," *ABC News*, November 13, 2014, http://abcnews.go.com/US/parents-ordered-pay-estranged-daughters-college-tuition/story?id=26889667.

Exodus 22:1–20

1. B. A. Morelli, "Fired on Facebook: What You Say CAN Hurt You," *Gazette* (Cedar Rapids, IA), October 4, 2014, http://thegazette.com/subject/news/fired-on-facebook-what-you-say-can-hurt-you-20141004.
2. "*Deepwater Horizon* Oil Spill," *Wikipedia*, last updated May 12, 2015, http://en.wikipedia.org/wiki/Deepwater_Horizon_oil_spill.
3. E. Ann Carson, "Prisoners in 2013," U.S. Department of Justice, Bureau of Justice Statistics, September 30, 2014, http://www.bjs.gov/content/pub/pdf/p13.pdf.
4. These comparisons only included countries with a population of more than 500,000 people. For more information on these data and further comparisons between countries and states, see http://www.prisonpolicy.org/global/#methodology.
5. Greg Vaughn recounts his experience with restorative justice in a video on the Restorative Justice Online website: http://www.restorativejustice.org/press-room/04av/rjvictimvaughn. The website has a number of powerful stories, some written, some on video, that could be displayed if your context allows.

Exodus 23:10–19

1. For recent discussions, see Cooper, "Once Again Seething"; Mealy, "You Shall Not"; Schorch, "'Young Goat'"; Welfeld, "You Shall Not."
2. The Directory for Family Worship, 1647 (modernized), available online at: http://www.christcovenantcullman.org/directory-modernized.pdf.

Exodus 23:20–33

1. The term *hatstsir'ah* is probably a generic word with a collective article, denoting hornets or large wasps. See Propp, *Exodus 19–40*, 290. *Tsir'ah* appears elsewhere only in Deut. 7:20 and Josh. 24:12, both of which strongly echo the present passage.
2. Sara Welch, Tracy Bloom, and Mark Mester, "Lifeguards Rescue Nearly 200 Swimmers as Dangerous Rip Currents Hit Beaches," KTLA, September 16, 2014, http://ktla.com/2014/09/16/lifeguards-makes-multiple-rescues-amid-dangerous-rip-currents-off-venice-beach/.

Exodus 24:1–18

1. "Golden Gate Bridge Research Library," Golden Gate Bridge website, http://www.goldengatebridge.org/research/.

Exodus 25:1–27:21

1. Learn more about the Mars One project here: http://www.mars-one.com.

Exodus 28:1–29:46

1. Michael Muskal, "Last FEMA Trailer Leaves New Orleans Six Years after Katrina," *Los Angeles Times*, February 15, 2012, http://latimesblogs.latimes.com/nationnow/2012/02/last-fema-trailer-leaves-new-orleans-six-years-after-hurricane-katrina.html.

Exodus 30:1–31:18

1. An online source like SpiritualGiftsTest.com is a great resource to use.

Exodus 32:1–33:6

1. Among the different scholars who support the idea of a pedestal are Albright, *From the Stone Age*, 299–301; Sarna, *Exploring Exodus*, 218; Weinfeld, *Deuteronomy 1–11*, 292.

Exodus 33:7–34:35

1. Dietrich Bonhoeffer, *The Cost of Discipleship* (New York: Touchstone, 1995), 44–45.

Bibliography

Recommended Resources

Alexander, T. Desmond. *From Paradise to the Promised Land: An Introduction to the Pentateuch*. 3rd ed. Grand Rapids: Baker Academic, 2012.

Alexander, T. Desmond, and David W. Baker, eds. *Dictionary of the Old Testament: Pentateuch*. Downers Grove, IL: IVP Academic, 2003.

Blackburn, W. Ross. *The God Who Makes Himself Known: The Missionary Heart of the Book of Exodus*. New Studies in Biblical Theology. Downers Grove, IL: IVP Academic, 2012.

Dempster, Stephen G. "Exodus and Biblical Theology: On Moving into the Neighborhood with a New Name." *Southern Baptist Journal of Theology* 12, no. 3 (2008): 4–23.

Leder, Arie C. "Reading Exodus to Learn and Learning to Read Exodus." *Calvin Theological Journal* 34, no. 1 (1999): 11–35.

Rosner, Brian S., and Paul R. Williamson, eds. *Exploring Exodus: Literary, Theological, and Contemporary Approaches*. Nottingham, UK: Apollos, 2008.

Select Bibliography

Albright, William F. *From the Stone Age to Christianity: Monotheism and the Historical Process*. Baltimore: Johns Hopkins Press, 1946.

Andersen, Francis I. *The Sentence in Biblical Hebrew*. Janua linguarum, Series practica, 231. The Hague: Mouton, 1974.

Avishur, Yizhak. "Treaty Terminology in the Moses-Jethro Story (Exodus 18:1–12)." *Aula Orientalis* 6, no. 2 (1988): 139–47.

Batto, Bernard F. *Slaying the Dragon: Mythmaking in the Biblical Tradition*. Louisville: Westminster John Knox, 1992.

Bietak, Manfred. *Avaris: The Capital of the Hyksos: Recent Excavations at Tell El-Dab'a*. London: British Museum Press, 1996.

———. "Perunefer." *Egyptian Archaeology* 34 (2013): 15–17.

Bimson, John J. *Redating the Exodus and Conquest*. Journal for the Study of the Old Testament Supplement Series 5. Sheffield: JSOT Press, 1978.

Boecker, Hans Jochen. *Law and the Administration of Justice in the Old Testament and Ancient East*. Translated by J. Moiser. Minneapolis: Augsburg, 1980.

Carpenter, Eugene E. "Exodus 18: Its Structure, Style, Motifs and Function in the Book of Exodus." In *A Biblical Itinerary: In Search of Method, Form and Content; Essays in Honor of George W. Coats*, edited by Eugene E. Carpenter, Journal for the Study of the Old Testament Supplement Series 240, 91–108. Sheffield: Sheffield Academic, 1997.

Cassuto, Umberto. *A Commentary on the Book of Exodus*. Jerusalem: Magnes Press, 1967.

Childs, Brevard S. *The Book of Exodus: A Critical, Theological Commentary*. Old Testament Library. London: SCM, 1974.

Cody, Aelred. "Exodus 18:12: Jethro Accepts a Covenant with the Israelites." *Biblica* 49, no. 2 (1968): 153–66.

Cooper, Alan. "Once Again Seething a Kid in Its Mother's Milk." *Jewish Studies, an Internet Journal* 10 (2012): 109–43.

Cross, Frank Moore. "The Song of the Sea and Canaanite Myth." In *Canaanite Myth and Hebrew Epic: Essays in the History of the Religion of Israel*, 112–44. Cambridge, MA: Harvard University Press, 1973.

David, Martin. "The Codex Hammurabi and Its Relation to the Provisions of the Law in Exodus." *Oudtestamentische Studiën* 7 (1950): 149–78.

Davies, Graham I. "The Exegesis of the Divine Name in Exodus." In *The God of Israel*, edited by R. P. Gordon, University of Cambridge Oriental Publications 64, 139–56. Cambridge, UK: Cambridge University Press, 2007.

———. "The Theology of Exodus." In *In Search of True Wisdom: Essays in Old Testament Interpretation in Honour of Ronald E. Clements*, edited by E. Ball, Journal for the Study of the Old Testament Supplement Series 300, 137–52. Sheffield: Sheffield Academic, 1999.

Day, John. *God's Conflict with the Dragon and the Sea: Echoes of a Canaanite Myth in the Old Testament*. University of Cambridge Oriental Publications 35. Cambridge, UK: Cambridge University Press, 1985.

Dever, William G. "Is There Any Archaeological Evidence for the Exodus?" In *Exodus: The Egyptian Evidence*, edited by Ernest S. Frerichs and Leonard H. Lesko, 67–86. Winona Lake, IN: Eisenbrauns, 1997.

Dozeman, Thomas B. *God on the Mountain: A Study of Redaction, Theology and Canon in Exodus 19–24*. Society of Biblical Literature Monograph Series 37. Atlanta: Scholars Press, 1989.

Driver, G. R., and John C. Miles. *The Babylonian Laws*. 2 vols. Ancient Codes and Laws of the Near East. Oxford: Clarendon, 1952.

Durham, John I. *Exodus*. Word Biblical Commentary 3. Waco: Word, 1987.

Fensham, F. Charles. "Did a Treaty between the Israelites and the Kenites Exist?" *Bulletin of the American Schools of Oriental Research* 175 (1964): 51–54.

Finkelstein, Jacob J. "The Ox That Gored." *Transactions of the American Philosophical Society* 71 (1981): 5–47.

Fouts, D. M. "A Defense of the Hyperbolic Interpretation of Large Numbers in the Old Testament." *Journal of the Evangelical Theological Society* 40, no. 3 (1997): 377–87.

———. "Numbers, Large Numbers." In *Dictionary of the Old Testament: Historical Books*, edited by Bill T. Arnold and H. G. M. Williamson, 750–54. Downers Grove, IL: InterVarsity, 2005.

Fretheim, Terence E. *Exodus*. Interpretation. Louisville: John Knox, 1991.

———. "Yahweh." In *New International Dictionary of Old Testament Theology and Exegesis*, 5 vols., edited by Willem VanGemeren, 4:1295–1300. Grand Rapids: Zondervan, 1997.

Galpaz-Feller, Pnina. "The Hidden and Revealed in the Sign of the Serpent (Exodus 4:2–5; 7:8–14)." *Biblische Notizen* 114/115 (2002): 24–30.

Garrett, Duane A. *Rethinking Genesis: The Sources and Authorship of the First Book of the Pentateuch*. Grand Rapids: Baker, 1991.

Gesenius, Wilhelm. *Gesenius' Hebrew Grammar*. Edited by E. Kautsch. Translated by A. E. Cowley. 2nd ed. Oxford: Clarendon, 1910.

Gispen, Willem Hendrik. *Exodus*. Bible Student's Commentary. Grand Rapids: Zondervan, 1982.

Grabbe, Lester L. *Israel in Transition: From Late Bronze II to Iron IIa (c. 1250–850 B.C.E.)*. Vol. 2, *The Texts*. Library of Hebrew Bible/Old Testament Studies 521. New York: T&T Clark, 2008.

Hamilton, Victor P. *Exodus: An Exegetical Commentary*. Grand Rapids: Baker Academic, 2011.

Heidel, Alexander. *The Babylonian Genesis: The Story of Creation*. Chicago: University of Chicago Press, 1951.

Hoffmeier, James K. "The Arm of God versus the Arm of the Pharaoh in the Exodus Narratives." *Biblica* 67 (1986): 378–87.

———. "Egypt, Plagues in." In *The Anchor Bible Dictionary*, edited by David Noel Freedman, 2:374–78. New York: Doubleday, 1992.

———. *Israel in Egypt: The Evidence for the Authenticity of the Exodus Tradition*. New York: Oxford University Press, 1996.

———. "What Is the Biblical Date for the Exodus? A Response to Bryant Wood." *Journal of the Evangelical Theological Society* 50 (2007): 225–47.

Hoffner, Harry A. *The Laws of the Hittites: A Critical Edition*. Leiden: Brill, 1997.

Hort, Greta. "The Plagues of Egypt." *Zeitschrift für die alttestamentliche Wissenschaft* 69 (1957): 84–103; 70 (1958): 48–59.

Houtman, Cornelis. *Exodus*. 4 vols. Historical Commentary on the Old Testament. Kampen: Kok, 1993–2002.

Humphreys, Colin J. *The Miracles of Exodus: A Scientist's Discovery of the Extraordinary Natural Causes of the Biblical Stories*. San Francisco: HarperOne, 2003.

———. "The Number of People in the Exodus from Egypt: Decoding Mathematically the Very Large Numbers in Numbers i and xxvi." *Vetus Testamentum* 48 (1998): 196–213.

———. "The Numbers in the Exodus from Egypt: A Further Appraisal." *Vetus Testamentum* 50 (2000): 323–28.

Hyatt, J. P. *Exodus*. New Century Bible. London: Oliphants, 1971.

Jackson, Samuel A. *A Comparison of Ancient Near Eastern Law Collections prior to the First Millennium BC*. Near Eastern Studies 10. Piscataway, NJ: Gorgias Press, 2008.

Jacob, Benno. *The Second Book of the Bible: Exodus*. Hoboken, NJ: KTAV, 1992.

Keener, Craig. *Miracles: The Credibility of the New Testament Accounts*. 2 vols. Grand Rapids: Baker Academic, 2011.

Keil, C. F., and F. Delitzsch. *The Pentateuch (Exodus-Leviticus)*. Biblical Commentary on the Old Testament in Ten Volumes. Edinburgh: T&T Clark, 1864.

Kitchen, Kenneth A. *On the Reliability of the Old Testament*. Grand Rapids: Eerdmans, 2003.

Kuntz, John K. *The Self-Revelation of God*. Philadelphia: Westminster, 1967.

Larsson, Göran. *Bound for Freedom: The Book of Exodus in Jewish and Christian Traditions*. Peabody, MA: Hendrickson, 1999.

Lerner, Phillip. "Redefining התלאה: An Assurance of Israel's Return to the Land in Jethro's Covenant." *Biblica* 87, no. 3 (2006): 402–11.

Levinson, Bernard M. "Is the Covenant Code an Exilic Composition? A Response to John Van Seters." In *In Search of Pre-Exilic Israel: Proceedings of the Oxford Old Testament Seminar*, edited by J. Day, Journal for the Study of the Old Testament Supplement Series, 272–325. London: T&T Clark, 2004.

Malul, Meir. *The Comparative Method in Ancient Near Eastern and Biblical Legal Studies*. Alter Orient und Altes Testament 227. Neukirchen-Vluyn: Neukirchener, 1990.

———. Review of *Inventing God's Law: How the Covenant Code of the Bible Used and Revised the Laws of Hammurabi*, by David P. Wright. *Strata: Bulletin of the Anglo-Israel Archaeological Society* 29 (2011): 155–59.

McEntire, Mark M. "A Response to Colin J. Humphreys's 'The Number of People in the Exodus from Egypt: Decoding Mathematically the Very Large Numbers in Numbers i and xxvi.'" *Vetus Testamentum* 49 (1999): 262–64.

Mealy, J. Webb. "You Shall Not Boil a Kid in Its Mother's Milk (Exod 23:19b; Exod 34:26b; Deut 14:21b): A Figure of Speech?" *Biblical Interpretation* 20, nos. 1–2 (2012): 35–72.

Milgrom, Jacob. "On Decoding Very Large Numbers." *Vetus Testamentum* 49 (1999): 131–32.

Motyer, J. Alec. *The Message of Exodus: The Days of Our Pilgrimage*. Bible Speaks Today. Downers Grove, IL: IVP Academic, 2005.

Newman, Murray Lee. *The People of the Covenant*. Nashville: Abingdon, 1962.

Niehaus, Jeffrey J. *God at Sinai*. Grand Rapids: Zondervan, 1995.

Noth, Martin. *Exodus: A Commentary*. Old Testament Library. London: SCM, 1962.

Otto, Eckart. Review of *A Law Book for the Diaspora: Revision in the Study of the Covenant Code*, by John Van Seters. *Review of Biblical Literature*. July 10, 2004. http://www.bookreviews.org/pdf/3929_3801.pdf.

Paul, Shalom M. *Studies in the Book of the Covenant in the Light of Cuneiform and Biblical Law*. Supplements to Vetus Testamentum 18. Leiden: Brill, 1970.

Propp, William H. C. *Exodus 1–18: A New Translation with Introduction and Commentary*. Anchor Bible 2. New York: Doubleday, 1999.

———. *Exodus 19–40: A New Translation with Introduction and Commentary*. Anchor Bible 2B. New York: Doubleday, 2006.

Rendsburg, Gary A. "An Additional Note to Two Recent Articles on the Number of People in the Exodus from Egypt and the Large Numbers in Numbers i and xxvi." *Vetus Testamentum* 51, no. 3 (2001): 392–96.

Roberts, J. J. M. "Hand of Yahweh." *Vetus Testamentum* 21, no. 2 (1971): 244–51.

Roth, Martha T. *Law Collections from Mesopotamia and Asia Minor*. Edited by Piotr Michalowski. Atlanta: Scholars Press, 1995.

Salmon, Wesley. "Religion and Science: A New Look at Hume's Dialogues." *Philosophical Studies* 33 (1978): 143–76.

Sarna, Nahum M. *Exodus*. JPS Torah Commentary. Philadelphia: Jewish Publication Society, 1991.

———. *Exploring Exodus: The Origins of Biblical Israel*. New York: Schocken, 1996.

Schorch, Stefan. "'A Young Goat in Its Mother's Milk'? Understanding an Ancient Prohibition." *Vetus Testamentum* 60, no. 1 (2010): 116–30.

Seitz, Christopher R. "The Call of Moses and the 'Revelation' of the Divine Name: Source-Critical Logic and Its Legacy." In *Theological Exegesis: Essays in Honor of Brevard S. Childs*, edited by Christopher R. Seitz and Kathryn Greene-McCreight, 145–61. Grand Rapids: Eerdmans, 1999.

Sivertsen, Barbara J. *The Parting of the Sea: How Volcanoes, Earthquakes, and Plagues Shaped the Story of Exodus*. Princeton, NJ: Princeton University Press, 2009.

Stuart, Douglas K. *Exodus*. New American Commentary. Nashville: Broadman & Holman, 2006.

Van Seters, John. *A Law Book for the Diaspora: Revision in the Study of the Covenant Code*. Oxford: Oxford University Press, 2003.

———. "Revision in the Study of the Covenant Code and a Response to My Critics." *Scandinavian Journal of the Old Testament* 21 (2007): 5–28.

Waite, Jerry. "The Census of Israelite Men after Their Exodus from Egypt." *Vetus Testamentum* 60, no. 3 (2010): 487–91.

Weinfeld, Moshe. *Deuteronomy 1–11*. Anchor Bible 5. New York: Doubleday, 1991.

Welfeld, Irving H. "You Shall Not Boil a Kid in Its Mother's Milk: Beyond Exodus 23:19." *Jewish Bible Quarterly* 32, no. 2 (2004): 84–90.

Wells, Bruce. "The Covenant Code and Near Eastern Legal Traditions: A Response to David P. Wright." *Maarav* 13, no. 1 (2006): 85–118.

———. "Exodus." In *Zondervan Illustrated Bible Backgrounds Commentary*, edited by John H. Walton, 1:160–283. Grand Rapids: Zondervan, 2009.

———. Review of *Inventing God's Law: How the Covenant Code of the Bible Used and Revised the Laws of Hammurabi*, by David P. Wright. *Journal of Religion* 90, no. 4 (2010): 558–60.

Wenham, J. W. "Large Numbers in the Old Testament." *Tyndale Bulletin* 18 (1967): 19–53.

Westbrook, Raymond. "Biblical and Cuneiform Law Codes." *Revue biblique* 92 (1985): 247–64.

———. "The Laws of Biblical Israel." In *The Hebrew Bible: New Insights and Scholarship*, edited by F. E. Greenspahn, Jewish Studies in the 21st Century, 99–119. New York: New York University Press, 2008.

Williams, R. J. *Hebrew Syntax: An Outline*. Toronto: University of Toronto Press, 1967.

Wood, Bryant G. "The Rise and Fall of the 13th Century Exodus-Conquest Theory." *Journal of the Evangelical Theological Society* 48 (2005): 475–89.

Wright, David P. *Inventing God's Law: How the Covenant Code of the Bible Used and Revised the Laws of Hammurabi*. Oxford: Oxford University Press, 2009.

———. "The Laws of Hammurabi as a Source for the Covenant Collection (Exodus 20:23–23:19)." *Maarav* 10 (2003): 11–87.

Zevit, Ziony. "Three Ways to Look at the Ten Plagues." *Bible Review* 6, no. 3 (1990): 16–23, 42, 44.

Index

Aaron, 15, 85, 149, 159
  assistance to Moses, 27, 29, 40, 41
  consecration of, 161
  and golden calf (bull), 173–74
Aaronic priests, 3, 22, 162–63, 185
Abraham
  covenant with, 17, 28, 35, 61
  father of many nations, 61
acacia wood, 155, 156, 185
Adam and Eve, 97, 138, 142
adultery, 103
Ahmose I, 8, 15, 66
Allais, Alphonse, 94
altar, 109, 165, 166
Amalekites, 85–86, 87
Amos, 133
Amram, 15, 41
ancient Near East
  law collections, 108, 112–13, 117, 122
  names of gods, 22
  vassal treaties, 96
angel, 54
angel of the Lord, 21, 66, 67, 142
animals
  care for, 136
  injuries caused by, 119
  injuries to, 119
  sacrifices of, 3, 163
  sexual relations with, 124
anointing oil, 166, 185
anxiety, 81
ʻapiru/ʻabiru, 10
apodosis, 116
ark of Noah, 15

ark of the covenant, 154, 167
Asherah, 141
asylum, 117, 120
atonement, 3, 54, 149, 150, 151, 154, 166
atonement cover, 155, 165
atonement payment, 166, 185, 192
Avaris, 9

Baal, 141
banner, 86
Bar Kokhba revolt, 100
Bezalel, 165, 166, 168, 184, 185
biblical theology, Exodus and, 6–7
blasphemy, 130
blood of Christ, 150
blood of goats and bulls, 150
blue laws, 120–21
Bonhoeffer, Dietrich, 181–82
Book of the Covenant, 2, 91, 96, 107–12, 114–
    15, 118, 128, 141, 148, 179
breastpiece, 160
bribe, 130
brick making, 10, 34–35
bride-price, 124
bronze altar, 156
bronze basin, 165, 166
bull
    as idol, 172
    as sin offering, 161
burning bush, 21–22, 24, 98
burnt offerings, 90, 148–49, 161

Caiaphas, 62
Cain, killing of Abel, 68
Canaan, nations of, 73

Canaanite religion, 141–42
capital punishment, 116, 120, 123
case laws, 89, 91, 116–20, 122–26
chariots, 66
cheap grace, 181–82
cherubim, 156
Christians, as countercultural, 145
church building, 157, 158
Churchill, Winston, 38
Church of Scotland, 139
circumcision, 28, 60–61
clean and unclean foods, 130
cleansing, 98, 149, 161
cloud, covered the tabernacle, 186
Code of Eshnunna, 115
Code of Hammurabi, 108, 112–13, 193
common good, 93
compassion, 129, 130, 131, 132, 138
complaining, 81
consecration, 3, 97–98, 148
cooperation, 93
coriander seeds, 79–80
counterfeit religion, 174–75
courtyard, for the tabernacle, 156
covenant
    breaking of, 173
    at Mount Sinai, 3, 4, 41
    obligations of, 96, 104, 128, 150
    renewal of, 179, 183
    sealing/ratification of, 147, 150
coveting, 103
creation mandate, 9, 11
crocodile, 28, 42
cursing father and mother, 117
curtains, in the tabernacle, 155–56

Day of Atonement, 165–66
debt slavery, 109, 110
delayed gratification, 19
Desert of Shur, 77
Desert of Sin, 78, 83
Deuteronomy, 3, 96
discouragement, 37, 38
disobedience, 174
Divine Warrior, 72, 74
Documentary Hypothesis, 2
Donne, John, 112
Duffin, Jacalyn, 44–45
dwelling place, 75

eagles' wings, 96
earthen altar, 109
Egyptian gods, 47
elders of the Israelites, 29
Eliezer, 90
Elim, 78
'elohim, 172

ephod of gold, 160
Etham, 66
exclusive commitment, 144
exile, 18, 90, 142
exodos (Greek word), 1
exodus, 64–69
    dating of, 5–6, 9
    historicity of, 5–6
    as new beginning for Israelites, 53
    as paradigm of salvation, 30, 99
    points forward, 71
exploitation, 10, 12, 16
"eye for an eye," 118

false prophets, 44
false religion, 144, 174–75
false testimony, 103, 130
false worship, 124, 173, 175, 176
fatherless, 129
fellowship offerings, 109, 148
fertility-cult practices, 141
Festival of Harvest (Weeks), 135, 137
Festival of Ingathering (Tabernacles), 135, 137
Festival of Unleavened Bread, 52–53, 54, 58, 135, 136–38, 180
finger of God, 42–43
fire, destroying another's property, 123
firstborn males, 3, 55, 58, 60, 62, 130
firstborn of Egypt, striking down of, 54–55
firstfruits, 137
Fleming, Alexander, 93
flies, 47–48
food, God's provision of, 79–81, 82
foreigners, 16–17, 129, 131, 135
Franklin, Benjamin, 87
freedom, to serve God, 111
frogs, 42
future life with God, 75

Garrison, David, 31
genealogical information, 39–40
generosity, 82, 132
Genesis, 2–3
genocide, 12
Gershom, 16–17, 28, 29, 90
glory of God, 69, 149
    fills the tabernacle, 186
    fills the whole earth, 187
    request by Moses to see, 178–79
gluttony, 81
gnats, 42
God
    anger with Israel, 172–73
    as compassionate and gracious, 50–51, 179, 180
    creation of cosmos, 168
    defeats powers of evil, 71

demands exclusive obedience of Israelites, 102
as divine warrior, 72, 74
dwells among Israel, 1, 4, 147, 154, 171, 183
faithfulness of, 17
goes ahead of Israel, 142–45
holiness of, 1, 24, 98, 99, 132, 162
honoring of, 132
as jealous, 103
justice of, 76, 133, 179
lordship of, 111
patience of, 50–51
presence of, 24
provides for and protects his people, 86
reassurances from, 37
reign of, 73
remembers his covenant, 35–36
as Savior and Judge, 92
self-revelation of, 25
sovereignty of, 68–69
testing/training Israel, 84, 108–9
willingness to forgive, 177, 180
gold, 154–55, 156
golden calf (bull), 97, 102, 107, 153, 171–75, 177, 178, 179
grace, 180–81
grace-gifts, 168, 169
gratitude, 74, 75, 81
greater exodus, 7, 30, 61
greediness, 81

hand of God, 23, 36, 72
Hansen's disease, 28
hard-hearted (English idiom), 29, 41, 49
Heidelberg Catechism, 82
Heine, Johann Heinrich, 182
higher criticism, 2
high priest, clothing of, 160, 162
holiness, 22, 99, 131, 150, 162, 166
associated with life, 130
holy dwelling, 72–73
holy ground, 21–22
holy nation, 97, 98, 131–32
Holy Place, 156
Holy Spirit, 145, 187
honoring father and mother, 103, 104, 117, 120
Horeb, 20, 84, 90
hornet, 143
"How Firm a Foundation" (hymn), 70
human life, value of, 119
Hur, 85, 149
Huram, 166
Hyksos, 8
hyssop, 54

"I AM," 22–23
idolatry, 145, 175

idols, 107, 109, 171–75
images, 102
immorality, 173
impartiality, 130, 132, 134, 138
incense, 166
incense altar, 165
infanticide, by Pharaoh, 10
Islam, 31
Israel, Israelites
consecration of, 56
as God's special nation, 95
as God's treasured possession, 5, 97, 174
grumbling of, 78, 79
memory of Egypt, 78
oppression in Egypt, 10
population growth of, 9, 11
put God to the test, 84
quarrel with Moses, 84, 87
as stiff-necked people, 174
tested by God, 78, 84, 108–9
worship God in song, 71
yearning to return to Egypt, 67

Jacob, 9,
twelve sons of, 160
Jebel Musa, 20
Jerusalem, 73
Jesus Christ
death of, 7, 99, 163
heals ten lepers, 75
as mediator of new covenant, 150
opens the way to God's presence, 162
as ransom, 62
resurrection of, 31, 32
return of, 188–89
signs of, 40, 50
as the spiritual rock, 85
transfiguration of, 180
Jethro, 16, 21, 29, 89
Jochebed, 15
John, signs of salvation in, 31
Joseph, 9
bones of, 66
Josephus, 42
Joshua, 85, 87
judges, 91
justice, 69, 76, 119, 125, 129–34, 193

kidnapping, 117
kingdom of God, 188
kingdom of priests, 97, 98
kinsman-redeemer, 60
knowing God, 4–5, 34, 90
knowledge, 166–67

Lake of Reeds, 4, 64–65, 72
lambs, as burnt offering, 162
lampstand, 155

land of Canaan, 25, 27, 36, 73, 142–43
law, 149
  enshrines value system, 120
leaders, limitations of, 92
lending with interest, 129–30
leprosy, 28
Levites, 3, 40–41
  consecration of, 61, 148
Leviticus, 3
lex talionis, 118
liberation from slavery, 36
"life for a life," 120
light and darkness, 69
locusts, 49
Lord's Prayer, 82
Lord's Supper, 150
love, for enemy, 130, 131
loyalty to God, 145
Luther, Martin, 169

magicians of Egypt, 42, 48
manna, 78–80
manslaughter, 117
Marah, 77–78, 84
marital rights, 110–11
marriage, 103
Massah, 84–85
meeting house, church building as, 158
mercy, 180
mercy seat, 155
Meribah, 84–85
Midian, 14, 15, 16–17, 90
midwives, 10
"milk and honey," 138
miracles, 43–44
Miriam, 15, 72, 74
Mischel, Walter, 19
moderation, in eating, 137
Molek, 141
monotheism, of Israel, 136, 143–44
moral symmetry, of divine justice, 119–20
Moses
  as author of Exodus, 2
  birth of, 14, 15
  calling of, 20–25, 27
  as Egyptian, 16
  hands held up, 85–86
  identity of, 14, 17–18
  ineloquence of, 27, 28–29, 40
  killing of Egyptian, 16
  mediation of, 177–78
  radiance of, 180
  reluctance to lead, 27, 29
  request to see God's glory, 178–79
  signs of, 30, 39
  tested by God, 78
  mosquitoes, 47

Most Holy Place, 156, 157
Mount Sinai, 1, 20–21, 29, 73
  covered with smoke, 98
  quaking of, 98
movement, in Exodus, 1
multiculturalism, 144
murder, 103, 104, 117

Nadab and Abihu, 149
name of God, misuse of, 102
Naomi, 129
nations, salvation of, 62
natural revelation, 5
negligence, 123
new covenant, 99–100, 104, 150, 151
new exodus, 61. *See also* greater exodus
new Jerusalem, 7, 18, 75, 98, 151, 156
new moon, 96
New Testament, and exodus story, 6
Nile, teeming with frogs, 42
no other gods, 102, 124, 143
numbers in Old Testament, 59, 192

obedience, 102, 152, 180–81
obligations. *See* covenant obligations
occult activity, 42
offerings, 130, 184
Oholiab, 165, 166, 168, 184
oil for tabernacle lamps, 156
omer, 80
onyx stones, 160
opposition to God's purposes, 36–37
oppression, 12, 16, 32
Origen, 170
Orwell, George, 19
overindulgence, 137
oxen, 123

papyrus basket, 15
parable of the growing seed, 188
parable of the talents, 139
parents, authority over children, 117, 120
Passover, 29, 52–56, 130
  centrality of, 3
  in John, 6
  as Old Testament paradigm for salvation, 43
  regulations for, 58, 60, 61–62
Passover lamb, 54, 56, 62–63
pastors, 157
patriarchs, 3, 17, 22, 35
peace offering, 148
Pentecost, 187
persecution, 37, 68, 69
Perunefer, 15
Pharaoh, 5
  as anti-God figure, 9, 11
  authority of, 33
  defeat of, 67–68, 71, 74

as deity, 33–34
hand of, 23
hardened heart of, 29, 41, 48, 49–50
hostility of, 68
intransience of, 55
stubbornness of, 28, 30, 34
Pharaoh's daughter, 15
pilgrimage feasts, 136–37
pillar of cloud/fire, 66, 67, 178
Pithom, 8
plagues. *See* signs and wonders
polytheism, of ancient Near East, 109, 136, 141, 143–44
poor, 36, 129–30, 132, 135, 136
possessions, of others, 123, 124–26
pregnant women, striking of, 118
premeditated killing, 117
priests, 157, 159
  clothing of, 160
  consecration of, 161, 162–63
primary case laws, 116
promised land, 22. *See also* land of Canaan
propitiation, 63, 192
protasis, 116
Puah, 12, 13
punishment, in case laws, 116, 119

quail, 79
Quakers, 158
quarreling, 117

ram, 161
Rameses, 8–9
Ramesses II, 9
ransom, 3, 60, 62, 149, 166, 168–69
reconciliation, 127
redemption, 36, 60
Red Sea, 4, 64–65. *See also* Lake of Reeds
repentance, 51
Rephidim, 83
responsibility, 93
rest, 79, 135, 136, 139
restitution, 123, 125–26, 127
restorative justice, 193
resumptive repetition, 40
Reuel, 16
rich young ruler, 17
Russell, Bertrand, 44

Sabbath, 79, 102–3, 104, 105, 120–21, 135, 136, 138–40, 153, 165, 167
  hope of, 140
  prophetic dimensions of, 139
sacrifices, 90–91
  to other gods, 124
salvation, 99, 180–81
sanctification, 148, 150, 151
sanctuary, 154
secondary case laws, 116

self-gratification, 175
self-promotion, 112–13
Sermon on the Mount, 131
servanthood, 18, 111–12
seventy elders, 149
severe combined immunodeficiency (SCID), 100
sexual relations, with animals, 124
Shiloh, 73
Shiphrah, 12, 13
signs and wonders, 39, 40, 41, 43–44, 46–48, 50, 85
silver, 154, 156
sin, and separation from God, 75
Sinai covenant, 95
  case laws in, 91
  ratification of, 153
  renewal of, 179, 183
sin offering, 161
skepticism, 30
skilled workers, 184
slavery, 109, 110
  deliverance from, 56
  in Egypt, 10
slaves, beating of, 117–18
smoke, covers Mount Sinai, 98
Soli Deo Gloria, 69
Solomon, 5
song of Miriam, 2, 71–75
"sons of Israel," 160
sorcery, 42, 48, 124
spiritual adultery, 145
sprinkling of blood
  on altar and people, 147, 149, 165
  on door frames, 54
Sproul, R. C., 51
Spurgeon, Charles, 76
staff, 28, 42, 85
stealing, 103
stealing animals, 123
stone tablets, 149, 173
substitution, 62, 63
swarms of flies, 47–48

tabernacle, 4, 148
  consecration of, 162, 185
  construction of, 16–66, 153–58, 168, 184–87
  diagram of, 155
  instructions for manufacture of, 2
  as microcosm of world, 167–68
  as temporary measure, 163–64
tablets of the covenant law, 165, 167
tebah, 15
Tell el-Dab'a, 9
temple, 142, 157, 186
ten Boom, Corrie, 12–13
Ten Commandments, 2, 96, 101–6, 117, 118, 143, 148, 167

tent of meeting (tabernacle), 157
tent of meeting (temporary), 156, 178
testimony, 93
theft, 125–27
theophany, 67, 98
thunder and hail, 48
Tolkien, J. R. R., 37
torah, 149
Tower of Babel, 11, 30
treasured possession, 5, 97, 174
treaty, 179
tree of life, 155
true worship, 175
trusting God, 80
truthfulness, 103, 130
tunic, 160
turban, 160
tyranny, defeat of, 68

uncleanness, 130, 148
understanding, 166–67

unity, 88
unleavened bread, 59, 161
Urim and Thummim, 160

virginity, 124

washing, of priest, 161, 166
"Waters of Meribah," 84
water turned into blood, 42
wealth, 169
Wellhausen, Julius, 2
widow, 129
wilderness, 77, 80
wisdom, 166–67
women, role in exodus story, 72
worship, 138, 139, 143

Yahweh, 23, 35
yeast, 137

Zacchaeus, 126
Zipporah, 28, 29, 90

Contributors

General Editors
Mark. L. Strauss
John H. Walton

Associate Editors, Illustrating the Text
Kevin and Sherry Harney

Contributing Author, Illustrating the Text
Adam Barr

Series Development
Jack Kuhatschek
Brian Vos

Project Editor
James Korsmo

Interior Design
Brian Brunsting

Cover Direction
Paula Gibson
Michael Cook